READING
WORKSHOP
Survival Kit

◆ ◆ ◆ ◆ ◆

GARY ROBERT MUSCHLA

**THE CENTER FOR APPLIED
RESEARCH IN EDUCATION**
West Nyack, New York 10994

Library of Congress Cataloging-in-Publication Data

Muschla, Gary Robert.
      Reading workshop survival kit : management techniques,
     reproducible worksheets, and 100 mini-lessons covering topics and
     skills in reading / Gary Robert Muschla.
         p.   cm.
     Includes bibliographical references (p.   ).
     ISBN 0-87628-592-2
      1. Reading (Elementary)—Problems, exercises, etc. 2. Reading
    (Secondary)—Problems, exercises, etc. I. Title.
    LB1573.M87   1997
    372.41′2—dc21   97-17265
                                          CIP

Acquisition Editor: *Susan Kolwicz*
Production Editor: *Zsuzsa Neff*
Formatting/Interior design: *Publications Development Company of Texas/Zsuzsa Neff
& Sandra Durrett*

© 1997 by The Center for Applied Research in Education

Printed in the United States of America.

10 9 8 7 6 5 4 3 2

ISBN 0-87628-592-2

ATTENTION: CORPORATIONS AND SCHOOLS

Prentice Hall books are available at quantity discounts with bulk purchase
for educational, business, or sales promotional use. For information, please
write to: Prentice Hall Career & Personal Development Special Sales, 240
Frisch Court, Paramus, NJ 07652. Please supply: title of book, ISBN
number, quantity, how the book will be used, date needed.

**THE CENTER FOR APPLIED
RESEARCH IN EDUCATION**
West Nyack, NY 10955
A Simon & Schuster Company

On the World Wide Web at http://www.phdirect.com

Prentice-Hall International (UK) Limited, *London*
Prentice-Hall of Australia Pty. Limited, *Sydney*
Prentice-Hall Canada Inc., *Toronto*
Prentice-Hall Hispanoamericana, S.A., *Mexico*
Prentice-Hall of India Private Limited, *New Delhi*
Prentice-Hall of Japan, Inc., *Tokyo*
Simon & Schuster Asia Pte. Ltd., *Singapore*
Editora Prentice-Hall do Brasil, Ltda., *Rio de Janeiro*

For Judy and Erin

About the Author

Gary Robert Muschla received his B.A. and M.A.T. from Trenton State College, and teaches at Appleby School in Spotswood, New Jersey. During his 22 years as a classroom teacher, he has specialized in language arts and has developed a reading workshop that is practical in its approach and effective in its results.

In addition to his years as a classroom teacher, Mr. Muschla has been a successful author. He is a member of the Authors Guild, the Authors League of America, and the National Writers Association.

Mr. Muschla is also the author of several other resources for teachers: *Writing Resource Activities Kit* (The Center for Applied Research in Education, 1989), *The Writing Teacher's Book of Lists* (Prentice Hall, 1991), *Writing Workshop Survival Kit* (The Center for Applied Research in Education, 1993), and *English Teacher's Great Books Activities Kit* (The Center for Applied Research in Education, 1994). With his wife, Judy, he has coauthored *The Math Teacher's Book of Lists* (Prentice Hall, 1995) and *Hands-On Math Projects with Real-Life Applications* (The Center for Applied Research in Education, 1996).

Acknowledgments

I'd like to thank William Skowronski, principal at Appleby School, for his support of both my efforts as a teacher and writer.

My wife, Judy, as always, deserves special thanks for her support of me in all I do, and especially for selecting the artwork that is found throughout this book.

My thanks also to Julia Rhodes, my language arts supervisor, whose knowledge and insights about the teaching of language are a valuable resource to me.

Very special and fond appreciation to Caroline Fitzgerald and Geri Priest, colleagues and friends, who read the manuscript of this book and provided helpful comments and ideas.

I'd also like to thank Susan Kolwicz, my editor, who continues to give me advice and suggestions which have greatly helped me in my work. Thanks also to Zsuzsa Neff, my production editor, whose efforts put this book into its final form.

Finally, my thanks to my students, who make my teaching experience rewarding and fulfilling.

About Reading Instruction

Reading is, without question, a fundamental skill in our society. Whether learning about a subject, understanding a road sign, or simply enjoying a good book, the opportunity and need for reading are just about everywhere. So vital is reading that the other subjects in school are largely dependent upon it. To master English, social studies, and science, a student must be able to read; even the typical math curriculum includes word problems that require competent reading skills if students are to find solutions.

Reading is a process composed of numerous skills that can be taught. No one is born with an innate ability to read, and not everyone learns to read in the same way. Underlying all of the methods for teaching reading, however, is the amount of time actually spent reading. Like most things in life where skills improve with practice, competency in reading increases in direct relation to how much a person reads.

While there are many approaches for teaching reading, one of the best is through a reading workshop, which, as presented here, is designed for students of varying abilities in homogeneous or heterogeneous groups. Your reading workshop will be built around reading, providing students with time to read, opportunities to react to their reading, and a chance to share their ideas. Your reading classes will become centers in which students read a variety of materials, analyze and discuss ideas, and learn about life and themselves through reading.

My best wishes to you as you share the wonderful experience of reading with your students.

Gary Robert Muschla

How to Use This Resource

Reading Workshop Survival Kit is divided into two major parts. Part I describes the organization of a reading workshop and offers classroom management strategies. Part II contains 100 mini-lessons that you can use in your reading workshop.

Part I is comprised of Chapters 1 to 3. Along with an overview and specific management techniques and suggestions, several methods of evaluation are discussed. Included in these chapters are reproducibles you may use with your students, depending upon their needs and abilities. (Of course, you may prefer to make transparencies of the reproducibles throughout the book and use them with an overhead projector.)

I recommend that you read through Part I first. This will familiarize you with the procedures of the reading workshop. You'll notice that the routines are flexible, and you may adapt them to satisfy your needs and curriculum.

Part II of *Reading Workshop Survival Kit* contains 100 mini-lessons divided into three sections: (1) Mini-lessons for Types of Reading and Related Topics, (2) Mini-lessons for Story Elements, and (3) Mini-lessons for Specific Reading Skills. The mini-lessons cover the topics and skills found in any comprehensive reading program. Each mini-lesson contains reading activities, and most include a writing activity that is an extension of the topic covered by the lesson. Many also provide reproducible worksheets. You will be able to use some of the worksheets throughout the year, with various stories. A good example is Worksheet 55–2, "Themes—An Author's Message," which is useful any time you are teaching the theme of a story. Designed to be used with various materials, the mini-lessons are entirely adaptable to different teaching styles and approaches. Moreover, each mini-lesson stands alone, permitting you to use the ones that fulfill your objectives. Each is set up in a clear, easy-to-read format, making implementation simple.

The management suggestions, mini-lessons, and activities included in this book will help to make your teaching in the reading workshop easier, more effective, and more enjoyable.

Contents

Part I

Management of the Reading Workshop

Chapter 1

An Overview of the Reading Workshop

There are many kinds of reading classes. What sets a reading workshop apart is its emphasis on reading. The largest amount of class time in the reading workshop is spent with students reading and responding to what has been read.

Obviously, "reading" is crucial to the success of any reading program; yet with the demands of adolescence—friends, relationships, sports, special activities, TV, multimedia computers, part-time jobs, and countless other things—unless students are given the opportunity to read in school, many don't have time. Reading assignments are glanced at, put off, or forgotten.

The reading workshop provides students with an environment in which reading is the priority. The class becomes a center where material is read and analyzed, and reactions to it are shared. Ideas and learning flourish.

READING IN THE READING WORKSHOP

In the typical reading workshop, reading is taught through the use of various materials—novels, nonfiction books, articles, short stories, poetry, magazines, and newspapers. Even basal reading programs may be easily incorporated into a workshop setting. The class revolves around reading and activities related to reading. See the "Elements of the Reading Workshop."

Students of high, average, and low abilities function equally well in reading workshops, which feature much cooperation, collaboration, and sharing. The classrooms are busy places where students work alone, interact with each other, and confer individually and in groups with the teacher. The entire class may listen to you present a mini-lesson, then read individually, or break into groups to discuss the novel that the class is reading. Depending on how you organize your classes, all students may be reading the same material, small groups of students may be reading a particular novel, or students may be reading different novels. Because the connection between reading and writing is so strong, writing topics

Elements of the Reading Workshop

Although reading workshops may differ because of the personality of the teacher and the particular needs of students, they share many of the following:

- Reading is paramount.
- Reading is respected and celebrated.
- Students have input into what they will read.
- Various materials—nonfiction books, articles, novels, short stories, plays, and poetry—are vital components of the class's reading experiences.
- Reading skills are taught in context and not isolation.
- Sufficient time is allotted for reading.
- Reading is emphasized as an important means of communication rather than an assortment of individual skills.

- Students are encouraged to become actively involved with their reading, thereby becoming critical thinkers.
- Students are encouraged to respond to what they read and share their ideas with others.
- Students assume responsibility for their learning.
- Students are encouraged to read at home as well as in school.
- Students are encouraged to read a variety of materials.
- Cooperation and collaboration are encouraged.
- The classroom is filled with books and reading materials. (If this is not possible, access to the library on a regular basis is provided.)
- Reading gives rise to writing.
- Language is used as a tool for learning even as it is being learned.
- Students and teachers become partners in learning.
- Goals and objectives are made clear to students.
- Students understand how they will be evaluated.
- Striving toward excellence is encouraged and applauded.
- A sense of belonging to a "reading" community is promoted.

often arise from your students' reading, making the workshop a site for learning language.

Of course, classroom rules, routines, and standards of behavior must be set and maintained. Methods of evaluation must be determined to ensure that course requirements are met. You must decide on how you will run your classes, based on the objectives and expectations with which you feel most comfortable. Through the effective management of your reading workshop, you will offer your students the wonder and power of reading in context and meaning.

TEACHER AND STUDENT ROLES IN THE READING WORKSHOP

Since the reading workshop is nontraditional in its structure, you and your students will assume new roles. No longer will you be just a provider of information, who lectures, leads discussions, and assigns specific chapters for reading homework; instead, you will be a manager of learning in your classroom. Much of your teaching will be via mini-lessons. You will work with the whole class, small groups, and individuals, although the greatest amount of class time will be spent with students reading. See "The Role of the Teacher in the Reading Workshop."

As a reading workshop teacher, you will become a facilitator and resource. Rather than "spoon-feeding" skills for reading in small, bite-sized pieces, you will guide your students as they explore literature for themselves. By presenting students with a setting in which they find meaningful uses for reading, you will be offering them the opportunity for learning through self-discovery.

During class your tasks will be many and varied. Based on how you structure your class, you might speak with individuals about the novels they are reading, or meet with small groups. You might ask probing questions of a student to help him see the author's purpose in a story, or you might listen to a student share her ideas about theme. From there you might join a discussion group and model the proper behavior for sharing thoughts and opinions about an author's use of symbolism. As your reading workshop evolves, the class becomes a place in which the opportunities for learning and individual growth are boundless.

The role of your students changes, too. In many reading classes, students are given an assignment to read for homework, which often includes answering some questions. The next day in class, the homework is collected and the material is discussed. In the reading workshop, however, students do much of their reading in class and become immersed in reading-related activities. They may maintain reading logs in which they record reactions to their reading, meet in discussion groups, or work on activities related to their reading. The reading workshop is a place in which some students discover "reading" for the first time.

In many reading workshops, as the students become more engaged with their work and assume more responsibility for their learning, they develop a sense of being a part of a "reading" community that shares a respect for language and learning. Motivation rises, behavior improves, and disruption is reduced. Gradually, teachers and students become partners in the experience of learning.

The Role of the Teacher in the Reading Workshop

Your role in a reading workshop will be a varied one. Each day you may be engaged in any or all of the following:

- Present a mini-lesson on a specific reading strategy or skill.
- Guide a literature discussion group.
- Work on developing an environment that exults reading.
- Encourage students in their reading.
- Support students in their efforts to identify a story's theme.
- Help a student select a book to read.
- Encourage a reluctant or uneasy reader.
- Teach reading test-taking strategies.
- Talk about an author with students.
- Tell students about one of your favorite books.
- Read a passage from one of your favorite books to the class.

- Read a favorite piece of poetry to your students.
- Answer specific questions about reading.
- Remind students of class rules and routines.
- Model behavior in a group.
- Maintain an orderly learning environment.
- Help students find a topic for writing that is related to what they are reading.
- Train parent volunteers to help maintain book inventories.
- Order books to build a classroom library.
- Offer the titles of some of your students' favorite books to the school librarian so that he or she may buy them for the school's library.
- Help students focus topics for research papers.
- Plan an interdisciplinary thematic unit with other teachers.
- Read professional journals to keep abreast of the latest research and trends in reading.
- Evaluate your teaching methods.

THE VALUE AND USE OF MINI-LESSONS

Much of your teaching in your reading workshop classes will be through mini-lessons. Since the major portion of class time should be spent allowing students to read and react to reading, mini-lessons offer an efficient way of teaching specific reading skills, techniques, and strategies. They provide a time at the beginning of the class when the students come together as an entire group.

Mini-lessons can be used with the whole class or small groups. If you find that a particular group is having trouble understanding point of view, for example, you might offer a mini-lesson on the topic to just these students. It makes little sense to spend the valuable class time of other students on a skill they have already mastered.

The typical mini-lesson lasts less than ten minutes and focuses on one skill. A mini-lesson might share a reading strategy, point out the use of imagery in novels, or discuss a particular genre. As you get to know your students and come to understand their strengths and weaknesses, you will likely design mini-lessons of your own suited to their specific needs. (Part II of this book offers 100 mini-lessons for your use. Using them will help ensure that you cover all the important reading skills contained in the typical reading program.)

While you may answer student questions during your presentation of a mini-lesson, you should avoid extending the lesson too long. Try to address questions that many students share during the lesson. It is usually better to answer questions that affect only a few students individually or in a small group after the lesson. This permits the other students to start their work. One of the values of mini-lessons is their short length, thereby providing students with class time to read.

While the information shared through some mini-lessons will be used right away, for example, the theme of a novel the class is reading, others, like the use of context cues, may not be used until students need that specific skill. You will find that once a mini-lesson has been presented, you will refer to it as necessary when you confer with students. As the year progresses, the information shared through mini-lessons will build an impressive wealth of knowledge about reading and language.

A FINAL WORD

Perhaps the greatest strength of a reading workshop is the time it gives students to read *and* react to reading. Rather than offering reading skills in isolation through worksheets and activities that provide little overall meaning, a reading workshop enables a teacher to offer reading to students through materials in which reading skills are taught in meaningful contexts. Reading thus becomes not a mere series of skills that must be mastered, but a means of communicating and sharing ideas.

Chapter 2

Managing the Reading Workshop

Like all classrooms, the success of a reading workshop depends to a large degree on effective management. Although the organization of a reading workshop is different from typical reading classes, your basic responsibilities as a teacher remain. You still must ensure a positive learning environment, teach skills, provide information, monitor and evaluate student progress, work closely with administrators and colleagues, and keep parents informed of their children's achievement. To all this the reading workshop adds the opportunity for you to enjoy much more personal interaction with your students.

Your reading workshop should be built around books, short stories, articles, and poetry—reading them, reacting to them, and sharing ideas about them. Achieving an atmosphere in which a variety of activities flourish is a key element to a successful reading workshop.

BUILDING A POSITIVE ATMOSPHERE

You start to build a positive classroom atmosphere the first day of school. As soon as your students hear they will be participating in a reading workshop, they will likely have many questions, particularly if they have only experienced traditional reading classes.

Begin the first day by offering a description of your reading workshop, emphasizing that the class will focus on reading and reading-related activities. Note some of the books, short stories, articles, and poetry students will read during the year. Explain that you will teach the same skills that are taught in traditional reading classes; however, you will teach skills through mini-lessons. This will provide more time for reading.

Describe a typical day in the reading workshop, and some of the activities students will be doing. Mention that they will read in class, work individually and in groups, and take part in discussions about their reading. Go over your schedule, and tell students if they will need any special materials, for example, spiral notebooks for reading logs. You should also explain your methods of evaluation. (See Chapter 3, "Evaluation.")

Because the structure of the reading workshop encourages students to assume more responsibility for their learning, it is important to discuss what you expect from your students in your reading workshop. You may wish to hand out copies of "Student Responsibilities in the Reading Workshop," and review the guidelines with your students.

If you teach in a district where you have flexibility in meeting the requirements of your curriculum, you may wish to ask your students for suggestions regarding materials to read. To help them clarify their thoughts about reading, distribute copies of "Reading Self-appraisal" and ask them to complete the questions. (Of course, you may use the self-appraisal as a guide and create your own according to your needs.)

The information obtained from the self-appraisal can be helpful in planning your course of study. Collect the self-appraisals and note common interests or trends. You may find that students have many of the same general interests, or you may find that different classes have specialized interests. For instance, if several students note science fiction as a favorite genre, you might wish to include science fiction stories and novels in your reading workshop. If mysteries are popular, you may wish to make mystery titles available. If several students mention that they like poetry, you might expand your poetry unit.

Whenever you can, foster and promote reading in your classroom. Sponsor special reading events like book exchanges or book talks in which students describe a favorite book. Actions such as highlighting the top authors of a specific genre, announcing a popular author's latest title, or displaying book reviews written by students can generate interest in reading.

The establishment of a positive reading environment begins the first day of school. When students understand a class's organization, their responsibilities, and their teacher's expectations, they are more likely to behave appropriately. For a concise list of steps you might take for developing and maintaining a classroom environment supportive of reading, see "Promoting a Positive Atmosphere in Your Reading Workshop."

SETTING UP YOUR CLASSROOM

The classroom that houses a reading workshop should be conducive to reading. While this is easier to accomplish if you have your own room, even teachers who travel from room to room throughout the day can take steps to ensure a successful reading experience in their classes.

In most classrooms a simple rearrangement of furniture can enhance a reading workshop. When reading or working individually, students may work at their desks. Tables are ideal for group work; however, if you don't have tables, you may simply have students push desks together. For whole class discussions, putting desks in an oval or semicircle tends to give everyone a feeling of inclusion without putting anyone in the front and center. Such arrangements help break down barriers and build a sense of a reading community.

Student Responsibilities in the Reading Workshop

The reading workshop offers you the exciting challenge of accepting new responsibilities for learning. To help make this class successful and meaningful for yourself and others, you should:

1. Come to class each day with your reading materials and be ready to read.

2. Read at home as well as in school.

3. Read a variety of materials—novels, nonfiction books, short stories, articles, newspapers, magazines, poetry, and plays.

4. Understand that reading is more than just an assortment of skills; it is a means of communication and sharing ideas.

5. Draw conclusions from your reading. Think about what you are reading, examine and analyze the ideas of authors, and compare them to your own.

6. Be willing to work with groups and discuss your ideas about what you have read.

7. Learn how to select reading materials that interest you.

8. Remember courtesy. Do not disturb others.

9. Do not do homework for other classes in reading workshop.

10. Expect that you will enjoy reading (even if you haven't before). If you are serious about reading, you will find books that thrill, fascinate, and interest you.

11. Accept the responsibility for completing assigned work and doing your best on tests and other forms of evaluation.

Reading Self-appraisal

Please answer the following questions. The information will help me to make this reading workshop more interesting and meaningful to you. (Use the back of this sheet if you need more room.)

1. Do you like to read? _____ Why or why not? _____

_____

_____

2. Check the types of materials you enjoy reading.

Novels _____ Short Stories _____ Magazines _____ Comics _____

Nonfiction books _____ Newspapers _____ Poetry _____

3. What is your favorite book? _____

Why is this your favorite? _____

_____

_____

_____

_____

_____

4. Who are your favorite authors? _____

_____

_____

What books written by them have you read? _____

_____

_____

5. Do you read mostly for pleasure or because you have to? _____

_____

6. Do you like poetry? _____ Do you have a favorite poet? _____ Who is he or she? _____

Why do you like this author's poetry? _____

_____

7. How many books did you read last year? _____

8. What kinds of books would you like to read in reading workshop? _____

_____

Promoting a
Positive Atmosphere in
Your Reading Workshop

You can promote a positive atmosphere in your reading workshop by doing the following:

- Make reading the priority of your classroom. Encourage reading. Provide time for reading.

- Make a variety of reading materials available.

- Make sure students understand their responsibilities.

- Encourage students to accept the responsibility for their learning.

- Establish and maintain effective routines. Remind students of the proper classroom procedures as necessary.

- Set and enforce clear standards of behavior.

- Model appropriate behavior in the reading workshop.

- Make sure students understand how they will be evaluated.

- Value everyone's opinion.

- Promote cooperation and the sharing of ideas.

- Read with and to your students, sharing your pleasure in reading.

- Maintain a belief that all students in your class can learn to read and express their ideas.

- Accept that learning is individual and that students will progress at their own rates.

- Make reading meaningful and demonstrate it to be an important part of life.

- Promote reading through special displays, events, and programs.

If you have a relatively small number of students and plenty of space, you can turn your classroom into a wonderful workshop. In a back corner you might set up a table and chairs for group meetings. In another corner, a few beanbags can make a fine silent reading niche, while other sections of the room may contain book shelves or newspaper and magazine racks.

Whatever type of classroom you have, fill it with as many materials for reading as you can. Make available as many books, magazines, and newspapers as possible; cover bulletin boards with information and posters about reading; and set up displays that highlight specific books and authors. Words should be everywhere.

Without question, some rooms and teaching schedules are easier to adapt to a reading workshop than others. However, with a little thought and effort, virtually all can be. It's not the physical arrangement that determines the true quality of a reading workshop, but the atmosphere and content of the class.

ORGANIZING YOUR DAY

Whether you are teaching in a situation where you have separate classes for reading, or must teach reading in combination with English, covering such subjects as writing and grammar, organizing your day effectively will result in a successful workshop. Obviously, if you teach only reading classes, your planning will be simpler. You can commit each class period entirely to reading and reading-related activities.

However, if your curriculum requires that you teach both reading and English in the same period that meets five times per week, you might decide to meet for reading workshop three times per week—perhaps Monday, Tuesday, and Thursday, or Monday, Wednesday, and Friday—and teach English skills on the other days. Of course, many of these skills overlap and you will be able to refer to them in either reading or English class. Reading and writing, for example, are closely related. When students are learning about theme in reading, that knowledge can be easily transferred to their writing assignments. Such overlap makes it easier to cover and reinforce skills throughout the year.

Another schedule you might use if you teach reading and English is to alternate units on reading and other course requirements. In this plan, you might read a novel, then do a two-week unit on subjects and predicates. Alternating reading and English requirements allows you uninterrupted time spans that provide continuity.

In many schools where reading and English are taught in separate classes, teachers enjoy the luxury of double periods. Double periods are ideal for teaching reading and English because they allow plenty of flexibility and time to concentrate on in-depth activities. If you teach reading and English to the same students in separate classes, a schedule allowing for back-to-back periods is a goal you should work to achieve.

Whichever schedule you use, provide a big chunk of time for reading during class. Unless students have time to read in school, they may not have the time at all. I like to set aside about half of the period for students to actually read and work on reading activities. That still gives me enough time to teach a mini-lesson, confer with individual students, and conduct a discussion, either with the whole class or through groups. Following is a sample breakdown of a 48-minute reading class period:

2 minutes—Students come to class and get ready to work.

8 minutes—Teacher offers a mini-lesson on plot, linking it to the novel students are currently reading.

25 minutes—Students read independently, write answers to questions the teacher assigned, or write reactions to their reading in reading logs. This is also a time individuals may quietly confer with the teacher.

10 minutes—Class discussion conducted by teacher (or students might assemble in prearranged groups for discussion of recently read material).

3 minutes—Closure and preparation to leave class.

The activities and times in the above example can be changed to fit your class's needs. For example, during the reading time, some teachers prefer that the room is silent, and everyone, including the teacher, reads. In other reading workshops, this time is spent with students reading independently, completing activities related to their reading, and writing in reading logs. The teacher may meet quietly with individuals or small groups to discuss the assigned reading, reteach a mini-lesson, or simply provide guidance.

As you plan your schedule, you should also allow time for reading-related activities and individual and group sharing. For example, there may be days when, after you complete your mini-lesson, the rest of the period is spent with a whole-class discussion of a book, sharing the results of group projects, or the completion of a special activity.

Effective time management is an important factor underlying the success of your class. Some reading workshops are tightly structured while others are forums in which different activities are going on at the same time. Your schedule and the routines and procedures you develop for your reading workshop should reflect your expectations as well as the needs of your students.

TEACHING METHODS IN THE READING WORKSHOP

Teachers utilize various methods for reading instruction. Most of these instructional strategies fall under the general category of guided reading, and virtually all work well in the reading workshop. During guided reading the teacher "guides" students—the entire class, groups of students, or individuals—through a variety of activities designed to help them find meaning in what they read, discover the author's purpose, and draw conclusions. Guided reading, in its many forms, is a major component of the reading workshop.

If you utilize whole-class guided reading in its purest form, all students will be reading the same material at the same time. Students will participate in the same activities, and discussions will involve everyone. Your teaching methods will likely include giving reading assignments, posing questions to be answered in reading logs, leading discussions, and using the mini-lessons of Part II of this book to teach or reinforce skills. Whole-class guided reading provides a teacher with more control and makes any class more manageable.

In small-group guided reading, students work primarily in groups. The groups in your class may all be reading the same book, or they might be reading different books. Although they may read and answer questions independently, discussions and other activities are conducted in the groups. If you rely on small-group guided reading, you would tailor your teaching and mini-lessons to each group.

Small-group guided reading offers several benefits. When students meet in groups to discuss their reading, discussions become shaped by the knowledge, attitudes, and needs of the group members. While all groups may start with the same topic, their analyses and conclusions may be quite different. Moreover, small-group guided reading enables you to respond to the needs of groups and individual students efficiently. If one group is having trouble understanding the theme of a story, you might sit in on their meeting and discuss theme in detail. Groups that understand theme might move on to other topics. Still another advantage of small discussion groups is the feeling of safety they provide. Some students, particularly shy ones, are often reluctant to offer their opinions and ideas to the whole class. Such students may be more willing to share their ideas in a small group, which they find less threatening. Finally, because groups are small, individual members have a greater opportunity to share their ideas.

Individual guided reading is another instructional method you might use in your reading workshop. In this program, students choose their own books and read at their own pace. Much of the monitoring of the student's progress is done through conferencing with the teacher. The teacher may guide the student by asking questions, offering reading strategies, and engaging in discussion according to the student's needs. Mini-lessons can be presented to the entire class. Even though the skills of the mini-lessons may not apply directly to what each student is currently reading, in time the skills will build into an impressive collection of information and be drawn upon as needed.

Individualized reading programs have both major benefits and potentially serious drawbacks. Perhaps the greatest advantage is that students may take greater responsibility for their reading and select books that truly interest them. In an individualized program good readers frequently seize the chance to devour books; they are not held back by slower readers or the curriculum.

Unfortunately, individualized reading programs are difficult to control. Reluctant readers may be hard to monitor, for the teacher is often under pressure to meet with all of his or her students in a timely manner. Also, because the teacher is dealing with so many books, it is impossible to be familiar with all of them, thus minimizing the effectiveness of instruction. Finally, if students are permitted to select their own books, they may choose books whose literary merit is questionable, or they may continually choose the same type of books. Think of the student who only wants to read gory horror stories or the student who hungers for one romance after another.

Many teachers rely on a combination of whole-class and small-group instruction in the reading workshop. This gives them various teaching options to cover material in fresh and stimulating ways. It also gives students the chance to interact as a class, while providing for the intimacy of group work. Choose the method or methods with which you feel most comfortable and you feel will be most beneficial to your students. Each method will provide your students with valuable reading experiences.

READING LOGS

An important part of the reading workshop is the reading log. Known by a variety of names—literature journals, response logs, and reading journals are just some—reading logs serve many purposes. Logs are a place students may record their reactions to reading. In their logs they may answer questions, make notes, write about their feelings or opinions, or include questions of their own about what they read. Because reading logs contain the responses and notes of students, they are essential to discussions and group meetings.

Reading logs can take many forms. While spiral notebooks work well for most classes, sections of three-ring binders, booklets, or sheets of composition paper stapled together to make a booklet are adequate. I instruct my students to use their reading logs only for reading. When making entries, they are to date and label their work, for example, Oct. 1, 1997, Ch. 4. If a student fills one notebook, he or she should number each additional one successively. This makes it easier to keep the logs in order.

Although the logs are primarily for the students, I collect them periodically, usually taking ten to twelve at a time. Reading some each day enables me to keep up with the students without making me feel overwhelmed. I don't grade logs, or correct grammar, spelling, or punctuation. (Grades are derived from other sources. See Chapter 3, "Evaluation.") If the logs are graded, many students start writing what they think will earn better grades—translated to what they think I want them to write—rather than offering their actual reactions to their reading. When students feel free to share their thoughts, they are more likely to analyze what they read more closely and take risks with their conclusions. You might wish to distribute and discuss copies of "Reading Log Guidelines" with your students. The sheet highlights important points about maintaining reading logs.

While reading logs may be used as a place for students to answer rather straightforward comprehension questions about their reading, they are ideal instruments for helping students to examine important issues or complex questions, especially open-ended questions whose answers depend on higher-level skills. Used properly, reading logs can help students react critically to what they read.

Presenting students with questions that require them to interpret and apply information stimulates them to go beyond reading for mere details to an in-depth analysis of meaning. A good time to do this is during the beginning of class, right after your mini-lesson. Present students with a question tied directly to their reading assignment, and instruct them to answer it in their reading logs. Encourage them to support their ideas with specific examples from their reading. Such questions can be a springboard for discussion or further activities. When students attempt to answer questions in their reading logs first, they come to discussions better prepared to talk about the situation, problem, or issue. For a list of higher-level questions for reading logs, see "Possible Questions for Reading Logs."

Reading Log Guidelines

1. Use a standard spiral notebook for your reading log. Put your name on it. Number your logs.

2. Bring your reading log to class each day.

3. Use your reading log only for reading workshop. Don't use it for other subjects.

4. Feel free to read at home and enter your reactions to your reading in your log.

5. Start entries for each book, article, short story, or poem on a new page. Keep your entries in order.

6. Date and label your entries. For example: Oct. 1, 1997, Ch. 4.

7. While you will answer questions in your log that I assign to your reading, you may also write about your ideas and opinions.

8. Always back up your ideas and opinions with facts. Cite specific page numbers.

9. Note that I will read your logs periodically. While I will not grade them, I may offer comments and suggestions. If you want, write brief notes to me in your log. I will respond and we can carry on a dialogue about your reading.

10. While I will respect the privacy of your ideas and opinions, remember that if I read something in your log that I feel endangers you or someone else, I must report it.

11. Be willing to share the ideas you record in your logs with your group and class.

12. Periodically review your log and see how you are growing as a reader.

Possible Questions for Reading Logs

Open-ended questions that require students to use higher-level skills such as interpretation and application are excellent for reading logs. You may use the following as they are, or as guides to write questions of your own.

Questions for fiction:

- What techniques does the author use to create a feeling of gloom and suspense in this chapter?

- What do you think the author's purpose was in writing this story? How has he or she changed your thinking about the subject?

- What were your emotions as you read this chapter? Why did you feel this way?

- What clues did the author offer to help you solve the mystery?

- How does the author's use of language, especially in dialogue, help to make this story realistic?

- How does the author show his or her characters to be individuals? What is unique about each one?

- Who is the point-of-view character in this story? How would the story change if the author used another character's point of view?

- How do the lead characters change in this story?

Questions for nonfiction:

- How did the author's style of writing help or hinder this work?

- How could you apply what you learned to your own life?

- If you had the opportunity, what questions would you ask the author about this topic?

- Did you find the author's arguments persuasive? Why or why not?

Reading logs are storehouses of students' reactions to what they read. At the end of the year, logs provide a detailed and interesting account of your students' reading experiences.

STRATEGIES TO ORGANIZE DISCUSSION GROUPS

Throughout the year you may wish to group students for discussion or cooperative activities. Unless you are faced with special circumstances, you should organize your groups by mixing abilities, genders, and ethnicities whenever possible.

For discussing reading, groups of five to eight work best. Less than five reduces the input for the discussion (especially if some students are absent), while more than eight can make a group unwieldy. Also, if you need to move furniture around, groups of more than eight can plunge you into a logistical nightmare of colliding tables, crashing desks, and overturned chairs.

The most effective groups tend to be those made randomly. A simple way to create groups is to count down the names in your roster (provided your roster is mixed between boys and girls). If you want to have six students in a group, the first six students are group one, the second six are group two, and so on. No matter how you organize groups, always reserve the right to adjust them when you feel necessary. For example, avoid placing a shy, "quiet" student in a group with four or five strong, opinionated personalities. Likewise, having too many exuberant individuals in a group can result in a free-for-all where everyone becomes more concerned with announcing his or her ideas than with what is being said. You should always avoid disruptive combinations. As the year goes on and you get to know your students, you'll know which combinations have trouble working together and you will be able to organize groups more effectively.

Be sure to rearrange your groups regularly, after every novel or unit, or every few weeks at the most. This gives students a chance to work with others whose personalities and viewpoints may be different from their own. In real life when people work in groups, personalities vary, and by allowing for this in your class you will be helping students to acquire skills that will serve them well throughout their lives. When it comes time to rearrange groups, you might rotate two or three students from one group to another. This reduces the time necessary for forming new groups.

INCORPORATING DISCUSSION GROUPS IN YOUR READING WORKSHOP

Discussion groups provide an excellent way for students to share their reactions about reading, and they are an important element of an effective reading workshop. The discussion group gives students a chance to share their ideas and opinions about reading.

In the beginning of the year, you will likely need to guide your groups and model appropriate group behavior. Unless students have participated in discussion groups before, they will probably have little idea of what is expected of them. As your students become more experienced with discussion groups, you may fade to the background and allow them to take over management of the group. Your role then becomes that of being an observer, who occasionally offers input or asks questions to help students gain a better understanding of their reading. You may wish to distribute and talk about "Discussion Group Guidelines," which highlights some of the important elements of effective discussion groups.

There are many ways to incorporate discussion groups in the reading workshop. You may have one group meet at a time (during which other students read and work quietly at their seats), or have all groups meet simultaneously. Depending on your schedule, the material students are reading, and the needs of your students, discussion groups may meet often, two or three times per week, once a week, or once every several days. Groups should meet only when the material they are reading warrants a discussion. If groups meet when they don't have a meaningful topic to discuss, the discussion will usually drift from that of the reading to the latest school gossip.

For the first few meetings, it is usually better to have one group meet at a time. This gives you a chance to sit in on it, offer guidance, and model appropriate behavior. After students understand the purpose and procedures of a discussion group, you may have all your groups meet at the same time. You would then circulate from group to group, monitoring the discussions and providing guidance as needed.

To facilitate a group's efficiency, you might assign specific tasks to students. One student might be the *Team Leader,* who has the responsibility of keeping the group focused on the discussion question; another student might be the *Recorder,* whose duty is to write down the ideas discussed by the group; a third student might be designated as *Spokesperson,* whose job is to share the group's opinions with other groups. These jobs should be rotated after every few meetings so that each member gets a chance to share in the responsibility for managing the group.

Some teachers prefer to utilize both group and whole-class discussions. Students may meet mostly in groups, but periodically the whole class takes part in a discussion about major events or issues in the book they are reading.

Unless your students are able to generate their own topics for discussion (after becoming comfortable with the procedures of your reading workshop, some students are quite capable of this), you will need to present them with discussion topics. You should develop questions around major themes and topics that give students the opportunity to draw upon material from their reading as well as their own values and experiences. While questions regarding theme, plot, characterization, and author's purpose often are good starting points for discussion groups, the best questions are those that require analysis and synthesis of ideas. The following are examples of group discussion questions. Note that they apply to specific novels.

- *Homecoming* **by Cynthia Voigt:** Dicey's "family" is quite different from the "typical" American family. With your group, decide how you would describe the "typical" American family today, and compare and contrast Dicey's "family" with it. Cite specific examples from the book to support your ideas.
- *The Outsiders* **by S.E. Hinton:** How has Ponyboy changed throughout the story? How is he different at the end of the story from the way he was at the beginning? Be sure to provide specific examples to support your conclusions.

Discussion Group Guidelines

Throughout this year you will be meeting in discussion groups where you will share your ideas and opinions about what you have read. The following guidelines will help your group to be successful.

1. Remember that the purpose of your group is to share your reactions and opinions about reading. Your discussion should remain focused on your topic.

2. Always bring your book and any notes to the group meeting.

3. Work together with other group members and strive to discover meaning in what you read.

4. Always be polite and considerate. Use your normal speaking voice.

5. Maintain an orderly discussion. While it is not necessary to raise your hand, you should not interrupt others or call out when you don't have the floor.

6. Speak clearly, and be ready to answer questions about your ideas.

7. Support your ideas with facts and specific examples from your reading. It's a good idea to write down page numbers of specific examples and bring them to the group.

8. After you have spoken, be willing to let others speak.

9. To help express your ideas clearly, use phrases like the following to start your statements:

   —I agree with you because . . .

   —I don't agree with that because . . .

   —I'm not clear about what you're saying . . .

   —I'm not sure about that, because . . .

   —In my opinion . . .

- ***The Contender* by Robert Lipsyte:** The title of the story has the obvious meaning of boxers "contending" in the boxing ring. How might the title also be applied to life? Back up your conclusions with examples from the book.

- ***A Separate Peace* by John Knowles:** Why do you think Knowles titled this book *A Separate Peace*? Give reasons for your opinion.

- ***I Know Why the Caged Bird Sings* by Maya Angelou:** Why do you think Maya Angelou wrote this book? Explain your reasons fully.

- ***The Pearl* by John Steinbeck:** What is the moral or lesson of this story? Use examples from the story to support your answer.

- ***The House on Mango Street* by Sandra Cisneros:** Describe Esperanza. Do you believe she is a keen observer of her world? Explain, using examples from the book to support your conclusions.

The average length of time for a discussion group to meet is about 10 to 15 minutes. If you go much beyond that, the group risks losing its focus. Sometimes, the topic a group addresses will require more than one session. That's fine. Suggest that the group's recorder write down what the group has covered so that the discussion can resume during the next class meeting. You might have groups discuss a topic one day, and report their conclusions to the class the next.

Having groups offer their conclusions to the rest of the class is a powerful method for sharing ideas. Because they tie into major issues, many discussion questions will have several possible answers based upon the experiences, values, and opinions of group members. Providing time for groups to share their ideas gives students a chance to see other views of the same question. Such exposure to new ideas often results in a reassessment of an individual's ideas, leading in turn to better understanding of a problem or issue.

As students gain confidence and learn the behaviors that will result in effective discussion groups, the quality of their discussions will improve, evolving from focus on the obvious literal elements of stories to the examination and interpretation of ideas. Students will begin making connections between their reading and their lives.

A FINAL WORD

A successful reading workshop in which students read a variety of materials and share their opinions and ideas about reading is generally a clear reflection of the management skills of the teacher. The importance of effective management to your reading workshop can't be overstated. Management is often the crucial difference between mediocre reading workshops and those that offer students reading experiences that help them to master essential reading skills and grow in their understanding of life.

Chapter 3

Evaluation

Evaluation can take many forms in your reading workshop. Tests, daily logs based on observation, reading conferences, portfolios, and completion of specific activities, reports, and projects are just some of the tools that can provide you with valuable information on how well your students are mastering the skills necessary for competent reading.

No matter which types of evaluative methods you select, they should be fair, have clear expectations, and note the growth, strengths, and weaknesses of students. Rather than focusing on the negative—what a student doesn't know—evaluation should focus on the student's overall progress and achievement.

READING TESTS

For most teachers, tests are a fundamental method of evaluation. Even if you may not feel that tests provide accurate measurements of student growth, your school district probably requires testing to help determine grades. When designed and administered properly, tests can be useful for evaluating the achievement of most students.

Your tests should be based upon the material that has been covered, as well as the abilities of your students. A typical, well-conceived reading test usually is a combination of fact-related questions—multiple choice, true/false, matching, and short answer—and open-ended essays that require students to use higher-level thinking skills in composing their answers. The best tests are weighted more heavily toward higher-level skills. When announcing an upcoming test, always explain what it will include so that students may be able to prepare for it.

If various groups of students in your workshop are reading the same material but at different times, you will need to develop a series of tests, one for each group. This will eliminate the potential problem of students from the first group telling others about specific questions on the test. While you should test the same skills and concepts, you should vary the format and questions enough so that no one has an advantage.

Although tests have drawbacks—some students just don't perform well on them—for most students tests can be solid indicators of progress. Tests can be important evaluative tools in your reading workshop.

DAILY LOGS OF STUDENT PERFORMANCE

Daily logs can also be an excellent instrument for evaluation. Attempting to write an accurate account of each student's daily performance in your class, however, can become a nightmare of clerical drudgery. Despite the best of intentions and efforts, many teachers who begin keeping daily logs eventually abandon them.

The key to maintaining daily logs is a system that is efficient, accurate, and manageable. You can create a log book for each of your classes by simply writing the title "Student Daily Log" on the top of a blank sheet of paper. Mark a spot for the name of the student at the top and photocopy as many sheets as needed, providing a sheet for each student. Storing the sets of log sheets for each class alphabetically in separate sections of a three-ring binder makes them readily accessible. Some teachers find it easier to use small, single binders for each class. Using binders of different colors makes class identification simple.

When you meet with a class, take its log sheets from the binder and put them on a clipboard. Carry the clipboard with you as you circulate around the room and work with individual students and groups. (If you have small binders for each class, you may prefer to keep the binder with you instead of using a clipboard.) Date your entries, and write brief notes describing the progress of students on their individual sheets. Be specific in your descriptions and try to focus on attitudes, actions, and outcomes that show the student's progress (or lack of it). If you write concisely, you will seldom use more than a few sheets for each student per marking period. Note the following sample entries:

4/19—Completed reading ch. 7; wrote opinion in log analyzing author's use of symbolism.
4/20—Met with group to discuss symbolism. Acted as group recorder.

These entries—which can be easily made while you are interacting with your students—show that this student is spending her class time productively. By the end of the marking period, such entries will create an impressive amount of anecdotal evidence detailing her progress.

The ideal, of course, is that you write descriptions like this for every student, every day. The reality is that you may not have enough time.

To cope with time constraints, some teachers focus their observation and record entries for five to ten students per class each day. The next day they would concentrate on other students. Of course, instances of exceptional work or a lack of progress on the part of any student should always be noted.

Another way to manage the problem of insufficient time for recording the daily performance of students is to let students log their own progress. Instead of you writing down what students are doing each day, have students keep their log sheets and record for themselves what they have accomplished. Given this responsibility, most students will record their activities honestly and correctly.

For those inclined to "fudge" a little, your circulation around the room is a strong encourager for accuracy. During class be aware of what students are doing and what they have written on their log sheets. If you find that students are not recording what you see, discuss your concerns with them.

If you permit your students to maintain logs of their class performance, you will need to work closely with them at the beginning of the year, informing them of the types of behaviors you will be looking for and showing them how to make accurate log entries. You should also collect their log sheets regularly, once every week or two. Not only does this encourage them to keep their logs up to date, but it enables you to review the logs and monitor their progress more closely. Having students record their own accomplishments frees you to work with groups and individuals on the mastery of reading skills.

Merely suggesting keeping daily logs of student performance to some teachers brings the immediate reply that logs are too time-consuming. Certainly, when logs are not managed efficiently, they can become overwhelming. However, when implemented in an effective manner, daily logs can provide consistent and detailed evidence of a student's progress in your class. Logs can also be the solid basis for scores for daily work that may be used in the determination of grades.

READING CONFERENCES

During your reading workshop, one of your most important tasks will be to meet with individuals and groups for conferences about reading. A reading conference need not be formal or long—sometimes a minute or two is enough—and it may take place at your desk, the student's desk, or a group's table. Conferences enable you and students to talk about reading in a manner that addresses their needs.

As you move around the room during your reading workshop, you will meet and speak with students. These meetings may turn in to conferences in which you pose questions, help them to master a skill, or discuss an issue with which students are having trouble. In some cases you might find that several students are having trouble with a particular aspect of a story, and you might address the problem through a mini-lesson designed for them. Some teachers set aside specific times for reading conferences, for example, scheduling a meeting with every student every few weeks or at least at the end of the marking period, while others prefer to utilize conferences as they are needed. Some teachers combine the plans, meeting as necessary throughout the marking period and scheduling a conference near the end in which overall progress throughout the marking period may be discussed.

Conferences provide you with an excellent opportunity to monitor and evaluate the growth of your students. As you speak with them, note clues that offer evidence of their strengths and weaknesses. Use conferences as a time to get to know your students as individuals and respond to their needs as readers.

Students will often initiate a conference by asking you a question. Sometimes the question is a simple one, perhaps about procedure, but sometimes it may reveal an underlying weak skill or confusion about reading that undermines comprehension. If this is the case, focus the conference on strengthening that skill and clarifying any confusion. It is best to limit a conference to one or two topics. Trying to do too much can overwhelm students and discourage them.

The most successful conferences are those that occur within an atmosphere of openness, support, and cooperation where students feel comfortable enough to discuss their problems in reading and work with you to solve them.

While some students will initiate a conference by asking a question, there will be students who, because of shyness or disinterest, will never raise a hand for help. You must seek out these students and talk with them about their work. Ask questions about their reading that requires them to give explanations. By drawing them out you will be more likely to uncover areas in which they need help. You can then direct the conference to address those areas.

Conferences provide a marvelous opportunity for you and your students to discuss reading. They are a powerful tool for evaluation.

PORTFOLIOS

During the past few years portfolios of students' work have become popular tools for evaluation. A portfolio is a collection of a student's work showing the student's achievement. You may compare it to an artist's portfolio that contains samples of pictures and drawings, but in this case the portfolio contains examples of reading work. Portfolios may include tests, book reports, research reports, special projects, and examples of daily work that show how students have mastered reading skills and class objectives.

For the actual portfolio, a large folder or envelope is useful. You may store the portfolios in boxes (organized alphabetically by class), or permit students to keep them. Allowing students to keep and maintain their portfolios not only relieves you of the task of storage but also the need to arrange access to the portfolios. Some teachers provide students with a list of work that should go in the portfolio, while others let students pick what they feel best highlights their achievement. A nice touch is to have students write an introduction and maintain a table of contents for their portfolios.

You should provide students with guidelines that highlight the criteria you will use in evaluating their portfolios. Criteria for evaluation should be based on your objectives for your students, and might include items like the following:

- Evidence of comprehension
- Evidence that indicates the understanding of specific concepts or issues
- The ability to analyze and organize information
- The ability to interpret information and draw conclusions
- The ability to support conclusions
- The ability to explain conclusions in writing
- Evidence of critical thinking
- Evidence of enthusiasm for reading

Because the greatest value in portfolios lies in their periodic review, you should set aside time throughout the year and check their portfolios with your students. Look for evidence of student growth and mastery of the class objectives. You may select work from portfolios that then becomes the basis for grades.

Over the course of the year, portfolios become an excellent means through which long-term growth can be examined and validated. Along with providing material for evaluation, portfolios offer students, teachers, parents, and administrators first-hand examples of student progress.

REPORTS, PROJECTS, AND SPECIAL ACTIVITIES

The reading workshop provides much flexibility for evaluation, and you may use various types of reports, projects, and special activities to assess your students' learning. Some teachers like to assign periodic book reports, some require research papers on a topic in literature, while others assign group projects in which students work together on a complex activity, for example, a debate over an issue brought out in their reading. These instruments can show student achievement as well as pinpoint areas in which students may need additional work.

An often overlooked method of evaluation focuses on the amount and quality of reading students do in your workshop. As students become accustomed to your reading workshop, many will begin reading more. Along with reading in school, they will read books outside of class. You will probably want to keep a record of these books, as well as give credit for your students' efforts.

A simple way to do this is to have them write summaries of the books they read. The "Book Summary Sheet" is useful for this. Make copies of the sheet available so that students have a ready supply and may take them as needed. When first explaining the summary sheet to your students, be sure to note that it is a guide and that not every question may pertain to their books. For example, question 4, which deals with characterization, will not apply to nonfiction titles. I also remind my students to select books that are on their "level." While I don't mind students reading challenging material, I discourage them from reading books several grade levels below their abilities. I explain that there is little purpose in reading "easy" books that won't hold their interest or strengthen their reading skills.

Summaries of books students read on their own are useful to you in many ways. They are evidence of work students have completed outside of class. Based on the quality of the summary, in most cases, you can tell if students truly understood and mastered the book (even if you are unfamiliar with it). Summaries may be graded, and may also be placed in portfolios as examples of student work.

Various types of evaluation are compatible with the concept of the reading workshop. You should select the methods that support your curriculum, satisfy your objectives for your classes, and meet the needs of your students.

GRADES IN THE READING WORKSHOP

No matter which methods of evaluation you use in your reading workshop, you will probably need to put grades on report cards. While the most common grading systems are based on percentages or an accumulation of points, just about any system can be used for the reading workshop.

Book Summary Sheet

Following are guidelines for writing a summary of the books you read.

1. At the top of the summary page, write your name, date, and class.

2. Write the title of the book, the author's name, publisher, place of publication, and date of publication.

   Answer the following questions. (Note: Not all questions may apply to your book.)

3. What is this book about? (For fiction, tell about the plot, including the central conflict. For nonfiction, tell about the book's major ideas.)

4. Describe the main characters. How did the characters change as the story went on? Which character did you find to be most interesting? Why?

5. Describe the setting.

6. What, if anything, did you learn from this book?

7. Did this book keep you interested? Why or why not?

8. What did you like most about this book? What did you like the least? Explain.

9. Would you like to read another book written by this author? Why or why not?

10. Would you recommend this book to others? Why or why not?

If you prefer to use percentages, you would determine grades from among your students' tests, projects, reports, research papers, and class participation. After identifying which components you will use for determining grades, you would decide how much of the total grade each component is worth. Some teachers break the percentages down into thirds: tests, reports and/or projects, and daily effort each count one-third of the student's total grade. Other teachers prefer grading systems that are more broad. Following is one that focuses on five components:

Tests—30%

Quizzes—20%

Reports—15%

Projects—15%

Daily Effort—20%

Such breakdowns can be adjusted, and you should develop a grading plan that satisfies the requirements of your curriculum and your objectives for your classes.

An alternative to a grading policy based on percentages is the point system. In this system, specific activities account for a certain number of points. The total points a student amasses during a marking period would correspond to a value on the report card. For example, reading a book might be worth 10 points; a satisfactory research project might be worth 20; a particular test average might be worth 15; and satisfactory class activities might be worth 15. Point systems may be set up to meet the needs of any classroom.

Whichever method you choose to determine grades, be sure to explain its requirements to your students. Only when students understand how they will be evaluated and graded are they able to make the appropriate effort to do well.

You should also consider explaining your grading policy to parents. Those parents not familiar with a reading workshop may feel uncomfortable unless they know what it is and what is expected of their children. You might explain your grading policy at back-to-school night and conferences with parents. You might also consider writing a brief description of your reading workshop, its expectations, and grading policy, and send copies home to parents at the beginning of the year. This helps to reduce any confusion and unwarranted concerns.

SELF-EVALUATION FOR TEACHERS

Because reading workshops vary in their structure, taking a form that best meets the needs of students and their teacher, you will find it helpful to evaluate how well your workshop is operating. Evaluating your workshop once or twice a year (at the mid-point and/or end) is a good way to review its effectiveness and determine if you have achieved the goals you have set for your classes.

Look upon self-evaluation as a means to improvement. By examining your attitudes, teaching techniques, and the procedures you have established in your reading workshop, you may identify areas that you can enhance to make your workshop even better than it is. Responding to the "Self-evaluation Questions for

Teachers" can help you analyze your reading workshop, and adjust your teaching strategies and methods as you feel necessary. The goal of your self-evaluation should be to grow in your teaching abilities and make your reading workshop exciting and challenging to your students.

A FINAL WORD

Evaluating a student's ability to read can be difficult, because many of the tools teachers use in evaluation are subjective. While test results can be useful, not all students who read proficiently do well on tests. Nevertheless, evaluation is essential in most classrooms if for no other reason than its use in the determination of grades. Achieving methods of evaluation that are fair, equitable, and consistent should be one of your priorities in developing your reading workshop. Evaluation based on specific objectives that arise from meaningful reading experiences will support your efforts to accurately measure the growth of your students. Used properly, evaluation can be an important tool as you help students master the skills needed for reading competence.

Self-evaluation Questions for Teachers

Answering the following questions can help you improve your reading workshop and make it an exciting and useful experience for your students.

- Are the procedures I have established clear, efficient, and supportive of a reading workshop? If not, how might I improve them?

- Have I provided a variety of reading materials in my reading workshop—novels, nonfiction books and articles, short stories, poetry, newspapers, plays? Am I providing meaningful material for my students to read?

- Have I made reading a priority in class?

- Have I managed to maintain a positive atmosphere in my reading workshop? How might I enhance the atmosphere for reading?

- Have I utilized the type of instruction most helpful to my students? What other types of teaching strategies might I use?

- Am I responding to the needs of my students as a class, in groups, and as individuals?

- Am I using conferences effectively?

- Do I notice enthusiasm for reading on the parts of my students? Are they reading more on their own?

- Am I providing my students with questions that focus on the higher comprehension skills of interpretation and application rather than mere literal comprehension?

- Am I supportive of the efforts of my students?

- Am I providing my students with mini-lessons that concentrate on specific skills? Do I tie those skills to what my students are reading, helping to make reading meaningful?

- Do I provide time for students to discuss their reading and share their ideas and opinions?

- Do I provide time for individual, collaborative, and cooperative reading activities?

- Are my methods of evaluation fair and consistent? Do my tests cover what I have taught?

- Have I managed to maintain effective communication with administrators, colleagues, and parents?

Part II

The Mini-lessons

The following mini-lessons are divided into three categories: (1) Types of Reading and Related Topics, (2) Story Elements, and (3) Specific Reading Skills. The lessons contain activities and reproducibles that enhance and reinforce information and skills. You should present the mini-lessons and any activities in a manner that best suits the needs of your students and satisfies the requirements of your curriculum.

The mini-lessons range from very basic to those that can be developed into great detail. Some—such as Mini-lesson 53, "What Makes a Good Lead?"—may be broken down into parts and presented in two or even three days. For example, you might offer general information about leads the first day, discuss leads for fiction on the second, and explore leads for nonfiction on the third. You have much flexibility in determining how to present the mini-lessons to your students.

Although there are 100 mini-lessons in Part II, you will likely find topics unique to your reading classes that you would like to present as mini-lessons. Many teachers, for example, offer mini-lessons about the lives of authors, highlighting the experiences of the author that may have influenced his or her writing. Feel free to use the mini-lessons of this book as guides in creating your own.

Mini-lessons
1 through 50
TYPES OF READING
AND RELATED TOPICS

MINI-LESSON 1:
FICTION AND NONFICTION

Prose can be divided into the broad categories of fiction and nonfiction. *Fiction* refers to those literary works produced by the imagination and includes novels, novellas, short stories, plays, and screenplays. *Nonfiction* is literary works that remain true to facts, and includes numerous types of books and articles such as essays, histories, biographies, autobiographies, and newspaper articles. Good readers are aware of the distinction between fiction and nonfiction, even if authors sometimes choose to blur the lines.

Procedure:

- Explain the difference between fiction and nonfiction.
- Note that stories are often based on facts. Historical fiction, for example, may depict an actual event with people who experienced the event as the characters of the story; however, many of the actions, emotions, and personalities of the characters may be the result of the author's imagination. Other stories, science fiction and fantasy, for instance, may be based on a few facts and much imagination.
- Emphasize that nonfiction depends entirely on facts, which can be verified. If any of the material is created from imagination, the piece is no longer nonfiction.

Activities:

1. Ask students to volunteer some examples of fictional and nonfictional works with which they are familiar.
2. Offer some of the books, stories, and articles students will read throughout the year as examples of fiction and nonfiction.

MINI-LESSON 2:
SHORT STORIES, NOVELLAS, AND NOVELS

Fiction may take the form of a short story, novella, or novel. The major difference between the forms is length.

Procedure:

- Explain the differences among the three forms of fiction.
  - —Short stories are short pieces of fiction, usually between 1,500 and 5,000 words. Because the author doesn't have much space to develop the story as a novel, which is much longer, the short story author often focuses on character, theme, and effect. Short stories usually center around one or two characters who face a problem in an extraordinary situation.
  - —Novellas, also known as novelettes, may be considered long short stories or short novels. They typically run between 7,000 and 15,000 words. Because they are longer than a short story, the author has the luxury to develop the story with greater detail.
  - —Novels are stories that may be several hundred pages. Many have involved plots, numerous characters, varying scenes, and significant details. Some novels have several themes.
- Point out that virtually all forms of fiction are built around plot, character, conflict, setting, and climax. Depending on the abilities of your students, you may need to explain the meanings of these terms. (Each of these elements is examined in detail via its own mini-lesson later in this book.)
- Provide examples of the three forms of fiction with the materials you use in your reading workshop.

Activities:

1. You may use this activity with either the whole class or with groups, provided students are reading the same story. Upon completion of the story, instruct students to evaluate its various elements, including character, plot, theme, setting, and conflict. To help students with their evaluations, distribute copies of Worksheet 2–1, "Evaluating Fiction." When students have finished the worksheets, conduct a discussion of the story with the entire class, or have students discuss the story in their groups. They should be prepared to give specific examples to support their views.

2. Encourage students to read a short story, novella, or novel of their choice. When they are done, have students meet in groups and share impressions of the stories they read with the other members of their group. Suggest that students concentrate on plot, theme, and characterization, citing specific examples from the story to support their ideas. They should also offer their opinion of their stories. This is an excellent way to help students become aware of good stories.

3. Select a short story to read to the class. When you read the story, be sure to add drama through inflection and tone. Afterward lead a class discussion

about its plot, theme, setting, conflict, and characters. (You may wish to read the story over the course of two or three days.)

Writing Activity:

- Instruct your students to select a character from the story they are currently reading and write a new adventure for the character. Encourage your students to concentrate on character development, plot, conflict, setting, and theme. Display the stories upon completion of the writing.

Name _____ Date _____ Section _____

Evaluating Fiction

Directions: Answer the questions below to help you analyze the story you are reading. Write your answers on another sheet of paper, and be ready to discuss your answers with your class or group.

Character:

1. Who are the main characters in the story?

2. Are the characters believable? Do they act and speak like real people? Give examples from the story.

3. Who is your favorite character? Why? Who is your least favorite? Why?

Plot:

1. What is the plot of the story?

2. Is the plot believable? Could it be improved? Explain.

Conflict:

1. What is the central conflict of the story?

2. Is the conflict strong enough to hold the reader's interest? Explain and give examples from the story.

Setting:

1. Describe the setting.

2. Is the setting realistic? Explain. What kinds of imagery words did the author use to create the setting?

Theme:

1. What is the theme of the story?

2. Does the story have more than one theme? If yes, what are they?

   What is your overall opinion of the story? Explain your answer.

MINI-LESSON 3:
THE ESSAY

The typical essay is an article in which the author discusses a specific topic. The purpose of most essays is to provide information. (Essays designed to influence or persuade readers to accept the author's position on an issue are editorials. See Mini-lesson 4.)

Procedure:

- Explain that most essays follow a general plan of introduction, body, and conclusion. The essay's main idea or purpose is stated in the introduction and explained in the body. The conclusion usually offers a final idea that supports the essay's main idea.
- Mention that good essays offer plenty of details in support of their main idea.
- Note that most essays are organized in logical patterns such as most important ideas to least important, cause and effect, or a chronological sequence.
- Also note that essays are usually written in a clear, concise style. Good essayists don't want to confuse readers with mile-long words and rambling, confusing writing.
- Mention that essays are often found in the op-ed pages of many newspapers and in many magazines.

Activities:

1. If students are currently reading an essay in class, discuss the purpose, strengths and weaknesses of the essay. You may wish to distribute Worksheet 3–1, "Essay Facts," which offers guidelines in analyzing essays. You may do this activity either with the whole class, or divide students into groups and let each group analyze the essay.

2. Instruct students to consult newspapers or magazines from home or materials in the school library. Ask them to find an example of an essay and bring it to class. (If they find an essay in the library, remind them that they will have to sign the source out. Inform the librarian ahead of time that your students will be searching for examples of essays; he or she may wish to assemble materials in advance.)

   In their groups, students should share their essays through reading and discussion, noting the main parts of the essays. The group should try to decide which essay they feel is the best. Provide time for groups to briefly report their results to the class.

Writing Activity:

- Encourage students to write an essay on a topic of their choice. Remind them to organize their essay with an opening that states the main point, a body that includes facts, explanations, and examples, and a conclusion that contains a final point or a brief summary of their main idea. Display the finished essays.

Name _____ Date _____ Section _____

Essay Facts

The typical essay is an article in which the author discusses a specific topic. Most essays are organized according to the following plan:

An *introduction* that states the main idea or purpose of the essay.

A *body* that develops the main idea with facts, details, and examples.

A *conclusion* that contains a final idea or briefly summarizes the essay's main idea.

Directions: You can use the information above to help you analyze essays. Select an essay you have read and answer the following questions. Use an additional sheet of paper if you need more space.

1. What is the purpose, or main idea, of the essay? _____

_____

_____

_____

2. What are some facts, details, or examples the author uses to support his or her ideas? _

_____

_____

_____

3. How does the author conclude the essay? _____

_____

_____

_____

4. Did you find this essay effective? Explain. _____

_____

_____

_____

_____

MINI-LESSON 4:
EDITORIALS

Editorials, sometimes referred to as persuasive or opinion essays, express an author's viewpoint about an issue or problem. (Sometimes a distinction is made between opinion and persuasive essays. In opinion essays the author attempts to convince the reader to accept his ideas, while in the persuasive essay he tries to get the reader to accept his ideas and take some form of action in support of them.) Editorials are most commonly found in newspapers and magazines in the "Letters to the Editor" pages.

Procedure:

- Explain that most editorials follow the typical essay structure of an opening, body, and conclusion.

- Note that the opening states the problem or issue and the author's position. The author develops his or her ideas in the body, offering facts, explanations, and examples. The conclusion emphasizes the main point of the editorial, and may call on the reader to take action of some sort.

- Mention that well-written editorials can be powerful tools for swaying public opinion.

Activities:

1. Working with the class as a whole, analyze an editorial students are currently reading. (You may also divide students into groups for this activity; however, then the members of each group will discuss the editorial among themselves. In this case, you may have each group report its conclusions to the class.) Discuss the purpose of the editorial, its main point, and the author's position. Examine how the author develops the essay, and decide if and how it influences the opinions of students on the topic. To help students with their evaluations, distribute copies of Worksheet 4–1, "Evaluating an Editorial."

2. Ask students to bring in an editorial page from a newspaper from home. Magazines that carry editorials may also be used. (You might ask your colleagues to bring in newspapers to make sure you have enough for your students.) Divide your students into groups, and instruct them to read and discuss the editorials. Each group may read several different pieces. They should read the editorials and analyze the effectiveness of each. Which editorial, in the group's opinion, is the strongest? Why? Provide time for groups to share their conclusions with the class. (You may also wish to hand out copies of Worksheet 4–1, which students might find helpful for this activity.)

Writing Activity:

- Ask your students to think about a problem or issue that is meaningful to them. Instruct them to research their topic, if necessary, to obtain facts and then write an editorial. To help your students generate possible ideas for topics, you may wish to conduct a class brainstorming session. Using the chalkboard or an overhead projector, ask your students to volunteer possible editorial topics. List the topics as fast as students suggest them. Don't bother expanding them; simply list them. Remind students to use an opening, body, and conclusion in writing their editorials. Upon completion of the activity, display the editorials.

Name _____ Date _____ Section _____

Evaluating an Editorial

Directions: Read the editorial you have been assigned, then analyze it by answering the questions below. Use an extra sheet of paper if you need more space for your answers.

1. Title of editorial: _____

Name of publication in which it appeared: _____

_____ Date: _____

2. What is the editorial about? _____

_____

_____

3. What is the author's position? _____

_____

4. What facts, examples, statistics, or explanations does the author use to support his or her position? _____

_____

_____

_____

5. Did the author change your opinion about the topic? Explain. _____

_____

_____

_____

_____

_____

_____

_____

_____

_____

_____

_____

_____

MINI-LESSON 5:
GENERAL INFORMATION ARTICLES

General information articles constitute a broad category, including subjects as varied as in-line skating and the latest medical breakthroughs to hot vacation spots and endangered species. Their primary purpose is to inform readers about their topic in an interesting and entertaining way.

Procedure:

* Explain that general information articles are found in countless magazines and include countless topics. Ask students if they know of any magazines that contain general information articles. Some magazines you might mention include: *Reader's Digest, Newsweek, Parade,* and *Life.*

* Explain that most general interest articles are organized in three parts: a *lead* in which the subject is presented, a *body* that provides explanations, details, and examples, and a *conclusion* that offers a final point and ties the article together.

* Note that the purpose of an informational article is to inform readers about a subject.

* Mention that the style of an informational article is based on its audience. An article written for high school students will have a different style from one written for adults.

* Explain that a special category of an informational article is the how-to article. This article explains how something can be done. Some example titles include "How to Make Homemade Pizza," "How to Get Straight A's without Trying," and "How You Can Earn Big Bucks Doing Odd Jobs." How-to articles are written in a clear, simple style in a voice that refers to the reader as "you."

Activities:

1. Prior to beginning this activity, ask students to bring in some magazines from home that contain general interest articles. You might also ask some of your colleagues to donate old magazines, or you may be able to obtain magazines from your school's library. Divide students into groups and have them review several informational articles. After reviewing the articles, students should discuss them and rank them according to quality. Distribute copies of Worksheet 5–1, "Ranking Informational Articles," to help students determine the quality of their articles. (Hand out a copy of the worksheet for each article the students will be working with.) Provide time for the groups to briefly share which articles they found to be of high quality.

2. Working individually, instruct students to select an informational article, read, and then summarize it. In their summaries they should include the topic, how the author developed the article, some facts or examples the

author included, and how he or she concluded the article. Students should also note what they learned from the article.

Writing Activity:

- Instruct students to select a topic of their choice and write an informational article. Remind them to begin their article with a strong lead, develop their topic in the body of their article, and provide a solid conclusion.

Name _____ Date _____ Section _____

Ranking Informational Articles

Directions: Answering the questions below will help you to determine the quality of an informational article. Use another sheet of paper if you need more space.

Title of Article: _____

_____

Publication: _____

Date: _____

1. Describe what the article was about. _____

_____

_____

_____

_____

_____

_____

_____

2. Did the article have an interesting lead? _____
Why or why not? _____

_____

3. Did the author use facts, details, or examples in the article? _____ Was the information he or she presented clear? _____ Explain. _____

_____

_____

4. Did the article have a strong conclusion? _____
Explain. _____

_____

_____

5. With 10 being the highest, how would you rate this article from 1 to 10? _____

MINI-LESSON 6:
NEWSPAPER ARTICLES

Newspapers offer a variety of articles, from straight news to comic strips. Despite the competition from TV, radios, and online news services, newspapers remain a major source of information. Some newspapers are written for a specific audience. *The Wall Street Journal,* for example, is a national newspaper written for businesspeople. Local papers are usually aimed at the people who live in particular towns. Other newspapers are written to appeal to general audiences across major regions, while some, like *USA Today,* are written for the entire country.

- Explain that most newspaper articles, especially straight news, are organized in an inverted pyramid. In this format, the most important information comes first. This allows busy readers—who may be scanning the paper at breakfast, or be on a commuter train to work—the opportunity to gain information by reading the first few paragraphs of articles. The structure of the inverted pyramid also permits editors to easily cut the final few paragraphs from articles if space becomes limited.

- Note that the lead of a newspaper article is crucial because it contains the most important information.

- Explain that the typical newspaper article is developed around the five W's and How.

  —Who is the article about?

  —When did the event happen?

  —Where did the event occur?

  —What happened?

  —Why did it happen?

  —How did it happen?

- Emphasize that the answers to these questions are usually contained in the lead or the first few paragraphs of the article.

- Note that most major newspapers have several different sections, including national news, local news, the financial section, fashion, TV and movie listings, sports, obituaries, comics, and classifieds.

- Mention that good newspaper writing is clear and concise and as objective as possible. Reporters should not include their feelings when reporting events.

Activities:

1. Ask students to bring newspapers from home to class. To ensure you have enough copies of newspapers, ask your colleagues to bring in some, too. Instruct your students to look through the newspapers they have and identify some of the different parts: main news, local news, sports, business (or financial section), fashion, TV and movie listings, entertainment section, various columns, comics, obituaries, and classified sections. Discuss the general content of the various sections. This activity will help to familiarize students with the many parts of newspapers.

2. This activity is designed for students working in groups. Each group will need at least one copy of a newspaper. With students working in their groups, instruct them to select three to five newspaper articles per group, read and analyze the articles, and decide if the articles answer the five W's and How. Allow time for each group to present its findings to the class. They will likely find that most articles use the inverted pyramid for organization. You may wish to distribute copies of Worksheet 6–1, "Analyzing a Newspaper Article," to help them in their efforts.

Writing Activity:

- Have your students write newspaper articles and publish them in a class newspaper. While students may create excellent newspapers in long-hand and line drawings, the use of computers and printers can help them to produce truly outstanding work. Most word-processing software offers a variety of fonts, print sizes, and clip-art that can be used to produce classroom newspapers of high quality. Following are some suggestions that will help you to make this an exciting and worthwhile activity.

  —If your students have a different teacher for English, you may wish to coordinate this project with him or her. Combining your skills and resources can result in an outstanding newspaper.

  —If you have access to a computer room in your school, consider reserving time for your students to write their articles on the equipment.

  —Before announcing the activity to your students, consider the types and lengths of articles you will accept. You may prefer that students do articles about local or school events, or you may permit them to write about any newsworthy topic. Tell students to keep the articles rather short, especially if this is the first time you are working on a class newspaper. This makes it easier for students to manage the organization of a newspaper article and also permits you to print more articles in a limited amount of space.

  —When you introduce this activity to your students, explain that they are to select a newsworthy event and write a newspaper article about it. Emphasize that their finished articles will be printed as a class newspaper.

  —Remind them to use the structure of the inverted pyramid. If they are writing about events that have occurred at school, they may be able to interview people and obtain quotes. Caution them that if they use the words of others, they should quote the individuals accurately.

  —If you are able to use word processors for writing the articles, add headlines to make your paper more attractive. You may also wish to add clip-art.

  —Upon completion of the writing, collect the articles and publish them in a class newspaper. Publishing may be done on a photocopier. Printing pages on both sides will save paper and result in a newspaper that looks more realistic. Produce enough copies for the class, as well as other students and faculty members.

  —Distribute copies to the students. You may also wish to display some copies in the school media center.

Name _____ Date _____ Section _____

Analyzing a Newspaper Article

Directions: Select a newspaper article. Read it carefully and then answer the following questions. Use another sheet of paper if you need more space.

1. What is the article about? _____

_____

_____

_____

_____

_____

_____

_____

2. Who is it about? _____

3. When did the event occur? _____

4. Where did it occur? _____

5. Why did it occur? _____

_____

_____

6. How did it occur? _____

_____

_____

_____

_____

_____

_____

_____

MINI-LESSON 7:
BOOK REVIEWS

A book review offers an analysis of a book, explaining what the book is about and usually offering the reviewer's opinion of it. Good reviews are written in an easy-to-read style.

Procedure:

- Explain that book reviews offer readers insightful information about a book, which provides the reader with facts that may help him or her decide if he or she wants to read it.

- Mention that many newspapers and magazines offer book reviews. An excellent source is the Sunday *New York Times Book Review.* In the *Times's* book review section, both fiction and nonfiction titles are reviewed.

- Note that a book review usually includes the title of the book, the author's name, publisher, copyright, number of pages, and retail cost.

- Explain that the elements of a book review for fiction may include a brief summary of the plot, and description of the main characters and their motivations. The author may also comment on what he or she feels are outstanding elements, such as superior writing style, surprising twists, or graphic violence, as well as offer his or her opinion of the overall book.

- Explain that nonfiction reviews differ from reviews of fiction titles in that the author discusses what the book is about and offers some of its most important points. The reviewer may also remark upon the book's general significance.

Activities:

1. Distribute copies of a book review (fiction) to the class. Also hand out copies of Worksheet 7–1, "Parts of a Book Review (for Fiction)." Instruct students to read the review and answer the questions on the worksheet. Conduct a class discussion in which you analyze the review.

2. Prior to beginning this activity, ask students to bring in copies of newspapers that contain book reviews. You may also ask your colleagues to bring in reviews. While working in groups, instruct your students to read several reviews. They should then discuss the reviews, comparing their organization and the authors' opinions. Based on the reviews, they should try to decide which book they would like to read most. Provide time for the groups to report their conclusions to the class. (You may also wish to hand out copies of Worksheet 7–1 for this activity.)

Writing Activity:

- Instruct your students to select a book, read it, and write a review. Suggest that they follow this plan for *fiction:*

—Summary of the plot.

—Description of the main characters and their motivations.

—Mention of any unique features.

• For *nonfiction,* students should review the book's main ideas and highlight some of its most important points. Encourage them to also comment on the book's general significance.

You may wish to display the reviews upon completion of the activity.

Name _____ Date _____ Section _____

Parts of a Book Review
(for Fiction)

Directions: Read a book review and answer the following questions. Use another sheet of paper if you need more space.

1. Title of book: _____

_____

Author: _____

Publisher: _____

Place of Publication: _____

Copyright Date: _____ Retail Price: _____

2. Briefly describe the author's summary of the book: _____

_____

_____

_____

_____

_____

_____

3. Who are the main characters? _____

_____

_____

4. Did the author describe any special elements of the book, such as great suspense, superior writing style, or excessive violence? _____ If yes, explain. _____

_____

_____

_____

5. Based upon this review, would you like to read this book? _____ Why or why not?

_____

_____

MINI-LESSON 8:
MOVIE REVIEWS

Movie reviews offer an analysis of a motion picture, most often including the author's opinion. Like a book review, a movie review analyzes plot and characters, but goes a step further to include cinematography. Movie reviews may be found in newspapers (in the TV and movie sections) and some magazines.

Procedure:

- Explain that a movie review summarizes the plot of a movie (usually without revealing the climax), describes the lead characters, and offers the author's impressions of the film's overall cinematography.

- Note that cinematography includes such elements as settings, scenes, costumes, special effects, musical score, etc.

- Mention that reviewers often include the rating of a movie, and their opinion of its general quality.

Activities:

1. Distribute a copy of the same movie review to each student. Also hand out copies of Worksheet 8–1, "Reviewing a Movie Review." Instruct your students to read the review, and then answer the questions on the worksheet. After students have completed the activity, conduct a class discussion that focuses on the structure and content of the review.

2. Ask students to bring in movie reviews from newspapers they have at home. You might also ask colleagues to bring in the movie sections of their newspapers so that you will be sure to have enough. Have students work in groups, and distribute several reviews to each group, about one per student. Instruct students to read the reviews and discuss them. In particular they should look for similarities and differences in the structures of the reviews, and try to determine which review is the best written. To help students in identifying similarities and differences among the reviews, distribute several copies of Worksheet 8–2, "Comparing and Contrasting Movie Reviews," to each group. At the end of the activity, provide time for groups to share their results with the class.

Writing Activity:

- Encourage students to watch a movie of their choice and write a review. (You might wish to put limitations in regard to rating.) Remind them to include details about the plot, characters, and any special elements the movie has. Display the reviews at the end of the activity.

Name _____ Date _____ Section _____

Reviewing a Movie Review

Directions: Read the movie review you have been assigned and answer the questions below. Use another sheet of paper if you need more space.

1. Name of movie: _____

Produced by: _____

Released by (Studio): _____

2. Briefly describe the plot of this movie (as explained in the review): _____

_____

_____

_____

_____

_____

_____

_____

3. Who are the main characters of the movie? _____

_____

_____

4. Does the movie have any exceptional features such as settings, costumes, or special effects? _____ If yes, explain. _____

_____

_____

5. Based on this review, would you like to see this movie? _____

Why or why not? _____

_____

Name _____ Date _____ Section _____

Comparing and
Contrasting Movie Reviews

Directions: While working with your group, use this sheet to help you compare and contrast movie reviews. Read each review your group has been given and note how it is structured. Try to determine which is the best written review.

Title of Movie: _____

1. Does the author describe the plot?   Yes _____   No _____

2. Does the author describe the characters?   Yes _____   No _____

3. Does the author offer an opinion on the casting; that is, if the actors and actresses chosen to play the roles of the characters of the story fit their parts?   Yes _____   No _____

4. Does the author offer an opinion on special features of the film such as great action, excessive violence, outstanding musical score, etc.?   Yes _____   No _____

5. Does the author offer an opinion on the settings, costumes, or scenery of the movie? Yes _____   No _____

6. Does the author offer an overall opinion of the quality of the film?   Yes _____ No _____

7. Based on a rating of 1 to 10, with 10 being highest, how would you rate this movie review?   _____

AROUND THE FILM WORLD

MINI-LESSON 9:
BIOGRAPHIES

A biography is the account of a person's life, written by another individual. It is different from an autobiography, which an individual writes about him- or herself.

Procedure:

- Define a biography for your students. To eliminate any confusion, note the difference between a biography and an autobiography.
- Explain that a biography may be very long and detailed, tracing a person's life from birth through childhood, adulthood, and death, or it may be relatively short and focus on a specific time or achievement of the subject's life.
- Mention that very short biographies are referred to as biographical sketches, and may be only a few paragraphs in length.
- Note that most biographers research their subjects with great care and write as objectively as possible. Some biographers, however, stray from facts, inject their own speculation, or draw conclusions from questionable sources. Readers should always remain vigilant when reading a biography that is not based entirely on verifiable facts.
- You might mention that most noteworthy people have been the subjects of biographies.

Activities:

1. For this activity, the whole class, or a group, must read the same biography. After students finish reading the biography, distribute copies of Worksheet 9–1, "Contributions," and instruct students to answer the questions. The worksheet will help students to focus their attention on the achievements of the subject of their biography. Upon completion of the worksheet, conduct a class discussion, or permit students to work in groups, and examine the accomplishments of the person they read about.

2. Instruct students to read a biography of their choice. (This activity works best if each student reads a different biography.) Upon completion of the reading, they are to prepare and give a two- to three-minute talk about their subject. They should focus their talk on their subject's accomplishments or contributions to society. They should also be prepared to answer questions from their classmates. This is an excellent activity for sharing information about the lives of people who have had an impact on society.

Writing Activity:

- After reading a biography, instruct your students to examine the accomplishments of their subject. What is their opinion of their subject's life? Has the subject made important contributions to society? What have been the results, if any? Students should write an essay about their subject, detailing the individual's achievements, and offer their opinions about this person. Display the essays upon completion of the activity. (You may wish to distribute copies of Worksheet 9–1, which may be helpful to students as they analyze and organize their thoughts for writing.)

Name _____ Date _____ Section _____

Contributions

Directions: Answer the following questions about the subject of the biography you read. Use an extra sheet of paper if you need more space.

1. Who is your subject? _____

2. Describe this person. _____

_____

_____

_____

3. What were his or her greatest accomplishments? _____

_____

_____

_____

_____

4. What effects have his or her accomplishments had on society? _____

_____

_____

_____

_____

_____

5. What is your opinion of this person? ____

_____

_____

_____

_____

_____

_____

_____

_____

MINI-LESSON 10:
AUTOBIOGRAPHIES

An autobiography is the account of an individual's life, written by the individual. Depending upon the person, autobiographies may be painfully honest, a thorough rearrangement of fact, or just about anything in between.

Procedure:

- Explain what an autobiography is, noting the difference between it and a biography. Because an autobiography is written by the subject about him- or herself, autobiographies can offer insights into an individual's life that biographies can't. Autobiographies can be excellent sources for research about an individual.

- Note that while many autobiographies are accurate records of the writer's life, some are not. Writing about one's own life tempts some authors to rewrite what actually happened. Readers must be aware of this possibility.

- Mention that, like biographies, autobiographies may cover a person's entire life (up to the point of its writing), or may focus on major events or accomplishments.

- You might wish to mention that the autobiographies of some famous people are ghostwritten. The person provides the ghostwriter with the information for the book, and the "ghost" writes it. The ghostwriter's name may or may not appear on the book.

- You might also wish to mention two examples of autobiographies:
  —Maya Angelou's *I Know Why the Caged Bird Sings,* in which she writes about her childhood.
  —Eudora Welty's *One Writer's Beginnings,* in which she writes about her start as a writer.

Activities:

1. After the class finishes reading the same autobiography, conduct a class discussion on the individual's life, noting both high and low points. Distributing copies of Worksheet 10–1, "Analyzing an Autobiography," will help students with this activity.

2. After reading the same autobiography, have students meet in their groups. Instruct them to discuss the subject and formulate at least three questions they would like to ask the author. Allow time for each group to share its questions with the rest of the class.

3. After the class, or a group, finishes reading the same autobiography, instruct students to meet in their groups and explore some of the major events in the subject's life. They should focus on these events and ask themselves how the subject's life would have changed had the event not worked out the way it did. What if, instead of an event having been a positive experience, it was a negative one? Or what if a negative experience that led to insight and

understanding had been positive? Students should discuss if, and how, changes in the events that shape a person's life might change the person.

Writing Activity:

• Encourage your students to write an autobiography. You may suggest that they write in general about their life, or focus on a major event or accomplishment. You may, of course, give them the option of how they would like to structure their autobiographies. Display the work of your students upon completion of the activity.

Name _____ Date _____ Section _____

Analyzing an Autobiography

Directions: Answer the following questions about the autobiography you have finished reading. Use another sheet of paper if you need more space.

1. Who is the autobiography about? _____

2. When was the subject born? _____

Where? _____

3. Briefly describe his or her childhood. _____
_____
_____
_____
_____
_____

4. Briefly describe his or her adult years. _____
_____
_____
_____
_____
_____

5. Describe any setbacks or disappointments this person suffered. _____
_____
_____
_____
_____

6. What was this person's greatest accomplishment? _____
_____
_____
_____
_____
_____

MINI-LESSON 11:
GENRE FICTION (OVERVIEW)

Genre fiction refers to various categories of novels. Sometimes, genre fiction is called *category fiction.*

Procedure:

- Explain that the word *genre* may be used to describe a general type of reading material, such as the novel or poem, or it may be used to describe a particular category within a major literary type.

- Point out that genre fiction refers to commercial novels. Some examples include: mysteries, romances, science fiction, fantasy, westerns, and historical novels.

- Note that the novels of each genre possess particular elements that define them as a part of the genre. Science fiction stories, for example, are usually set in the future in which advanced technology is an important part of the plot. Mysteries are stories in which an investigator attempts to solve a crime or mystery. Romances are stories in which the relationship between two characters is central to the storyline.

- Mention that most of the novels published each year are examples of genre fiction.

Activities:

1. Instruct your students to work in groups. Ask them to brainstorm a list of novels with which they are familiar, organizing them according to category. Warn them that they may have trouble placing some novels in specific categories because not all novels fit neatly into a single category. Students should discuss the novels and decide why each novel belongs in a particular category. Hand out copies of Worksheet 11–1, "Categories of Fiction," which lists six popular genres, including criteria for selecting stories for each. Students should compose their lists of titles on a separate sheet of paper. Upon completion of the activity, each group should report to the class the category into which they were able to place the most novels.

2. While working in groups, instruct your students to think of the stories they've read. What types of stories (genres) do they like? Students should share their favorite genres and stories with the members of their group. Provide time for groups to report to the class which genres their members like the best. You might ask your students why they believe some genres were found to be more popular than others.

Name _____ Date _____ Section _____

Categories of Fiction

Directions: On a separate sheet of paper, list as many novels as you can according to the categories (genres) on this sheet. Include both the title of the novel and its author, if possible. Use the criteria below each genre to help you select novels for the separate categories.

Romance

These stories may have plenty of action and suspense, but above all they are love stories.

Adventure

The action in these stories is almost nonstop. In most adventure novels the lead characters overcome incredible obstacles.

Science Fiction

These stories are usually set in the future where technology is highly advanced. Space travel may be common, as are aliens.

Fantasy

Magic and the supernatural are important parts of fantasies.

Westerns

These stories are set in the Old West and may include cowboys, pioneers, and Native Americans.

Historical

These stories are set in a specific time in the past. The setting is necessary to the story.

MINI-LESSON 12:
STORIES OF ROMANCE

The modern romance has evolved into one of the most popular categories of fiction. Romances may have adventure, danger, and plenty of action, but they always revolve around the development of a love relationship between the lead characters.

Procedure:

- Explain that the modern romance features a female lead character and her developing relationship with a man. Most, quite simply, are a good love story.
- Note that most romances follow a general formula in which two lead characters face great obstacles before their love triumphs. The moral of most romances is that love wins out over all problems and hardships.
- Point out that settings may vary from current times to the past. Settings are usually detailed and scenes may be elaborate.
- Emphasize that most romances employ elements of adventure, mystery, and suspense, but all of these elements add to the plot of the developing relationship.
- Note that romances today are written for a wide range of audiences, including young adults. Some noteworthy romances for young adults include:

  —*The Death of the Heart* by Elizabeth Bowen

  —*Flambards* by K.M. Peyton

  —*Princess Amy* by Melinda Pollowitz

  —*P.S. I Love You* by Barbara Conklin

  —*Rebecca* by Daphne du Maurier

- You might mention that gothic romance is one of the most popular versions of the romance story. Gothic romance relies heavily on adventure and mystery; the use of an old mansion or castle that contains old mysteries is a common setting. Some examples of gothics include:

  —*Jane Eyre* by Charlotte Brontë

  —*Sense and Sensibility* by Jane Austen

  —*Wuthering Heights* by Emily Brontë

- You might also mention that while most romances end with the lead characters finding true love and happiness, some romances end in tragedy. William Shakespeare's *Romeo and Juliet* and Erich Segal's *Love Story* are good examples. However, such stories usually leave the reader with the feeling that despite the tragedy, the love between the characters is noble and lasting, transcending even death.

Activities:

1. If students are reading the same novel, have them meet in groups and discuss if and how the author uses various elements—such as mystery, adventure, danger, and suspense—to help develop the love relationship of the lead

characters. Distribute copies of Worksheet 12–1, "There's More to Romance Than Romance," to help students organize their ideas. Allow time for groups to share their findings with the class.

2. This activity, which is aimed at students of the upper grades, utilizes both the reading of a romance novel and the story's movie adaptation. *Jane Eyre, Wuthering Heights,* or *Romeo and Juliet* are good stories to use for this activity, although any good romance will do. Instruct your students to read the novel, and then show the movie adaptation to the class. (I suggest that you preview any movie before showing it to your class to make sure it is appropriate for your students.) Ask your students to look for similarities and differences in development. They should especially note the differences, and be prepared to discuss whether the changes in the movie version of the story added to or detracted from the original story. Students should also speculate on why any changes were made. Handing out copies of Worksheet 12–2, "The Novel Versus the Big Screen," can help students with their note-taking. Conduct a class discussion upon completion of the activity. (*Note:* This worksheet may be used to compare any novel with its movie adaptation.)

Writing Activity:

• This activity may be developed as a long-term project. Modern romances are a relatively new genre in literature. The word romance was first used for Old French, which was a language derived from "Roman" Latin. Eventually the term came to be used to describe any work written in French, especially stories of knights and their adventures. In time, the stories, now called romantic fiction, changed and focused more on life that differed from ordinary life. For this activity, instruct your students to trace the development of the romance story, from the past to its current form. They should write a detailed report based upon their research.

Name _____ Date _____ Section _____

There's More to Romance Than Romance

Directions: Although romance stories focus on the developing love relationship between the lead characters, their authors include many other elements to make the stories interesting. After you have read a romance, write examples from the story showing how the author used mystery, danger, suspense, or adventure to keep readers interested. Use another sheet of paper if you need more space.

Title: _____

Author: _____

1. Briefly describe the plot of this story. _____

_____

_____

2. Examples of mystery: _____

_____

_____

3. Examples of danger: _____

_____

_____

4. Examples of suspense: _____

_____

_____

_____

5. Examples of adventure: _____

_____

_____

_____

Name _____ Date _____ Section _____

The Novel Versus the Big Screen

Directions: After reading a novel, watch its movie adaptation and compare the stories by answering the questions below. Use another sheet of paper if you need more space.

Title of novel: _____

Title of movie: _____

1. Does the movie contain the same characters?_____

If no, explain. _____

_____

_____

_____

_____

_____

2. Have any scenes or events been changed? _____

If yes, how? _____

_____

_____

_____

_____

3. Why do you think changes are sometimes made when a novel is produced as a movie?

_____

_____

_____

4. Which version of this story, the novel or the movie, did you like better? _____

Explain. _____

_____

_____

_____

_____

MINI-LESSON 13:
STORIES OF ADVENTURE

Adventures focus on heroes or heroines who must fight villains and overcome dangers as they accomplish a crucial mission or reach an important goal. Modern adventure stories almost always include elements of romance. Not only does the lead reach his or her goal, but he or she wins the heart of the love interest as well.

Procedure:

- Explain that the modern adventure story is built around a lead, usually a male, who must accomplish an important task or reach a goal. Along the way he is faced with obstacles and must battle evil in the form of a villain.

- Note that adventure stories include elements of other types of stories, such as romance or mystery.

- Point out that the plot of adventures tends to be fast-paced with plenty of action. The lead characters are usually handsome, beautiful, and courageous; they are created in a way that makes it easy for audiences to identify with them and root for them.

- Note that the typical theme of an adventure story is good versus evil.

- Mention that Robert Louis Stevenson was one of the first authors to write what are considered to be modern adventures. *Treasure Island, Kidnapped,* and *The Master of Ballantrae* are among his best works. Today, adventure stories are common in novels, on TV, and in the movies. You might ask your students to name some.

- You might also mention that adventure stories have their roots in the epics and myths of ancient times. One can imagine people of those days huddled around a fire, listening to the village storyteller relate a tale of hardship and triumph.

Activities:

1. As the class, or a group, is reading the same adventure, instruct students to focus their attention on the lead characters. In most adventure stories, the leads are easy for the reader to like. The lead male character is usually handsome; the female lead is beautiful. Both are courageous and strong-willed. Instruct your students to note specific instances of how the lead characters of their story are appealing. Distribute copies of Worksheet 13–1, "True Heroes and Heroines," to help students with this activity. Upon conclusion of the activity, conduct a class discussion, or have students meet in their groups and discuss their ideas.

2. After reading an adventure story of their choice, students are to meet in groups and offer a summary of their stories to the group's members. They should include the plot, characters, and conflict in their summaries. This activity works best when students read different stories.

3. In virtually every adventure story, the lead characters have a clear goal. For this activity, students who are reading the same story are to meet in groups and discuss how the character's goal is a driving force of the novel. Encourage them to cite specific examples that support their ideas.

Writing Activity:

• After reading an adventure story of their choice, instruct your students to write a letter to a friend, explaining why their friend should or should not read this book.

Name _____ Date _____ Section _____

True Heroes and Heroines

Directions: Answer the questions below about the characters in the adventure story you have read. Use an extra sheet of paper if you need more space.

Title of story: _____

Author: _____

1. Briefly describe the plot of the story. _____

_____

_____

_____

_____

_____

2. Describe the male lead character's appearance. _____

_____

Describe his personality. _____

_____

_____

_____

3. Describe the female lead character's appearance. _____

_____

Describe her personality. _____

_____

_____

_____

_____

4. What are the most appealing qualities of the lead characters? _____

_____

_____

_____

MINI-LESSON 14:
MYSTERIES

Mysteries, sometimes called detective stories or whodunits, are stories in which an investigation is central to the plot. Many famous detectives have been created by the world's mystery authors.

Procedure:

- Explain that mysteries are a major genre in literature. Mysteries may be divided into several categories— the hard-boiled detective story, the secret agent story, and the crime story that may be investigated by the police, a private eye, or a nonprofessional sleuth.

- Explain that the major feature of the mystery is the reader's involvement in trying to solve the mystery. Clues are offered throughout the plot that enable the reader to try to figure out the solution along with the story's hero or heroine.

- Note that red-herrings, or misleading clues and innocent suspects, are often used to confuse and challenge the reader.

- Emphasize that mystery writers use words that paint vivid images in the minds of their readers. The authors strive to create a mood that fits the plot of the mystery.

- You might mention that Edgar Allan Poe is considered to be the father of the modern mystery. His story "The Murders in the Rue Morgue" is a classic mystery.

- Note some of the mystery world's most famous detectives and their authors:
    —Sherlock Holmes (Sir Arthur Conan Doyle)
    —Hercule Poirot (Agatha Christie)
    —Miss Jane Marple (Agatha Christie)
    —Mike Hammer (Mickey Spillane)
    —V.I. Warshawski (Sara Paretsky)
    —Nick and Nora Charles (Dashiell Hammett)
    —Philip Marlowe (Raymond Chandler)
    —Virgil Tibbs (John Dudley Ball)
    —Brother Cadfael (Ellis Peters)

Activities:

1. This activity is designed for students reading the same mystery. Upon completion of their reading, instruct students to note the place they solved the mystery. They should list several clues that they used to solve the mystery, and also note any red-herrings they found. Conduct a discussion either with the class, or have students meet in groups to discuss the story, especially noting the places individuals were able to solve the mystery. They should consider the question: Why might readers solve the mystery at different

places? Distribute copies of Worksheet 14–1, "Taking the Mystery Out of Mystery," to help students with their work.

2. This activity may be done with either the whole class, a group reading the same mystery, or students reading different mysteries. As students read the mystery, instruct them to pay close attention to the author's use of imagery, and how he or she uses imagery to create the mood of scenes. Hand out copies of Worksheet 14–2, "Mood and Mystery," and encourage students to note examples of imagery words and mood as they read the mystery. Either conduct a whole class discussion about imagery and mood, or permit students to meet in groups and discuss the topic. If students have read different mysteries, they may share what they found in the mystery they read.

Writing Activity:

- Students are to select a famous mystery author such as Sir Arthur Conan Doyle, Agatha Christie, or Mickey Spillane, research his or her life, and try to find out why he or she became a writer of mysteries. Was there an event in his or her life that set the author on a course to write mysteries? Instruct your students to write a biographical sketch in which they address this subject. Display the writings.

Name _____ Date _____ Section _____

Taking the Mystery
Out of Mystery

Directions: Answer the questions below, then be ready to discuss your answers with your class or group. Use an extra sheet of paper if you need more space.

1. At what point in the story were you able to solve the mystery? _____

_____

_____

2. List at least three clues that helped you to solve the mystery. (Include the numbers of the pages on which they are found.) _____

_____

_____

_____

_____

_____

_____

_____

_____

_____

_____

3. List any red-herrings you found. (Include their page numbers.) _____

_____

_____

_____

_____

_____

_____

_____

Name _____ Date _____ Section _____

Mood and Mystery

Directions: Authors of mysteries create mood by carefully choosing words that paint sharp images in the minds of their readers. Select a scene in the mystery you are reading that you feel contains strong, clear images. Answer the questions below, and be ready to discuss your answers with your class or group.

1. Briefly describe the scene. _____

_____

_____

_____

_____

2. Describe the mood of this scene (suspenseful, terrifying, dangerous, etc.). _____

_____

_____

3. List some of the words that the author uses to create this mood. _____

MINI-LESSON 15:
SCIENCE FICTION

Science fiction (SF) is a major genre in fiction. As our world becomes more dependent on science and technology, it is likely that SF will continue to enjoy broad popularity.

Procedure:

- Explain that SF stories are usually set in the future, have a strong technological element, and often include alien characters. You might mention that the "Star Trek" series and "Star Wars" trilogy are examples of SF. (Although students may be more familiar with the TV shows and movies, numerous novels have been written for these series.)

- Note that SF is distinct from fantasy, which usually includes elements of magic.

- Mention that the best SF stories have strong, distinct characters and solid plots. Some stories assume epic proportions, such as Frank Herbert's *Dune.*

- Point out that aliens frequently are major characters in SF. They can assume the roles of heroes or villains.

- Note that settings are usually detailed. Authors must define their worlds clearly if readers are to find them believable.

- Explain that many SF stories are based on scientific principles. When new physical laws are introduced to stories, they are usually based on current physics, or at least theoretical assumptions. Sometimes, however, SF authors invent entirely new worlds. When they do, these places must remain consistent to the author's conception.

- You might like to mention that Jules Verne *(Twenty Thousand Leagues Under the Sea* and *From the Earth to the Moon)* and H.G. Wells *(The Time Machine* and *The War of the Worlds)* were the first two modern SF authors.

- You might also mention how SF authors often have an uncanny ability to predict the future. For example, lasers were used in SF as deathrays long before they became a reality. Wireless communications devices, used by planetary explorers, have become a fact in our cellular phones. The computers that charted the way to the stars in early SF stories are now on our desks.

Activities:

1. This activity works best when students are reading the same story, and may be used either with the whole class or with groups. Distribute copies of Worksheet 15–1, "The Elements of Science Fiction," and instruct students to identify examples of these elements in their stories. Upon completion of the activity, you may conduct a class discussion, or encourage students to discuss their results in their groups.

2. Have students meet in groups to briefly share a favorite SF story they've either read or watched on TV or in the movies.

3. Distribute copies of Worksheet 15–2, "Some Popular Science Fiction Novels." Instruct students to select a novel from the list (or you may permit them to choose another novel), read the book, and provide an oral report about it to their group or the class.

4. Suggest that students watch one of the "Star Wars" or "Star Trek" movies and compare the story to the novel. You might wish to distribute copies of Worksheet 12–2 (from mini-lesson 12), which students may find helpful.

Writing Activity:

• Instruct your students to select a SF novel. (If the class or a group is currently reading one, you may use that novel.) Ask students to look for ways the author has created a distinct setting for the story, and write an essay detailing how he or she has used the setting to make the novel more realistic. Students should use examples from the story to support their ideas.

Name _____ Date _____ Section _____

The Elements of Science Fiction

Directions: Answer the questions below that highlight the major elements of science fiction (SF) stories. Use an extra sheet of paper if you need more space.

1. *SF stories usually take place in the future.* When does your story take place? _____

_____

2. *Many SF stories take place on other worlds.* Where does your story take place?_____

_____

3. *Advanced technology plays an important role in the story.* Give some examples of technology in your story. _____

_____

_____

_____

_____

4. *Aliens or other life forms may be central characters.* Describe any aliens in your story.

_____

_____

_____

5. *Many SF stories have interplanetary or interstellar space travel.* Does yours?_____

If yes, explain. _____

_____

_____

_____

_____

_____

_____

_____

Name _____ Date _____ Section _____

Some Popular Science Fiction Novels

The following list offers some popular science fiction novels. There are many others.

The Hitchhiker's Guide to the Galaxy, Douglas Adams

The Martian Chronicles, Ray Bradbury

Fahrenheit 451, Ray Bradbury

Childhood's End, Arthur C. Clarke

The City and the Stars, Arthur C. Clarke

The End of Eternity, Isaac Asimov

The Long Tomorrow, Leigh Brackett

Walk to the End of the World, Suzy McKee Charnas

The Sirens of Titan, Kurt Vonnegut

Dune, Frank Herbert

Juniper Time, Kate Wilhelm

The Wanderer, Fritz Leiber

The Dancers at the End of Time, Michael Moorcock

The Dream Master, Roger Zelazny

Downward to the Earth, Robert Silverberg

Woman on the Edge of Time, Marge Piercy

The Guardians, John Christopher

Journey beyond Tomorrow, Robert Scheckly

Stand on Zanzibar, John Brunner

Time Out of Joint, Philip K. Dick

The Inheritors, William Golding

No Enemy But Time, Michael Bishop

Gods of the Riverworld, Philip Jose Farmer

The Year of the Quiet Sun, Wilson Tucker

Way Station, Clifford D. Simak

Jurassic Park, Michael Crichton

Have Space Suit—Will Travel, Robert A. Heinlein

A Stranger in a Strange Land, Robert A. Heinlein

A Journey to the Center of the Earth, Jules Verne

The Time Machine, H.G. Wells

MINI-LESSON 16:
FANTASY STORIES

Fantasies are stories that include events and characters that go beyond reality. Fantasy stories may be set in distant times or places, or may be set now in rather typical situations.

Procedure:

- Explain that fantasy is a broad category of fiction in which magic—or belief in the unreal—is essential to the plot.
- Note that fantasies come in many forms. Some of the most common include:
  - Heroic fantasy, sometimes called low fantasy. These stories are set in old, usually forgotten, civilizations on Earth or elsewhere. Sword and sorcery are major parts of the story in which the hero or heroine battles evil.
  - High fantasy, which are stories that have powerful psychological implications.
  - Contemporary fantasy, in which ordinary people find themselves confronting magic or situations beyond reality.
- Note that the theme of most fantasies is good versus evil.
- Point out that authors must create the worlds of their fantasy stories with great detail. The "unreal" situations they present to the reader must seem entirely believable.
- You may wish to mention that some fantasies, particularly heroic fantasies, often evolve into series.
- You may also wish to note the following examples of fantasy novels and their authors:
  - *Alice's Adventures in Wonderland* by Lewis Carroll
  - *Charlotte's Web* by E.B. White
  - *A Wrinkle in Time* by Madeleine L'Engle
  - *The Sword in the Stone* by T.H. White
  - *The Chronicles of Narnia* by C.S. Lewis
  - *A Wizard of Earthsea* by Ursula K. LeGuin
  - *The Illustrated Man* by Ray Bradbury
  - *Something Wicked This Way Comes* by Ray Bradbury
  - *The Lord of the Rings* Trilogy by J.R.R. Tolkien
  - *Animal Farm* by George Orwell (note that this is also considered to be one of the world's greatest satires)
  - *Watership Down* by Richard Adams
  - *Slaughterhouse-Five* by Kurt Vonnegut
  - *The Indian in the Cupboard* by Lynn Reid Banks

Activities:

1. This activity will work well if the class, or a group, is reading the same story. Ask students to note the author's use of magic or events that are beyond our normal reality. They should ask themselves how he or she makes these events believable to the reader. Hand out copies of Worksheet 16–1, "The Reality of the Unreal," to help your students with their ideas. At the end of the activity conduct a discussion with the class in which you examine how authors of fantasies achieve believable settings and events, or permit students to discuss their findings in their groups.

2. This activity is designed for students working in groups, with each group reading a different fantasy. Upon completing the story, the members of each group are to select what they feel are some of the best scenes, and then read excerpts of the story to the class. They should also provide a brief report about the story.

Writing Activity:

- Suggest that students write a different climax for a fantasy they read. Their new climax should be a logical development of the plot.

Name _____ Date _____ Section _____

The Reality of the Unreal

Directions: From the fantasy you have read, select a scene in which magic, or an event that is beyond our normal reality, occurs; then answer the questions below. Use another sheet of paper if you need more space.

1. Title of story: _____

Author: _____

2. Describe the event you have selected. _____

_____

_____

_____

_____

_____

_____

_____

_____

_____

3. Do you feel the author made this event believable? _____ If yes, how? If not, why not?

_____

_____

_____

_____

_____

_____

_____

_____

_____

_____

MINI-LESSON 17:
HORROR STORIES

Horror stories are immensely popular; just think of all the novels Stephen King has sold. So popular is this genre that many horror novels are eventually made into movies.

Procedure:

- Explain that the typical horror story has a plot in which the lead characters fight evil that manifests itself as a supernatural force. Evil may be in the form of a ghost, demon, gremlin, vampire, werewolf, or other strange creature.

- Explain that horror stories have their basis in superstition and the fears people have of death and evil. One of the original horror stories is the legend of the vampire. Vampires, known as the "undead," survive by drinking the blood of the living. Bram Stoker's novel, *Dracula,* was based on the legend. The vampire legend has been used in numerous stories and movies.

- Note that while horror stories may also include elements of romance, mystery, and adventure, the focus of the plot is the battle against evil in a reality that is unreal.

- Mention some examples of horror stories. You might wish to include the following:

  —*Frankenstein* by Mary Shelley

  —*The Strange Case of Dr. Jekyll and Mr. Hyde* by Robert Louis Stevenson

  —"The Turn of the Screw" by Henry James

  —*Carrie* by Stephen King

  —*The Shining* by Stephen King

  —*Haunted* by R.L. Stine

  —*Something Wicked This Way Comes* by Ray Bradbury

- You might mention that many of Edgar Allan Poe's stories were forerunners of today's horror. His story "The Fall of the House of Usher"—with its apprehension, uncertainty, and fear—is an excellent example of classic horror.

Activities:

1. This activity may be used with either the whole class or groups, provided students are reading the same horror story. Instruct your students to note the ways the author creates a believable setting for the action. In horror, authors must convince their readers to accept belief in the unreal; otherwise, readers will not enjoy the story. Distribute copies of Worksheet 17–1, "Believing in Horror," to help students clarify their ideas. At the end of the activity, conduct a class discussion analyzing the author's techniques in creating a believable "reality," or have students discuss the topic in their groups.

2. This activity may be used with the entire class, or groups, provided students are reading the same story. Have students meet in their groups and

briefly discuss the story they read, sharing what they felt were its most frightening scenes. Ask them to try to identify how the author made the scenes frightening; for example, through suspense, terrifying images, scary situations, or unnerving settings. If the class has read the same story, conduct a class discussion that focuses on some of the most frightening scenes of the story. If the groups have read different stories, provide time for each group to report to the class and briefly summarize the story its members read, highlighting the most frightening scenes. Groups might like to read excerpts from their stories.

3. Instruct your students to read Edgar Allan Poe's "The Fall of the House of Usher." (This story may be found in virtually any collection of Poe's writings.) Ask students to focus their attention on how Poe achieves the mood of the story, which includes such emotions as terror, fear, apprehension, and melancholy. Conduct a class discussion or have students meet in groups to discuss the topic.

4. You might like to show students the original *Dracula* or *Frankenstein* movies, and conduct a class discussion comparing the horror movies of the past with those of today.

Writing Activity:

- Horror stories are designed to scare people. A good horror can even cause nightmares. Instruct students to write an essay on the question: "Why are horror stories popular?" Or, put another way, why do people enjoy being scared? You may suggest that students write the essay primarily from their own ideas or opinions, or (especially for advanced students) suggest that they research the topic first. Display the essays upon completion of the activity.

Name _____ Date _____ Section _____

Believing in Horror

Directions: Readers must be willing to believe in the unreal (at least during the time they are reading) if they are to enjoy horror stories. Authors can help their readers accept the events presented in the story by carefully altering reality. Note how the author of the story you are reading does this, then answer the questions below. Use another sheet of paper if you need more space.

1. How does the author use the setting to help alter

reality in the story? _____

_____

_____

_____

_____

_____

_____

2. What elements of the plot does he or she use to help shape reality? _____

_____

_____

3. How do the characters, especially evil ones, add to the reality of the story? _____

_____

_____

_____

_____

4. Is the reality believable? Why or why not? _____

_____

_____

_____

_____

MINI-LESSON 18:
HISTORICAL NOVELS

Historical novels are stories set in the past. The setting becomes the foundation for the plot.

Procedure:

- Explain that historical novels comprise a large category of fiction. The stories are set in a specific time and place that become the background for the action.

- Explain that historical novels usually are set during times of conflict, particularly when cultures are in collision. The characters not only are affected by the historical events, but may themselves influence the outcome of the events.

- Emphasize that historical novels are founded on solid historical facts. While the novelist may take liberties with some of the characters, he or she usually doesn't alter history (at least in any major way).

- Mention that historical novels often are centered in a social context, showing people affected by the mores and customs of their societies. Nathaniel Hawthorne's *The Scarlet Letter* is a good example.

- While there are countless historical novels, you might wish to mention some of the more noteworthy and their authors, including:

  —*The Three Musketeers* by Alexandre Dumas

  —*The Hunchback of Notre Dame* by Victor Hugo

  —*The Last of the Mohicans* by James Fenimore Cooper

  —*A Tale of Two Cities* by Charles Dickens

  —*Gone with the Wind* by Margaret Mitchell

  —*Centennial* by James Michener

  —*Shogun* by James Clavell

  Some historical novels of particular interest to students include:

  —*The Red Badge of Courage* by Stephen Crane

  —*My Brother Sam Is Dead* by James Lincoln Collier

  —*The Winter Hero* by James Lincoln Collier

  —*The Sign of the Beaver* by Elizabeth George Speare

  —*The Fighting Ground* by Avi

  — *The Slave Dancer* by Paula Fox

  —*Roll of Thunder, Hear My Cry* by Mildred D. Taylor

- You might mention that some historical novels cover a grand scale. An example here is *War and Peace* by Leo Tolstoy. Some consider this novel to be one of the best novels ever written. The story is an epic of Russian society in which the lives of five aristocratic families are traced through the years just before and after the Napoleonic invasion. The book includes 559 characters, and accurately relates historical figures, battles, and events.

Activities:

1. After reading the same historical novel, students should meet in their groups and discuss how the events of the story affected the major characters. They should explore what the characters were like before the event, and how the event changed them, if at all. Distribute copies of Worksheet 18–1, "The Impact of History," to help your students with their ideas. Allow time for group sharing at the end of the activity.

2. This activity is designed for groups that are reading different novels. Each group is to research the time in which their novel takes place, and plan a panel discussion in which they report on various aspects of society at that time. They should include topics such as government, the local economy, religion, family life, food, health, and recreation. Provide time for each group to present its findings.

3. Many of the popular historical novels have been made into movies. You might like to have students watch the movie adaptation of a historical novel and compare and contrast it to the original story. Distribute copies of Worksheet 12–2 to help students with their ideas.

Writing Activity:

- Upon completing the reading of a historical novel, students are to select an event of the story that has historical importance. They are to research the event, and write an essay describing it. In their essay they should note how accurately the event was related in the novel. Display the finished essays.

Name _____ Date _____ Section _____

The Impact of History

Directions: In most historical novels, the characters are living at a time of great conflict, and they are changed by the events they experience. Select two characters of your story. Then answer the following questions below to identify how the characters changed in the story. Use another sheet of paper if you need more space.

1. Name of character: _____

a. Traits at the beginning of the story: _____

_____

_____

_____

_____

_____

b. Traits at the end of the story: _____

_____

_____

_____

_____

_____

c. Major cause(s) for the changes: _____

_____

_____

2. Name of character: _____

a. Traits at the beginning of the story: _____

_____

_____

b. Traits at the end of the story: _____

_____

_____

c. Major cause(s) for the changes: _____

_____

_____

MINI-LESSON 19:
WESTERNS

Westerns are a special type of adventure story with a good portion of history mixed in. The western, based on the settlement of the Old West, is a uniquely American story.

Procedure:

- Explain that westerns are stories that take place in the American West during the days the frontier was being settled. They typically focus around a hero who is in conflict with a protagonist—an outlaw, gunslinger, settlers, cattle barons, or Indians.

- Point out that the central conflict in a western can take several forms; for example, hostilities between pioneers and Native Americans, ranchers and farmers, marshal and outlaws, or cowboy and crooked saloon owner. There are many variations. The major appeal of the western is fast action and the conflict between the good guys and the bad guys.

- Emphasize that the setting, particularly the landscape, is symbolic and may play an important part in the story. Sometimes the land is at the heart of the central conflict. It is the place where the frontier and civilization collide, and the hero frequently finds himself as the defender of the frontier.

- Mention that westerns were originally published as "dime" or "pulp" novels, because of the cheap quality of paper that was used in printing them. This allowed publishers to mass-produce the novels and make them available to millions of readers.

- You might mention that James Fennimore Cooper's writings—*The Deerslayer, The Pathfinder,* and *The Last of the Mohicans*—in which the setting was the frontier, led to the western as a genre.

- Also, you might mention some of the most popular authors of westerns, including:
  —Zane Grey, whose *Riders of the Purple Sage* is considered to be a classic western
  —Max Brand, who wrote 120 westerns
  —Louis L'Amour, who wrote more than 80 westerns
  —Larry McMurtry, who wrote *Lonesome Dove,* which was made into the popular TV mini-series

Activities:

1. After the class has finished reading the same western, conduct a discussion that focuses on the primary conflict and how it sustains the pace of the novel. Hand out copies of Worksheet 19–1, "The Ways of the Old West," which will help students with their ideas.

2. For this activity, students may read the same western or different ones. After reading the novel, students are to meet in groups and discuss why the

western has been, and remains, a popular genre. Provide time for each group to share its conclusions with the class.

3. Americans often identify with cowboys. We admire their courage, their taming of the frontier, their yearning for "open spaces." After reading a western, have your students meet in groups to discuss the question: "How much, if at all, has the reality, stories, and myths of the Old West played a role in shaping America's culture?" Provide time for groups to share their conclusions with the class.

4. For this activity, students may work individually or in groups. Instruct them to research the life of some of the great authors of westerns. In particular they should focus on whether the author learned about the West from first-hand experience, hearsay, or research. Students should prepare and present a short oral report of their findings. You may focus a culminating discussion on how important first-hand experience is to writing.

Writing Activity:

• After reading a western, students should research the historical period in which it was set and determine how accurate the story is at portraying the real West. They should write a brief report.

Name _____ Date _____ Section

The Ways of the Old West

Directions: Westerns are fast-paced and have plenty of action and conflict. Answer the questions below to help you identify how the central conflict sustains the action in the story you are reading. Use another sheet of paper if you need more space.

1. Title of novel: _____

Author: _____

2. Briefly summarize the story. _____

_____

_____

_____

_____

_____

3. What is the central conflict? _____

_____

_____

_____

_____

_____

_____

_____

_____

4. Why is conflict necessary to the story? _____

_____

_____

_____

_____

_____

_____

_____

MINI-LESSON 20:
COMEDY

A comedy is a story that has humor. Comedies have been around a long time. They were as popular among the Ancient Greeks and Romans as they are with people today.

Procedure:

- Explain that comedies are stories in which achieving humor is one of the purposes of the author.
- Note that comedy may be light (in which the humor is of a silly, light-hearted nature) or dark (in which the humor arises from serious themes).
- Mention that satire is frequently used as a vehicle for humor. Satire is the use of irony or wit to expose human follies or vices.
- Note that comedy often plays a part in other types of stories. Thus we have romantic comedies, comedies that take place in historical settings, comedies that are set in the Old West, and even comedies in outer space.
- You might note that *Don Quixote* by Miguel de Cervantes, because of its satirical treatment of knights and ladies, is felt by many to be one of the first of the modern comedies. The book was published in the early 17th century.
- Perhaps mention some comedies in which your students might be interested, including:
  —*The Princess Bride* by William Goldman
  —*The Hitchhiker's Guide to the Galaxy* by Douglas Adams
  —*The Prisoner of Zenda* by Anthony Hope
  —*The Merchant of Venice* by William Shakespeare
  —*The Adventures of Huckleberry Finn* by Mark Twain

Activities:

1. After students have finished reading the same comedy, have them work in groups and select what they believe is the story's funniest scene or event. They should try to decide why this scene is funny, and how the author creates humor. Distributing copies of Worksheet 20–1, "The Humor in Comedy," will help students with their ideas. Allow time for the groups to report their conclusions to the class.

2. This activity works best if groups are reading different comedies. After finishing the stories, students are to meet in their groups, select what they feel is one of the story's funniest scenes, and plan to act it out. (Caution them to select scenes that can be easily acted out in the classroom.) Encourage them to make and use minor props if you wish. To make it easier for students to act out the scene, you may suggest that they use their books for the dialogue. Permit time for students to act out their scenes for the class.

3. After reading a comedy, have your students meet in groups and discuss why comedy is so popular. After all, comedy appears in stories, in stage plays, and on TV and in the movies. Why do people seem to enjoy a good laugh? Permit time for groups to share their conclusions with the class.

Writing Activity:

- Satire is often a key component of comedy. Indeed, many authors are known more as satirists than comedy writers. A few of the best known are Miguel de Cervantes, Jonathan Swift, H.L. Mencken, and George Orwell (for *Animal Farm*). Instruct your students to research a satirist and write a brief report about this author.

Name _____ Date _____ Section _____

The Humor in Comedy

Directions: Select what you feel is the funniest scene in the book you are reading, then answer the questions below. Use another sheet of paper if you need more space.

1. Title of book: _____

Author: _____

2. Describe what you feel is this book's funniest scene. _____

_____

_____

_____

_____

_____

3. What made this scene so funny? _____

_____

_____

_____

_____

4. Did the author use the characters' actions, dialogue, or situations (or all three) to create the humor? _____

Explain. _____

_____

_____

_____

_____

_____

_____

_____

_____

_____

_____

_____

MINI-LESSON 21:
AMERICAN FOLKLORE

American folklore may best be described as a collection of stories, legends, tall tales, proverbs, and songs that, through a mix of fantasy, fact, and symbolism, gives a unique insight to the people who created it. Most libraries contain several volumes of folklore.

Procedure:

- Explain that folklore expresses and celebrates past experiences of the American people. Sometimes these experiences are greatly fictionalized in folklore.

- Note that folklore heroes were often symbols. Paul Bunyan, for example, is a symbol for hardy loggers. John Henry symbolizes the sturdy laborers whose jobs were threatened by the machine age. Old Stormalong represents sailors.

- Mention that folklore often includes animal characters that possess human traits and attributes.

- Explain that many stories of folklore are also examples of tall tales, stories in which exaggeration is a major element.

- Note that folklore, which was originally passed down through oral tradition, often changed over time. Thus, some stories have many variations.

- Point out that because folklore is an expression of a people at a particular time, it often includes the prejudices and biases of that time. What is considered poor taste today may have been acceptable then.

- If you wish, distribute copies of Worksheet 21–1, "Folklore Characters." This list may be used as an introduction to some of the best-known stories of American folklore, or as a take-off point for a general discussion.

Activities:

1. This activity may be used with the entire class or with groups. After reading the same examples of folklore, conduct a class discussion or have students meet in their groups to explore how folklore represents a people's past. For example, how does folklore offer details about the way people lived at that time? Distribute copies of Worksheet 21–2, "Folklore—A Window to the Past," to help students explore their ideas.

2. Instruct your students to read several examples of American folklore and decide on a favorite. Students should then meet in groups and discuss the examples they read, which pieces they liked best, and why. They should look for similarities between the favorite pieces. Did they tend to like the same kinds of folklore? If yes, why might that be? Provide time for groups to share their findings with the class.

3. While some of the characters of American folklore are entirely fictional (Pecos Bill), many were real people (Daniel Boone). Others were symbols for

groups of people (Paul Bunyan). Hand out copies of Worksheet 21–1, "Folklore Characters," and ask your students to select one and research if the character was a real person, if he or she was fictional, or if the character is a symbol for a group. Students should research the background of the character as well as read one of the stories about him or her. They should also try to determine how true the story is. Ask students to share their findings with the class via a brief oral report.

Writing Activity:

- Instruct students to select a character of folklore and write a new tale. A twist for this activity might be to bring the character to the present and write about his or her reactions to life today in the context of a tall tale. Display the stories upon completion. You may wish to hand out copies of Worksheet 21–1, "Folklore Characters," and permit students to choose a character from the list.

Name _____ Date _____ Section _____

Folklore Characters

Following are well-known characters of American folklore. Some are fictional, while others were real people. Some are symbols for groups of people. Many of these characters appear in several stories, and sometimes a story may have several variations. How many of their stories do you know?

Johnny Appleseed—planted apple trees throughout the Midwest

Clara Barton—founder of the Red Cross

Sam Bass—a good outlaw

Judge Roy Bean—frontier judge

Bonnie and Clyde—outlaws

Bowleg Bill—sea-loving cowboy

Buffalo Bill—plainsman, frontier scout, showman

Pecos Bill—cowboy, known for riding cyclones and similar accomplishments

Billy the Kid—young outlaw

Daniel Boone—pioneer, scout, frontiersman

Lizzie Borden—accused axe murderer

Jim Bridger—scout, frontiersman

Paul Bunyan—lumberjack

Kit Carson—scout, frontiersman

Casey at the Bat—baseball slugger who struck out

Davy Crockett—frontiersman, congressman, Alamo hero

Wyatt Earp—marshal

Febold Feboldson—pioneer

Mike Fink—frontiersman

Bill Greenfield—a great liar

The Hatfields and McCoys—feuding neighbors

John Henry—railroad man

Wild Bill Hickok—frontier scout and marshal

Doc Holliday—doctor and gunslinger

Mose Humphreys—firefighter

Johnny Inkslinger—bookkeeper

Jesse James—outlaw

Calamity Jane—adventurous woman of the west

Casey Jones—railroad engineer

Joe Magarac—early steelworker

Florence Nightingale—nurse

Annie Oakley—sharpshooter

Molly Pitcher—female patriot

Sacajawea—Native American guide to Lewis and Clark expedition

John Smith and Pocahontas—English captain saved by this Native American princess

Old Stormalong—sailor

Sojourner Truth—liberator

Name _____ Date _____ Section _____

Folklore—A Window
to the Past

Directions: Folklore is often based on the legends, customs, and traditions of a people. It can provide a fascinating look at the past through the stories, songs, and expressions of the people who lived during that time. Answer the questions below and try to determine how the folklore you read can be a window to the past. Use another sheet of paper if you need more space.

1. Title of folklore: _____

2. About when does this piece of folklore take place? _____

3. Where does it take place? _____

4. Describe the main characters. _____

_____

_____

_____

_____

_____

5. Summarize this piece of folklore. _____

_____

_____

_____

_____

_____

_____

6. What examples of how life was like at that time are contained in the folklore? _____

_____

_____

_____

_____

MINI-LESSON 22:
MYTHOLOGY (OVERVIEW)

Every land has its mythology. Although the stories may differ, most share common themes. Myths may try to explain creation, events in nature, religion, life and death, or record the adventures of heroes or great changes in society.

Procedure:

- Explain that myths were created by ancient people, who had little understanding of science. Most myths are stories that attempt to provide answers to the big questions of life, such as the creation of the universe, the origin of people, death, and the cycles and phenomenon of nature. Some myths tell of heroes who overcame great struggles or describe the cultures and traditions of a people.

- Note that although English readers are usually most familiar with Greek, Roman, and Norse mythology, because those peoples had great influence on Western traditions, every country throughout the world has its own mythology.

- Point out that many myths attempt to explain nature by representing nature with gods. Sun gods, moon gods, sea gods, storm gods, and gods of the harvest are common in many myths.

- Explain that some myths from cultures around the world show striking similarities. A good example is the myth telling of a great flood, after which only a few people survived. This story, in one form or another, appears in the mythology of Native Americans, the Bible, and many other cultures. Some researchers believe there may have been a great flood in antiquity, and that these myths recount the event.

- Note that the study of mythology can provide a wondrous glimpse to the life of an ancient civilization, because myths often incorporated the context and conventions of the times in which they were created. Myths usually express the general beliefs, values, and customs of the people who invented them.

- Mention that myths were originally passed down orally from one generation to the next. Many were changed over time, and today there may be several variations of some myths.

Activities:

1. After the class, or a group, reads a myth, students are to analyze the myth and explain its meaning. Hand out copies of Worksheet 22–1, "Making Meaning of Myths," to help your students with their analyses. Conduct a class discussion examining the myth, or let students work in groups to discuss the myth.

2. For this activity, have your students work in groups. Instruct each group to select a different mythology. Some possible choices include myths of the Egyptians, Greeks, Romans, Norse, Native Americans, Indians (Asia), Chinese, Japanese, or Pacific Islanders. The groups are to read and research

several examples of the mythology they selected, then prepare and present an oral report about these myths to the class.

3. The myth of a great flood that destroys most of humankind is found among many cultures throughout the world. Working in groups, students are to investigate and research the Myth of the Great Flood. Students should find as many stories of the great flood as they can, compare the stories, and speculate how and why various cultures would invent similar myths. Was there in fact a great flood long before history was recorded? After students have found sufficient information, you might like to organize a debate on the topic—The Great Flood: Fact or Fiction. Instead of a debate, you might simply have groups report their conclusions to the class.

Writing Activity:

• Ancient myths attempted to explain and answer questions for which there were no answers; for example, how was the universe created, or what happens after death? Such questions still have no clear answers. Instruct your students to write a modern myth in which they try to answer a question for which they seek the answer. Upon completion of the activity, display the myths or ask volunteers to read their myths to the class.

Name _____ Date _____ Section _____

Making Meaning of Myths

Directions: After reading a myth, answer the questions below. Use another sheet of paper if you need more space.

1. Name of myth: _____

2. What country (or land) does it come from? _____

3. Briefly describe the myth. _____

_____

_____

_____

_____

4. What do you think the purpose of this myth was? _____

_____

_____

_____

_____

5. Is modern science able to explain what this myth tries to understand? _____

Explain. _____

_____

_____

_____

_____

_____

_____

_____

_____

_____

MINI-LESSON 23:
GREEK MYTHOLOGY

Perhaps more so than the myths of any other people, Greek mythology is a reflection of the ancient Greeks and their philosophies. Greek myths are truly rich in language and marvelous in imagination.

Procedure:

- Explain that Greek mythology focused on the great questions of life that Greek thinkers pondered. Forces of nature were given personalities and were worshipped as gods.

- Note that the Greeks were one of the first people to worship gods that had their own image. (You might mention that this is known as *anthropomorphism,* meaning in the "form of human.") Many of their myths are about gods and demigods whose powers extend beyond those of mortals. Although the Greek gods were stronger and more beautiful than mortals, they had human weaknesses such as jealousy, anger, and spite. The gods lived on Mt. Olympus and often interfered with the affairs of mortals.

- Emphasize that many of the Greek myths attempted to explain nature. Zeus, the highest of the gods, hurled thunderbolts. Apollo drove his golden chariot (the sun) across the daytime sky. One of the most obvious of the nature myths is that of Demeter and her daughter Persephone. Demeter was the goddess of grain. One day Hades, the god of the Underworld, abducted Persephone and took her to his Underworld palace. In mourning for her daughter, Demeter did not bring forth the spring. Crops failed and starvation came to the Earth. When Apollo learned that Hades held Persephone captive, he told Zeus, who sent Hermes to order Hades to let the girl go. Hades knew he must obey Zeus; however, he tricked Persephone by enticing her to eat pomegranate seeds, which were known as the seeds of the dead. Thus, although Persephone was permitted to rejoin her mother, she was required to spend a part of the year with Hades in the Underworld. This is the time of the year the world endures winter.

- Mention that the Greeks were an artistic and creative people. Because of this, some scholars believe that some Greek myths may have been invented simply for entertainment. The story of Jason and his quest for the Golden Fleece might fall into this category. Of course, the story might also relate the adventures of a hero who sailed to a distant land for some reason (although not a golden fleece). The stories are so old, and so much has been lost, that no one can be sure.

- If you wish, you might mention some of the following major gods of Greek mythology to your students:

  —Zeus, high god, known as the Thunderer

  —Apollo, god of light and song; drives the chariot of the sun across the sky

  —Aphrodite, goddess of love

  —Hermes, messenger of the gods

—Hephaestus, god of fire

—Artemis, moon goddess, and goddess of vegetation

—Ares, god of war

—Athena, goddess of wisdom

—Hera, wife of Zeus

—Hades, god of the Underworld

Activities:

1. This activity is designed for the whole class or for students working in groups. Students are to read and analyze a Greek myth. They should try to determine what the story tries to explain or symbolically represents. Distributing copies of Worksheet 23–1, "Understanding Greek Mythology," will help students to explore their ideas. Upon completion of the worksheet, conduct a class discussion or let students work in groups to analyze the myth.

2. The Greeks were a bright people, who were inventive storytellers. Most of their myths are excellent stories. They contain notable characters, conflict, excitement, and suspense. Because their gods were much like the Greeks themselves, gods and mortals often played a role in Greek myths, resulting in a blend of reality and the supernatural that made entertaining stories. Instruct your students to read several Greek myths, then meet in groups and discuss how real events are blended with the supernatural in Greek mythology. Students should focus on the humanlike characteristics of the Greek gods and demigods. For each myth, they should list examples of real and supernatural events, and discuss how these elements are combined to create suspense and interest. You might also suggest that each group try to decide on a favorite myth. Provide time for each group to share its findings with the class.

Writing Activity:

• The mythology of a people is the result of that people's culture. Instruct your students to research the early Greeks. What type of people were they? Where did they come from? Suggest that your students examine the early Greeks' form of government, their beliefs, traditions, and customs. They should try to answer the question of how Greek culture gave rise to their mythology. Students should write about their findings in a report.

Name _____ Date _____ Section _____

Understanding Greek Mythology

Directions: Answer the questions below about the Greek myth you read. Use another sheet of paper if you need more space.

1. Name of myth: _____

2. Describe the main characters in this myth. _____

_____

_____

_____

_____

3. Briefly describe what happens in this myth. _____

_____

_____

_____

_____

_____

_____

_____

_____

_____

_____

_____

4. What do you think the purpose of this myth was? _____

_____

_____

_____

_____

_____

_____

_____

MINI-LESSON 24:
ROMAN MYTHOLOGY

Unlike the Greeks, whose intellectual curiosity and inventiveness produced mythology rich in language and spirit, the Romans were a practical people whose purpose was to build an empire. Their mythology can be described as a mosaic, with elements borrowed from the many people they conquered. Many of the gods the Romans worshipped came from Greece. In many cases, only the names were changed.

Procedure:

- Explain that Roman mythology is largely comprised of elements from people found throughout the ancient Mediterranean world. As Rome expanded its imperial rule, it incorporated the myths and gods of the people it conquered with its own.
- Note that Greek influence was very strong in early Rome. Greek civilization flourished before Rome, and its mythology came to dominant that of Rome. Many of Rome's myths are similar to those of Greece.
- You might mention some of the major gods of Greece and their counterparts in Roman mythology:
  —Zeus became Jupiter
  —Hera became Juno
  —Ares became Mars
  —Athena became Minerva
  —Aphrodite became Venus
  —Hermes became Mercury
  —Artemis became Diana
  —Hephaestus became Vulcan
  —Hades became Pluto (although in the latter Greek period he was often called Pluto)
  —Apollo remained Apollo
- Note that Roman mythology conformed to the needs of the Roman spirit and state. The Roman gods were practical gods, protectors to whom Romans paid tribute and offered sacrifices in exchange for favors.
- Point out that as the empire expanded, Rome added more gods and myths.

Activities:

1. This activity may be done with either the class or groups, provided students have read the same myth. Upon reading a Roman myth, students are to analyze it and try to determine its meaning. Distribute copies of Worksheet 24–1, "Understanding Roman Myths," which will help your students to organize their thoughts. Upon completion of the activity, conduct a class discussion or have students work in groups to analyze the myth.

2. For this activity, students should work individually. Considering that Romans were a practical people, instruct your students that they are to select a Roman myth, and create a poster with a slogan describing it. Encourage them to be creative and artistic. Display the posters at the end of the activity.

Writing Activity:

• Students are to select a Roman myth, research it, and try to determine its origin. Was it originally Roman, or did the Romans borrow it from another culture? Students should write a report tracing the development of the myth they selected, including a summary and what they feel the myth means. Display the reports upon conclusion of the activity.

Name _____ Date _____ Section _____

Understanding Roman Myths

Directions: Answer the questions below about the Roman myth you read. Use another sheet of paper if you need more space.

1. Name of myth: _____

2. Describe the main characters. _____

_____

_____

_____

_____

_____

3. Briefly describe the myth. _____

_____

_____

_____

_____

_____

_____

_____

_____

_____

_____

_____

4. What do you think the purpose of this myth was? ____

_____

_____

_____

_____

MINI-LESSON 25:
NORSE (GERMANIC) MYTHOLOGY

Norse mythology is most often associated with the Scandinavian countries. The myths, however, originally were of the Teutons, a Germanic people who inhabited much of Northern Europe. The Teutons eventually became divided into three great groups: the Goths, located to the east, the West Germans, of whom the Anglo-Saxons occupied England, and the northern tribes of the Teutons who populated Scandinavia. It is mostly through the Scandinavians that the myths have come down to us, although they were once shared by all Germanic groups.

Procedure:

- Explain that Norse mythology is a reflection of the rugged lands and long dark winters of Northern Europe, the land inhabited by Germanic people.

- Note that like the myths of other people, Norse myths try to answer the great questions of life, creation, death, and events of nature.

- Explain that Norse myths center around heroes and reflect a warrior culture. After all, these people were the ancestors of the Vikings and the sackers of Rome.

- Point out that Norse myths almost always include gods and supernatural beings, including elves, water-sprites, wood-sprites, dwarfs, and giants. Norse gods were humanlike, mortal, and often suffered greatly.

- You might mention that Norse mythology contains much tragedy. Even the gods are doomed to die, to be defeated at the end of the world by the Frost Giants. This final battle was called Ragnarok.

- You might wish to note some of the important gods of Norse mythology, including:

  —Odin, the highest of the gods, who was a great warrior and possessed much wisdom

  —Thor, the Thunderer, a storm god, who was perhaps the greatest warrior in Norse mythology; he wielded a magic hammer that, after being thrown, returned to him like a boomerang

  —Tyr, god of war and treaties

  —Frey, god of the sun and rain

  —Freyja, goddess of love and beauty

  —Frigga, Odin's wife

  —Hel, goddess of death

  —Loki, the evil one

  —Balder, god of light

- You might mention that some of the names of the days of our week are based on Norse mythology. (Note that English is a Germanic language.)

  —Odin (who was also known as Wotan): Wednesday

  —Thor: Thursday

—Tyr: Tuesday

—Frigga: Friday

Activities:

1. This activity may be done with the whole class or with groups. After students have read the same myth, they should analyze and explore its meanings. Hand out copies of Worksheet 25–1, "Exploring Norse Mythology," to help your students focus and organize their ideas. After students have completed the worksheet, either conduct a class discussion or have students work in groups to discuss the myth.

2. This activity is designed for groups. Instruct your students to conduct a study of Norse mythology. They are to create a chart in which they describe the various gods and supernatural beings that appear in Norse myths in a Who's Who in Norse Mythology. Permit time for students to present their charts to the class.

Writing Activity:

- After students have read several Norse myths, instruct them to select one that they find most interesting. They are to summarize it, explain what they believe the purpose of the myth was, and tell why they liked this myth.

Name _____ Date _____ Section _____

Exploring Norse Mythology

Directions: After reading a Norse myth, answer the questions below. Use another sheet of paper if you need more space.

1. Name of myth: _____

2. Describe the main characters of this myth. _____

_____

_____

3. Describe any supernatural beings in this myth. _____

_____

_____

_____

4. Briefly describe the myth. _____

_____

_____

_____

_____

_____

_____

_____

5. What do you think the purpose of this myth was? _____

_____

_____

_____

_____

_____

_____

_____

_____

_____

_____

MINI-LESSON 26:
MYTHOLOGY OF NATIVE AMERICANS

The myths of Native Americans are as varied as the Native Americans themselves; however, there are common themes and symbols. Like the myths of other cultures, myths of the Americas try to explain creation, the origin of humans, death, and events in nature.

This mini-lesson addresses general information about Native American mythology. It provides a good starting point from which you can lead your students into the study of specific myths among particular tribes or groups.

Procedure:

- Explain that the mythology of Native Americans is extensive, stretching from the Inuit of the far North to the tribes of South America.

- Emphasize that nature is a recurring theme in Native American mythology. A good example is a myth of the Abnaki Indians of North America. A young man encountered a woman with long golden hair. She told him that if he followed her instructions, she would remain with him. She said that he should make a fire and scorch the ground. He was then to drag her over the burned ground so that her golden hair would be intertwined with the corn seeds for harvesting. When the Abnaki see the silky styles on a cornstalk, they know the woman with the golden hair has not forgotten them. The myth attempts to explain the origins of corn.

- Explain that totems are an important part of many Native American cultures. The totem, which represents a being or a force of nature, is worshipped and respected. In return, the totem provides help and protection. Totems are often looked upon as the ancestor of a clan, group, or individual. In some of the advanced cultures, such as the Mayas and Aztecs, totems eventually evolved into various gods, which were often associated with nature.

- Explain that the myths of the tribes of the Americas were strongly influenced by their environment. The Inuit, for example, live in a harsh, savage land, and their myths are frequently concerned with the destiny of the individual and survival against the elements. Myths of the Plains Indians are influenced by the vast lands on which they live, and the greatness of nature is a frequent theme. The sun, earth, moon, morning star, wind, fire, and thunder are some of their gods. In Mexico, the sun was worshipped, because the sun is essential to the growing of crops.

Activities:

1. This activity is designed for the class or for groups, provided students read the same myth. After reading the myth, have students analyze it and try to determine its meaning. Hand out copies of Worksheet 26–1, "Myths of the Americas," which students will find helpful in their analysis. After students have completed the worksheet, conduct a class discussion or have students meet in groups to analyze the myth.

2. This activity is designed for students working in groups. Because the myths of Native Americans are likely to be somewhat unfamiliar to many of your students, instruct groups to read several myths (perhaps one by each member of the group), summarize them, and then share the summaries orally with the class. Having each group read myths from a different tribe or civilization will add interest to the activity.

3. Students should work individually or in pairs for this activity. Students are to read a myth in which a totem or symbolic figure plays a prominent role. They should either draw or create a model of the totem or symbolic figure. Provide time for students to show their work to the class, and also briefly summarize the myth they read. (Consider collaborating with your students' art teacher for this activity. She or he can work with students on the drawings and models, while you can focus on the myths.)

Writing Activity:

• For this activity, students should read a myth and rewrite it for the benefit of younger students. You might wish to arrange for your students to read their rewritten myths to younger students. Young children enjoy having older students read to them. (Of course, this arrangement can work both ways, and you may wish to welcome students of younger grades into your class to read some of *their* writing to *your* students.)

Name _____ Date _____ Section _____

Myths of the Americas

Directions: Answer the questions below about the Native American myth you read. Use another sheet of paper if you need more space.

1. Name of myth: _____

_____

2. Who were the people who created this myth? _____

_____

Where did they live? _____

_____

3. Describe the main characters of this myth. _____

_____

_____

_____

4. Briefly summarize this myth. _____

_____

_____

_____

_____

_____

_____

_____

5. What do you think the purpose of this myth was? _____

_____

_____

_____

_____

MINI-LESSON 27:
THE MYTHOLOGY OF AFRICA

The mythologies of the peoples of Africa place nature at the center of worship. Along with nature worship, many African myths contain powerful themes of sorcery and magic.

African mythology is a huge topic and this mini-lesson is designed only to be an introduction. You may use it as a springboard to study the myths of specific cultures or regions in Africa. A good time to study African mythology in reading is when students are studying Africa in social studies.

Procedure:

- Explain that Africa is a large continent populated with many people. The great size of Africa and its varied inhabitants have given rise to an extensive mythology.

- Explain that many myths tell of events of life or nature. The Malagasy of southwest Madagascar have myths that tell of rain, the appearance of humans on the Earth, and death. The Zulus have myths about the origin of the world.

- Note that many myths of Africa personify forces in nature—the sun, moon, sky, mountains, rivers, etc., giving them human attributes.

- Note that in some cultures myths tell of gods. The Masai, for example, have a myth that tells of a single god.

- Explain that magic and sorcery are recurrent themes in many African myths. Amulets and talismans are used to protect their owners against such things as disease, injuries, thieves, and murderers, or to increase good fortune. In Angola, for example, fetishes—roughly carved statues of wood—are thought to give protection from evil spells. In many myths magicians and sorcerers have great powers over nature.

- Mention that many myths contain references to the existence of the soul after death. The souls of the dead often transmigrate into the bodies of animals, or may even be reincarnated in plants.

Activities:

1. This activity is designed for the whole class or groups, provided students have read the same myth. After students have read the myth, they are to analyze it. Hand out copies of Worksheet 27–1, "The Myths of Africa," to help students clarify their ideas. Upon completion of the worksheet, conduct a discussion with the class or have students work in groups to analyze the myth.

2. For this activity, instruct your students to work in groups. Each group should focus on a different region of Africa and read several of that region's myths. Suggest that they choose from among the following:

   —Myths of Southeastern Africa (including Madagascar)

   —Myths of the Peoples of the South

—Myths of Central Africa

—Myths of Uganda

—Myths of the Sudan

—Myths of Guinea

After conducting their research, students should prepare an oral presentation for the class.

Writing Activity:

• Instruct students to write an informational article about magic. Although magic plays a prominent role in some African myths, historically, belief in magic is found throughout the world. Encourage students to investigate the historical roots of magic and determine what people hoped to achieve through the use of magic. Upon completion of their articles, conduct a class discussion and display the work of your students.

Name _____ Date _____ Section _____

The Myths of Africa

Directions: Answer the following questions about the African myth you read. Use another sheet of paper if you need more space.

1. Name of myth: _____

2. What people told this myth? _____

In what region of Africa did they live? _____

3. Describe the main characters of this myth. _____

_____

_____

_____

_____

_____

4. Briefly describe the myth. _____

_____

_____

_____

_____

_____

_____

_____

_____

_____

5. What do you think the purpose of this myth was? _____

_____

_____

_____

MINI-LESSON 28:
MYTHOLOGIES OF ASIA

Asia is an enormous continent populated with many people. The mythology of Asia is as diverse as its people.

This mini-lesson is a general survey that focuses on Indian, Chinese, and Japanese mythology. Even as a survey, the mini-lesson contains a lot of material and you may wish to divide it into three separate lessons. Of course, you may use it as an introduction and follow it with more lessons on the mythologies of specific Asian cultures.

Procedure:

- Explain that great empires and cultures have flourished in Asia throughout history. Every culture has its own mythology.
- If you wish to focus on Indian mythology, note the following:
  - India is a country comprised of people of many historical roots, including Aryan invaders from the northwest who settled in the upper valley of the Indus River between 3000 and 1500 B.C., Dravidians who had already achieved a rather advanced culture by this time, and many lesser-known groups and tribes.
  - Indian mythology arose from the many different peoples who lived in India over a long period of time. Thus, Indian mythology is very complex, and often includes stories of warriors, gods, and demons.
  - Much of what we know about early Indian mythology comes down to us in the Vedas, a collection of sacred writings from about 1200 B.C. The Vedas contain information on Indo-Aryan social practices, religion, culture, and mythology.
  - Vedic hymns of a later period contain references to Hinduism, a major religion in India.
  - Buddhism, one of the world's major religions, also has its beginnings in Indian mythology.
- If you wish to focus on Chinese mythology, note the following:
  - There are many divinities in Chinese mythology. Chinese gods watched over virtually every aspect of life. For example, there were gods of happiness, gods that took care of people, gods that were concerned with wealth, and so on. There were also many nature divinities, including the sun, moon, rain, thunder, and wind.
  - Many Chinese gods are deified men. The highest of the gods are surrounded with courts and have their own palaces.
  - From ancient times, Chinese governments have been highly organized. This is reflected in many of the myths about their gods. Chinese gods often act more like bureaucrats than they do gods. They have clearly defined powers, and keep records and accounts. They may be promoted or demoted, depending on their performance.

- If you wish to focus on Japanese mythology, note the following:

  —It is thought that the ancestors of the Japanese invaded the island from Korea, engaging in war with the people already there. Japanese myths include elements from these days, long before recorded history.

  —Japanese myths tell of the origin of the world, origins of the gods, and try to answer the same questions of nature that puzzled other ancient people.

  —Japanese myths were preserved by *katari-be,* reciters, whose function was to recite ancient legends at important festivals.

  —The Japanese deified aspects of nature, which they called *kami,* meaning, "beings more highly placed." Rivers, mountains, even great men could be kami.

  —Japanese gods have bodies like humans and are endowed with all human qualities—good and bad. The gods are not all-powerful.

Activities:

1. This activity may be used with the whole class or with groups. After reading the same myth, students are to analyze and discuss it. Distribute copies of Worksheet 28–1, "Asian Mythology," to help them with their ideas. Upon completion of the worksheet, conduct a class discussion or have students meet in groups to analyze the myth.

2. Working in groups, students are to select one of the major regions of Asia—for example, India, China, or Japan—and read several examples of that region's mythology. Groups should summarize the myths they read, and then share them orally with the class.

3. Working in groups, students are to select one of the major regions of Asia, research the region, and try to determine how the area's history affected its mythology. Each group should prepare an oral presentation for the class.

Writing Activity:

- Instruct your students to compare some myths of Asia with myths of ancient Greece. They should summarize the myths they select, and note similarities and differences in a brief report.

Name _____ Date _____ Section _____

Asian Mythology

Directions: Answer the questions below about the Asian myth you read. Use another sheet of paper if you need more space.

1. Name of myth: _____

2. What people told this myth? _____

What modern country do they live in? _____

3. Describe the main characters of this myth. _____

_____

_____

_____

_____

4. Briefly describe this myth. _____

_____

_____

_____

_____

_____

_____

_____

_____

5. What do you think the purpose of this myth was? _____

_____

_____

_____

_____

MINI-LESSON 29:
POETRY (OVERVIEW)

Poetry is language laden with imagery and emotion. Unlike prose, the words of poetry are filled with power and meaning, often assuming a musical or rhythmical quality. Poetry is found in cultures throughout the world.

Procedure:

- Explain that poetry probably developed as a form of early storytelling. Long before writing, people told stories of great events, successful hunts, and memorable battles. They chanted during religious ceremonies, using rhythmical patterns and rhymes to help them remember the words better. Eventually, some of the stories were sung.
- Explain that there are many kinds of poems. Some of the best-known English poems include narratives, epics, ballads, and sonnets. Poems may be written in lyrical form, free verse, blank verse, or in special patterns.
- Explain the difference between *rhythm* and *rhyme,* which students often find confusing. *Rhythm* refers to the pattern of stressed and unstressed syllables in the lines of a poem. *Rhyme* refers to the repetition of sounds, and, along with rhythm, may give a poem a musical quality. There are various rhyme patterns, including end rhyme (words at the end of lines rhyme), internal rhyme (words within lines rhyme), and beginning rhyme (words that begin sentences rhyme). The most common is end rhyme.
- Note that because most poems are shorter than stories, poets choose their words carefully and try to create strong images in the minds of their readers. They often use figures of speech such as similes, metaphors, and personification to paint vivid images. (See Mini-lesson 73, "Figures of Speech.")
- Mention that poems are written in lines, which are usually organized in stanzas.
- Explain that the term *poetic license* refers to poets taking liberties with the rules of standard English to enhance the meaning of a poem. A good example is a poem that does not have any punctuation.

Activities:

1. This activity is designed for the class or for groups. After reading the same poem, students are to interpret it. Distribute copies of Worksheet 29–1, "Making Sense of Poetry," which will help your students clarify their ideas. After students have finished the worksheet, conduct a class discussion or have students meet in groups to discuss the poem.
2. This activity works well with groups. Ask students to obtain a copy of a favorite poem—they might have a copy at home or they may need to obtain a copy from the library—and read it to the members of their group. Encourage them to put "feeling" in their words. After reading their poems, students should share with the other members of their group why these poems were favorites.

3. Read some poems of your favorite poet to the class. Most students who lack an appreciation of poetry often have had little experience with it. Sometimes, merely listening to someone read a meaningful poem can show the listener the power of poetry and the emotion it can evoke.

4. Distribute copies of Worksheet 29–2, "Some Poets of Distinction." Most students know of few good poets. Although the list of outstanding poets on this handout is by no means complete, it offers poets who have achieved recognition. Providing this list to students may inspire some of them to seek the works of these authors in the library or bookstore.

Writing Activity:

• Encourage students to write a poem on a topic of their choice in whatever form they wish. Conclude the activity with a session in which your students read their poems to the class or to their groups. Consider displaying the poems.

Name _____ Date _____ Section _____

Making Sense of Poetry

Directions: Answer the following questions about the poem you read. Use another sheet of paper if you need more space.

1. Title of poem: _____

Author: _____

2. Does this poem have rhythm? _____ Does it have rhyme? _____ Explain the effect the rhythm and/or rhyme have on the poem. (If the poem does not have rhythm or rhyme, tell why you think its author did not use these elements in the poem.) _____

_____

_____

_____

_____

_____

_____

_____

3. What mood or feelings does this poem arouse in the reader? _____

_____

_____

4. How does the poet achieve this mood? _____

_____

_____

5. What do you think the poet's purpose was in writing this poem? _____

_____

_____

Name _____ Date _____ Section _____

Some Poets of Distinction

William Wordsworth

While no list can claim to contain the world's "best" poets, this one certainly contains some of them. You are encouraged to find the works of these poets in your library or bookstore. You will also find many of their poems in various anthologies.

Anna Akhmatova (Russian)
Vincente Aleixandre y Merlo (Spanish)
Dante Alighieri (Italian)
Louis Aragon (French)
Margaret Atwood (Canadian)
Matsuo Basho (Japanese)
Charles Baudelaire (French)
Stephen Vincent Benet (American)
Gottfried Benn (German)
Giovanni Boccaccio (Italian)
Elizabeth Barrett Browning (English)
Gwendolyn Brooks (American)
William Cullen Bryant (American)
Lewis Carroll (English)
Jean Cocteau (French)
Hart Crane (American)
e.e. cummings (American)
Emily Dickinson (American)
Gunnar Ekelof (Swedish)
Robert Frost (American)
Federico Garcia Lorca (Spanish)
Allen Ginsberg (American)
Heinrich Heine (German)
Friedrich Holderlin (German)
Langston Hughes (American)
Victor Hugo (French)
John Keats (English)
Jean de La Fontaine (French)
Henry Wadsworth Longfellow (American)

Joachim Maria Machado de Assis (Brazilian)
Vladimir Mayakovsky (Russian)
Edna St. Vincent Millay (American)
Szeslaw Milosz (Polish)
Eugenio Montale (Italian)
Pablo Neruda (Chilean)
Octavio Paz (Mexican)
Fernando Pessoa (Portuguese)
Sylvia Plath (American)
Edgar Allan Poe (American)
Vasco Popa (Yugoslavian)
Alexander Pushkin (Russian)
Arthur Rimbaud (French)
Carl Sandburg (American)
Robert Service (Canadian)
William Shakespeare (English)
Sara Teasdale (American)
Alfred, Lord Tennyson (English)
Dylan Thomas (Welsh)
Paul Verlaine (French)
Robert Penn Warren (American)
Walt Whitman (American)
John Greenleaf Whittier (American)
Richard Wilbur (American)
William Carlos Williams (American)
William Wordsworth (English)
William Butler Yeats (Irish)
Yevgeny Yevtushendo (Russian)

MINI-LESSON 30:
NARRATIVE POEMS

Narrative poems tell a story. Most likely the origins of narrative poems are deep in prehistory when storytellers repeated tales of great men and events.

Procedure:

- Explain that narrative poems, much like fiction, tell a story. Narrative poems have a plot, action, setting, characters, and usually dialogue. Rhythm and rhyme are also important elements.
- Note that narrative poems generally take one of two forms: the epic (see Mini-lesson 31) and the ballad.
- Explain that an epic is a long poem about a hero's adventures and deeds. Good examples are Homer's "The Iliad" and "The Odyssey."
- Explain that a ballad is a form of verse that is designed to be sung or recited. Ballads are much shorter than epics and are written in a regular rhythm and rhyme. They are usually dramatic and focus on a short episode. Good examples of ballads are "The Ballad of Casey Jones," "John Henry," and "The Streets of Laredo." Ballads often are based on folk culture.

Activities:

1. This activity can be used with the whole class or with groups, provided students have read the same narrative poem. After reading the poem, instruct your students to analyze it, paying close attention to the poem's plot, characters, and setting. Hand out copies of Worksheet 30–1, "Analyzing Narrative Poems," to help your students with their ideas. Upon completion of the worksheet, conduct a class discussion or have students meet in groups to discuss the narrative.

2. Students should work in groups for this activity. Have groups select a narrative and create a storyboard of at least six frames that represent six actions or scenes described in the narrative. For this activity you might consider using Longfellow's "Paul Revere's Ride" or a similar narrative that has various scenes. Storyboards can help students reflect on and visualize the imagery of the narrative. Oaktag or poster paper may be used for the storyboards. Suggest that students plan their scenes on scrap paper before working with the material that will be their finished product. Planning their storyboards on scrap paper reduces the chances for mistakes later. Provide time for students to show their storyboards to the class. You may also wish to display them.

3. Have students work in pairs or groups of three and do dramatic readings of a ballad of their choice.

Writing Activities:

1. Working individually or in pairs, instruct students to write a ballad. Some possible topics include:

—Exploits of the School Football Team

—The Student Who Didn't Study Enough

—The Science Experiment That Didn't Work

—The Computer That Crashed

—The Secret of the Student with Pink Socks

At the end of the activity, permit time for students to read their ballads to the class.

2. Encourage your students to write a narrative poem on a topic of their choice. They might consider selecting a real-life hero they know of, or a sports star, celebrity, or fictional character to take the hero role in their narrative. Either provide time for students to read their narratives to the class, or display the poems upon completion of the activity.

Name _____ Date _____ Section _____

Analyzing Narrative Poems

Directions: Narrative poems tell a story. They have a plot, conflict, characters, and settings. Answer the questions below about the narrative poem you read. Use another sheet of paper if you need more space.

1. Title of poem: _____

_____

Author: _____

2. Describe the setting of this poem. _____

_____

_____

_____

_____

_____

_____

3. Describe the main character(s) in this poem. _____

_____

_____

_____

4. What problem, conflict, or obstacle does the main character(s) face? _____

_____

_____

_____

5. Briefly summarize the plot of this poem. _____

_____

_____

_____

_____

MINI-LESSON 31:
EPIC POEMS

Epic poetry, a form of the narrative poem, tells a long story. In the past, *epic* referred only to poetry, but in recent years the word has been loosely applied to any story that is extensive in scope and detail.

Procedure:

- Explain that epic poems usually are accounts of heroes or people of high rank who encounter adventures or struggles on a grand scale.

- Note that epic poetry most likely arose out of the myths, legends, and traditions of primitive people. The oldest versions of these stories were passed down orally from generation to generation.

- Emphasize that epic poems have strong plots, heroic characters, conflict, excitement, adventure, detailed descriptions, and strong imagery. Many epics also contain examples of powerful symbolism.

- Note that epic poetry is found in cultures throughout the world. You might want to mention some examples:

  —The "Epic of Gilgamesh." This is the earliest epic in western civilization, told before 3000 B.C. It came down to us from the ancient Sumerians of Mesopotamia.

  —"The Iliad" and "The Odyssey" by Homer. "The Iliad" is the story of the Trojan War, and "The Odyssey" is the story of Odysseus and the adventures he encountered on his voyage home after the war.

  —The "Ramayana" and "Mahabharata" of India. These epics recount the struggles of Aryan invaders with the original inhabitants of ancient India.

  —The "Aeneid" by the Latin poet Virgil in the first century B.C. tells of the founding of Rome.

  —"Beowulf." This Old English epic tells of a heroic warrior.

  —"The Song of Roland." This epic relates the tragedy of a great warrior of medieval France.

  —"The Song of the Niebelungs." Written around 1200 A.D. by an unknown German author, this story is based on several ancient German and Scandinavian legends. It tells of knights and their ladies, loves, and battles. The hero of the epic is Siegfried.

  —"Paradise Lost." Written by John Milton, this epic tells of Lucifer's fall from heaven.

Activities:

1. This activity can be used with the whole class or with groups, provided students have read the same epic poem. After reading the epic, instruct students to review it and focus on its plot, characters, conflict, and setting. Also ask them to consider if rhythm and rhyme enhance the poem. Hand

out copies of Worksheet 31–1, "The Story in the Epic," which will help students organize their ideas. After students have completed the worksheet, conduct a class discussion or have students meet in groups to discuss the epic they read.

2. This activity is designed for groups. Instruct each group to read a different epic. They are to discuss the epic among themselves, summarize it—focusing their summary on the elements that make it a good story, such as plot, conflict, characterization, and setting—and present an oral report to the class. Encourage them to read excerpts of their favorite parts. (*Note:* Try to steer students away from epics that might be too difficult for them.)

3. Your students should work individually or in pairs for this activity. Epic poems contain many of the customs and traditions of the people during the time in which the story is set. Instruct your students to research the setting of the epic they are reading. They should try to discover how people lived then and create a model depicting their way of life. Some suggestions for models might be a representation of a village, a warrior's helmet, a royal crest, or a symbol that represents the hero of the epic. Display the models upon completion of the activity. (You might want to collaborate with your students' art teacher on this project. He or she might be willing to manage the work necessary for completing the models, and you can manage the reading and comprehension of the epics.)

Writing Activity:

• Instruct students to select a favorite scene of an epic they read, and rewrite this scene in prose. Encourage them to note how different the story becomes. Display the writing of your students upon completion.

Name _____ Date _____ Section _____

The Story in the Epic

Directions: Epic poems tell a story of great deeds. They have heroes, conflict, strong plots, and detailed settings. Answer the questions below about the epic you read. Use another sheet of paper if you need more space.

1. Title of epic: _____

Author: _____

2. When does this epic take place? _____

Where does it take place? _____

3. Describe the main character(s). _____

_____

_____

_____

4. What is the main conflict of this story? _____

_____

_____

5. Briefly summarize this epic. _____

_____

_____

_____

_____

_____

_____

_____

_____

_____

_____

_____

_____

MINI-LESSON 32:
LYRIC POEMS

Lyric poems are the most common form of English poetry. Long ago, lyric poems were meant to be set to music and accompanied by a lyre, a stringed instrument related to the harp. Lyres were popular in ancient Greece.

Procedure:

- Explain that, in the past, lyric poems were written as songs. A song is a lyric poem adapted to music.

- Emphasize that lyric poems are very common in English literature. They are the most frequently written and read poems.

- Note that lyric poems are usually shorter than narrative or dramatic poetry. They are designed to express the poet's thoughts or feelings on a subject.

- Mention that lyric poems create mood through vivid images, descriptive words, and the musical quality of their lines. Images are often designed to appeal to the senses. Two examples are "Harlem Night Song" by Langston Hughes and "Blue Butterfly Day" by Robert Frost.

- Note that of the many types of lyric poems, three well-known forms are sonnets, odes, and elegies. You might wish to mention the basic elements of each.

  —A sonnet has 14 lines. Sonnets come in various rhyme patterns, although the English and Italian forms are the most common. The *English sonnet,* which is the form Shakespeare used, uses this rhyme pattern:

  abab cdcd efef gg

  The *Italian sonnet* is quite different. It is divided into an octave (the first 8 lines) and a sestet (the next 6 lines). The rhyme pattern is as follows:

  abbaabba cdecde **or** cdccdc **or** cdedce

  The octave offers a problem or a reflection on an ideal and the sestet resolves the problem or realizes the ideal.

  —An *ode* is a poem usually addressed to a person, thing, or quality. William Wordsworth's "Ode to Duty" is an example.

  —An *elegy* is a poem written about death or in the memory of someone. William Cullen Bryant's "Thanatopsis" with its death theme is a good example. Dylan Thomas's "Do Not Go Gentle into That Good Night" is another.

- Mention that many other poems—for example, narrative poems—often have lyrical qualities.

Activities:

1. This activity may be used with the whole class or with groups. After reading the same lyric poem, students should analyze it, focusing especially on its lyrical qualities. Distribute copies of Worksheet 32–1, "Poems That Could Be Songs," to help your students with their ideas. Upon completion of

the worksheet, conduct a class discussion or have students meet in groups to discuss the elements of the poem.

2. This activity is designed for students working in groups. Instruct your groups to read several examples of lyric poems, then select one that they feel exhibits distinct lyrical qualities. They should analyze this poem and discuss how rhythm, rhyme, and appeal to the reader's senses enhance the poem. After their discussion, they should share their results with the class.

3. William Shakespeare is unquestionably one of the greatest writers in English literature. Encourage your students to conduct an independent study of Shakespeare's sonnets. Instruct them to select a favorite sonnet and read it to the class.

4. Ask your students to think of some of their favorite singers or music groups. Encourage them to obtain the lyrics for some of the songs their favorite singers have recorded. (You might wish to remind them that any lyrics they bring in should be appropriate for the classroom.) Ask them to read the lyrics of these songs to the class. It's likely that the lyrics will possess a rhythmical, poetic quality. At this point you might conduct a class discussion or organize a debate on this topic: "Are the writers of song lyrics actually poets?" (Students who claim they "hate" poetry, but who like current, popular songs might find this to be a dilemma.)

Writing Activity:

• Instruct your students to write a lyric poem on a topic of their choice. You may encourage them to write a sonnet, ode, or elegy; however, for many students, any poem with lyrical qualities should be acceptable. At the end of the activity, collect the poems and publish them in a class anthology of lyric poetry.

Name _____ Date _____ Section _____

Poems That Could Be Songs

Directions: In the past, lyric poems were meant to be set to music and accompanied by an instrument. Even today a song is a lyric poem adapted to music. Answer the following questions about the lyric poem you read. Use another sheet of paper if you need more space.

1. Title of poem: _____

_____

Author: _____

2. Briefly describe what this poem is about. _____

_____

_____

_____

_____

_____

3. Explain how the rhythm and/or rhyme affect the lyrical quality of this poem. _____

_____

_____

_____

_____

_____

4. Lyric poems often create mood through the poet's use of vivid images and descriptive words. Give some examples of descriptive words and phrases the poet used in this poem.

_____

_____

_____

_____

MINI-LESSON 33:
BLANK VERSE

Blank verse originally was modeled after the poetry of the ancient Greeks and gained a popular English following with William Shakespeare. Blank verse is most often used in narrative or dramatic poems.

Procedure:

- Explain that blank verse is poetry written in unrhymed lines of iambic pentameter. Each line of blank verse is composed of ten syllables of alternating stress of accent.

- Point out that although blank verse is used most often with narrative or dramatic poems, it is a versatile form that lends itself to various types of poems.

- Mention that much of Shakespeare's drama is written in blank verse. *Hamlet* is an excellent example. John Milton's *Paradise Lost* is another. You might wish to read excerpts of these or other works to show your students examples of blank verse.

Activities:

1. Since Shakespeare popularized blank verse in English literature, a study of some of his works is an excellent way to familiarize your students with this poetic form. Assign the reading of *Hamlet*. As students read the play, be sure to point out how this work is written in blank verse. You might wish to have students meet in their groups, select excerpts of scenes they particularly enjoy, and do a dramatic reading for the class. Perhaps they'd like to act out the scenes. To help students in their study of the play, you may wish to distribute copies of Worksheet 33–1, "The Story of *Hamlet*." After students have finished reading the play, you may conduct a class discussion or have students work in groups to discuss the play and Shakespeare's use of blank verse.

2. Encourage students to obtain examples of poems written in blank verse. They may wish to check their school or local library for poems written in blank verse. Instruct them to read several examples of blank verse, choose one they like, and read it to the class. Provide time for students to read the poems to the class.

Writing Activity:

- Instruct students to write a poem using blank verse. Remind them that blank verse is unrhymed iambic pentameter. Have a poetry reading at the end of the activity.

Name _____ Date _____ Section _____

The Story of *Hamlet*

Directions: Answer the following questions about *Hamlet*. Use another sheet of paper if you need more space.

1. Describe Hamlet's meeting with the ghost. _____
_____

_____

2. What does Hamlet decide to do after he meets the ghost? _____
_____

_____

3. Do you think his plan was a wise one? _____ Explain. _____
_____

_____

4. How does Claudius try to eliminate Hamlet? _____
_____

_____

5. Describe the climax of the play. _____
_____

_____

6. This story is written in blank verse. Explain how you think the story would have

changed if it had been written with rhyme. _____

_____

_____

_____

_____

_____

_____

_____

MINI-LESSON 34:
FREE VERSE

Free verse has been widely used by many poets in the 20th century. It enables poets to write about a great variety of subjects with various tones and effects.

Procedure:

- Explain that free verse refers to poetry that does not follow a conventional pattern of rhythm or stanzas.
- Explain that free verse usually has an irregular rhyme pattern or no rhyming at all. Rhythms result from sounds, words, phrases, and stanzas. Sometimes, free verse may sound like ordinary speech.
- Note that free verse has become quite popular in the 20th century. Many poets prefer it to other forms.
- Mention that free verse "frees" the poet from concentrating on rhythm and rhyme, which often restrain ideas or force the use of certain words in particular places. This is most apparent in the poet being forced to select words for ending rhyme.
- While many poets write in free verse, you might like to mention that Walt Whitman was one of the first major poets to use this form. His "Song of Myself" is an excellent example.

Activities:

1. This activity may be used with the whole class or with groups, provided students read the same poem. After reading a poem written in free verse, instruct students to analyze it, focusing their attention on how the use of free verse supports the author's purpose in the poem. Distribute copies of Worksheet 34–1, "Poetic Freedom," to help your students clarify their ideas. Upon completion of the worksheet, conduct a discussion with the class or have students meet in groups to discuss the poem.

2. Read one or more examples of poems written in free verse to your students. Free verse poems are found in numerous anthologies. Be sure to add feeling and tone to your voice. Discuss the meanings of the poems with your students.

3. For this activity students should work in groups. While in their groups, have students read several examples of both lyric and free verse poetry. They should then discuss the poems, focusing on the following:

—Which poems are more pleasing to the ear?

—Which poems have more imagery?

—Which poems inspire more emotion?

—Could any of the lyric poems be rewritten successfully as free verse poems? Why or why not?

—Could any of the free verse poems be rewritten successfully as lyric poems? Why or why not?

Writing Activity:

- Ask your students to write a poem in free verse on topics of their choice. Encourage them to pay close attention to imagery and emotion in writing. Either permit time for a poetry reading session, or publish the poems of your students in an anthology of free verse.

Name _____ Date _____ Section _____

Poetic Freedom

Directions: Free verse refers to poetry that does not follow a conventional pattern of rhythm or stanzas. Answer the questions below about the free verse poem you read. Use another sheet of paper if you need more space.

1. Title of poem: _____

Author: _____

2. What is the subject of this poem? _____

_____

_____

3. Free verse poems are known for their strong imagery. Describe some examples of

imagery in this poem. _____

_____

_____

_____

_____

_____

_____

_____

4. How do you think the use of rhythm or rhyme would have changed this poem? _____

_____

_____

_____

_____

_____

_____

_____

_____

_____

MINI-LESSON 35:
LIMERICKS

Although trained as an artist who specialized in drawings and paintings of natural history, Englishman Edward Lear is best remembered for popularizing the limerick. In 1882 Lear was invited by the Earl of Derby to come to his estate and create drawings of the Earl's private collection of animals. While there, Lear became a favorite of the Earl's nieces, nephews, and grandchildren by entertaining them at first with his comic pictures and then with silly, nonsensical poems. Lear most often wrote these poems in a form that became known as the limerick.

Procedure:

- Explain that a limerick is a short, humorous poem of five lines. It has a special rhyme pattern: the first, second, and fifth lines rhyme, as do the third and fourth. Limericks also have a unique cadence that is quickly mastered and recognized.
- Emphasize that the silliness of the content, the cadence, and rhyme make limericks funny, especially to children.
- Mention that most libraries have collections of limericks written by Lear as well as many other authors. Limericks are timeless in the pleasure they offer.

Activities:

1. Obtain several examples of limericks, and have students meet in groups and read them. Have each group select some of their favorite limericks and read them to the class.
2. Read several examples of limericks to your students. Point out the ryhme pattern and the special cadence. Note how these poems are silly and often nonsensical. Conduct a discussion on how such nonsense poems can be entertaining and amusing.

Writing Activities:

1. Encourage your students to write limericks of their own. Remind them to follow the rhyme pattern and cadence that are unique to limericks. Also remind them that limericks are humorous. Permit time for students to read their limericks to the class or their groups.
2. Edward Lear was a talented, remarkable man. Instruct your students to research his life and write a biographical sketch, highlighting his achievements. Display the writing of your students.

MINI-LESSON 36:
CONCRETE POETRY

Concrete poetry is frequently thought of as being a modern form of poetry. This form, however, dates to at least the 17th century when the English poet George Herbert used the concept of the concrete poem with his "The Altar," which was an altar-shaped poem. Today many authors have created concrete poems.

Procedure:

- Explain that concrete poems are poems that take the shape of their subject. Thus, a concrete poem about a tree is written in the form of a tree.
- Note that although George Herbert, an English poet, used the form in the 17th century, concrete poems have only become popular during the latter part of this century.
- Mention that concrete poems may be about anything. They are simple and artistic. They hardly ever have rhyme.
- You might wish to mention that concrete poems may be found in various books and anthologies. Two good ones are *Concrete Poetry* edited by Mary E. Solt and Willis Barnstone (Indiana University Press, 1969) and *An Anthology of Concrete Poetry,* edited by Emmett Williams (Something Else Press, 1967).

Activities:

1. Have students meet in their groups and read several examples of concrete poems. Remind them to pay attention to the artistic patterns.
2. Working with the entire class, read and discuss concrete poems.

Writing Activity:

- Instruct your students to pick a subject and write a concrete poem about it. Suggest that students first write their poem on a standard sheet of paper; then, once it is in finished form, redo the poem on poster paper. This will enable them to create a large version of their poem. Suggest that they use markers to highlight their poem. Display the posters upon completion of the activity.

MINI-LESSON 37:
THE POETRY OF NATIVE AMERICANS

The poetry of Native Americans is a broad subject, because virtually every culture created poems. This mini-lesson merely highlights some major points about the poetry of Native Americans, and may be used as an introduction to the study of the poetry of particular cultures.

Procedure:

- Explain that Native Americans created poems for many reasons, including:
  —To praise their gods
  —To ask their gods for help in life
  —To describe or celebrate the wonders or powers of nature
  —To record the history of the tribe
  —To record great events
  —To record the adventures of heroes
  —To explain natural phenomenon (often as part of their mythology)
  —To describe battle and war
  —To express an idea or observation
- Explain that many poems were created to be chanted to the rhythmic accents of drums, especially poems that were recited at ceremonies.
- Note that the poems of Native Americans are expressive, and full of human emotion and spirit.
- Point out that in most Native American cultures any individual could create poems. Poems were not the domain of a special group of "poets."
- Mention that Native American poems frequently are difficult to translate into English. Elements such as rhythm and imagery are hard to translate directly. Also, many modern readers of these poems do not have the background or cultural perspective that would enable them to fully appreciate the poetry. Thus, much of the beauty and power of the poems of Native Americans is lost during translations.
- You might mention that while there are many sources of Native American poetry, perhaps one of the best is *American Indian Prose and Poetry: An Anthology,* edited by Margot Astrov (The John Day Company, 1972). Good books for background on Native Americans include:
  —*Indian Heritage, Indian Pride* by Jimalee Burton (University of Oklahoma Press, 1974).
  —"Native Americans Resource Library," a series of four volumes written by Dana Newmann (The Center for Applied Research in Education, 1995, 1996, 1997). The series focuses on Indians of North America: Volume 1, *Desert Indians;* Volume 2, *Plains Indians;* Volume 3, *Coastal Indians;* and Volume 4, *Woodlands Indians.*

Activities:

1. This activity is designed to be used with the whole class or groups, provided students have read the same poem. After students have read a poem of Native Americans, instruct them to analyze it. What do they believe was the purpose of the poem? What does it mean? Hand out copies of Worksheet 37–1, "Native American Poems," which will help your students with their ideas. Upon completion of the worksheet, conduct a class discussion or have students meet in groups to discuss the poem.

2. This activity is designed for group work. Each group is to select a region of North America, Central America, or South America, and choose a major culture to research. Students should attempt to find out how the people of this culture lived, and how their way of life influenced their poetry. Each group should prepare an oral report—including examples of poetry—which group members will present to the class. Suggest that students consider cultures from the following regions:

    —The Arctic

    —The Subarctic

    —The North American Plains

    —The North American East Coast Woodlands

    —The North American West Coast

    —The North American Southwest

    —Mexico and Central America

    —The Amazon Basin

    —The West Coast of South America

Writing Activity:

*   Instruct your students to study a particular Native American culture or tribe. Students are to imagine that they are a member of that tribe or group, then write a poem celebrating or describing some aspect of their life as Native American.

Name _____ Date _____ Section _____

Native American Poems

Directions: Answer the following questions about the Native American poem you read. Use another sheet of paper if you need more space.

1. Title of poem (if any): _____

2. From what Native American culture or tribe does this poem come? _____

_____

3. What is the subject of this poem? _____

_____

_____

_____

4. Describe some examples of imagery in this poem. _____

_____

_____

_____

_____

_____

5. What do you think the purpose of this poem was? _____

_____

_____

_____

_____

_____

_____

_____

_____

_____

MINI-LESSON 38:
THE POETRY OF AFRICAN-AMERICANS

Both the oral and written literature of African-Americans has been influenced by race and the unique experiences of African-Americans in the United States. The influence of their experiences is vividly expressed in their poetry, which often focuses on the attempt to examine their dual African and Western heritages.

Procedure:

- Explain that African-American poetry explores and celebrates African-American heritage, culture, and condition in American society.

- Point out that African-American poetry frequently is a result of conflicting heritages—that of African culture and Western (English) culture. The influence of these cultural heritages results in poetry that often focuses on the place of African-Americans in contemporary American society.

- Caution your students that African-American poetry is best understood by interpreting it in the light of history and its purpose.

- Mention that Phillis Wheatley was the first slave and the second woman in colonial America to publish a book of poems: *Poems on Various Subjects: Religious, and Moral* (1773).

- Mention the Harlem Renaissance. This was a period in the 1920s that witnessed an explosion of African-American poetry, led by Langston Hughes and Countee Cullen. (In general, this was a time of major achievement in virtually all areas of literature and the arts by African-Americans.)

- Mention that by the 1940s African-American poets had gained distinction through the work of various authors, including Robert Hayden, Margaret Walker, and Gwendolyn Brooks. Brooks, for her *Annie Allen* (1943), was the first African-American to win the Pulitzer Prize for Poetry.

- Mention that by the 1970s and 1980s a new generation of African-American poets rose to prominence, including Alice Walker, Rita Dove, Christopher Gilbert, Cornelius Eady, and Maya Angelou. Angelou read her poem "On the Pulse of Morning" at President Bill Clinton's first inauguration in 1993.

- You might tell your students that there are many books containing the work of both African-American and African poets. Some good ones include:

  —*Every Shut Eye Ain't Asleep: An Anthology of Poetry by African Americans Since 1945,* edited by Michael S. Harper and Anthony Walton (Little, Brown and Company, 1994)

  —*The Heinemann Book of African American Poetry in English,* selected by Adewale Maja-Pearce (Heinemann, 1990)

  —*The Penguin Book of Modern African Poetry,* edited by Gerald Moore and Ulli Beier (Penguin Books, 1984)

  —*The Heritage of African Poetry: An Anthology of Oral and Written Poetry,* edited by Isidore Okpewho (Longman, 1985)

Activities:

1. This activity is designed for the whole class or for groups, provided students have read the same poem. After reading a poem written by an African-American poet, instruct your students to interpret the poem and try to identify its meaning and the author's purpose. Distribute copies of Worksheet 38–1, "An African-American Poem," which will help your students with their ideas. Upon completion of the activity, conduct a class discussion or have your students meet in groups to discuss the poem.

2. This activity works best when students meet in groups. Encourage your students to obtain various examples of African-American poetry. You might suggest that students check for poems in the school or local library. While in their groups, students are to read several poems and discuss what they mean. They should compare the poems according to style, imagery, and the author's purpose. After they have read and discussed several poems, they should select a few they like the best and read these to the class. Provide time for groups to read their favorite poems to the class.

3. This activity is also designed for groups. Have groups review several traditional African-American folk songs, spirituals, and modern poetry. Compare them. In what ways, if any, are the spirituals and folk songs similar to the modern poems? How are they different? What might explain the differences? Organize panel discussions where each group presents its conclusions to the class.

4. Have students work in groups and compare examples of the poetry of African-Americans to the poetry of Africans who reside on the continent. Instruct students to compare the themes, structures, and purposes of these poems. Each group should prepare an oral presentation for the class.

Writing Activity:

- The poetry of African-American poets often reflects the influence of the dual culture of African roots and Western heritage. Instruct your students to write an essay on how these dual heritages may affect African-American poets. Display the essays upon completion of the activity.

Name _____ Date _____ Section _____

An African-American Poem

Directions: Answer the following questions about the poem you read. Use another sheet of paper if you need more space.

1. Title of poem: _____

Author: _____

2. What is the subject of this poem? _____

_____

3. Describe the structure of this poem. (For example, does it have rhyme, a specific rhythm, or special pattern?) _____

_____

_____

_____

_____

_____

4. What do you think this poem means? _____

_____

_____

_____

_____

_____

5. Why do you think the author wrote this poem? _____

_____

_____

_____

_____

MINI-LESSON 39:
JAPANESE POETRY—FREE VERSE, TANKA, AND HAIKU

Poetry enjoys great importance in Japanese culture and is recited at various occasions and celebrations. Most Japanese poems are short and written in free verse, or in the form of tanka or haiku.

You might wish to divide this mini-lesson into two or three parts, especially if you wish to conduct a detailed study of Japanese poetry, spending a day each on free verse poems, tanka, and haiku.

Procedure:

- Explain that poetry is very popular in Japan. Many Japanese read and write poetry. Many magazines in Japan are devoted to publishing poetry.
- Note that few Japanese poems use rhyme. Rather, they are based on a syllable count.
- Point out that most Japanese poems are examples of refinement and craftsmanship. Perfection is always sought.
- Emphasize that free verse, tanka, and haiku are the most common forms of Japanese poetry.
- If you wish to focus on *tanka,* note the following:
  —Tanka can be traced to the 7th century A.D. Examples of tanka were often recited at the court of the emperor.
  —A tanka is a poem of five lines, based on a specific syllable count. The first line has five syllables, the second has seven, the third has five, and the fourth and fifth have seven each. The total number of syllables in a tanka is 31.
  —Tankas do not have rhyme.
  —Subjects vary, ranging from nature to love to the ponderings of the poet.
  —The poet, Tsurayuki Ki, is considered by many in Japan to be the master of tanka.
- If you wish to focus on *haiku,* note the following:
  —Haiku emerged in the 16th century.
  —Haikus are poems of three lines with a specific syllable pattern. The first line has five syllables, the second has seven, and the third has five.
  —Haikus do not have rhyme.
  —These poems usually focus on an aspect of nature, suggesting a mood or image.
  —The traditional haiku consists of contrasting images, one of time or place and the other of a vivid observation. The purpose of a haiku is to evoke mood and emotion.
  —The poet, Basho, is regarded by many Japanese as one of the greatest writers of haiku.
- You might mention that most libraries carry several anthologies of Japanese poetry. Following are two examples:

—*Anthology of Modern Japanese Poetry,* translated and compiled by Edith Marcombe Shiffert and Yuki Sawa (Charles E. Tuttle Company, 1972)

—*The Penguin Book of Japanese Verse,* edited by Brownas Geoffrey and Anthony Thwaite (Penguin Books, 1964)

Activities:

1. While working in groups, students are to read several examples of tankas or haikus. They should share their impressions of the poems, focusing their discussion on the imagery and emotion the poems evoke.

2. Read several examples of tankas or haikus to your class. Conduct a discussion about their purpose, and what the poet is trying to communicate to his readers.

3. While working in groups, instruct your students to read several examples of free verse poems written by English and Japanese authors. Students should compare the poems and look for similarities and differences. How do the subjects compare? How do the styles compare? How do the imageries compare? Provide time for students to share their findings with the class in an oral presentation.

Writing Activities:

1. Instruct students to write a tanka. Remind them to follow the structure of five lines and a syllable count of 5, 7, 5, 7, 7 for the lines. Encourage students to write more than one.

2. Instruct your students to write a haiku. Remind them to follow the three-line structure with the syllable count of 5, 7, 5. Encourage your students to write several haikus.

3. Upon conclusion of their writing, you might have your students read their examples of tanka or haiku to the class, or compile their poems and publish them in a class magazine.

4. As an extension of these writing activities, perhaps you can have students work with their art teacher to create bamboo brush paintings to illustrate their poems.

MINI-LESSON 40:
ANTHOLOGIES, SEQUELS, TRILOGIES, AND SERIES

While your students will most likely be familiar with novels and short stories, which they read in basal texts when they were younger, the terms *anthology, sequel, trilogy,* and *series* may be unfamiliar. Because so many stories fit into these categories, a mini-lesson explaining them may be well worth a few minutes of class time.

Procedure:

- Explain that within the field of literature, students will undoubtedly come across the terms anthology, sequel, trilogy, and series. Define each.

—*Anthology:* a collection of selected stories written by various authors. Sometimes an anthology is a collection of the writings of one author. Anthologies are sometimes referred to as collections. Some examples include:

> *Short Circuits: Thirteen Shocking Stories by Outstanding Writers for Young Adults,* edited by Donald R. Gallo
>
> *The Norton Anthology of Short Fiction,* edited by R.V. Cassill
>
> *Masters of Fantasy,* edited by Terry Carr and Martin Harry Greenberg

—*Sequel:* a story that is complete in itself, but that continues the storyline from a previous story and usually has the same characters. Sequels may consist of several books. Some good examples include:

> *Alice's Adventures in Wonderland* and its sequel *Through the Looking Glass* by Lewis Carroll
>
> *Dicey's Song* and its sequel *The Homecoming* by Cynthia Voigt
>
> *Lonesome Dove* and its sequel *The Streets of Laredo* by Larry McMurtry
>
> *The Adventures of Tom Sawyer* and its sequel *The Adventures of Huckleberry Finn* by Mark Twain
>
> *Anne of Green Gables,* which has several sequels, written by Lucy Maud Montgomery

—*Trilogy:* a group of three separate novels related in subject or theme. Frequently the same characters appear in all three stories. Some good examples include:

> *The Lord of the Rings* trilogy by J.R.R. Tolkien
>
> *The Earthsea* trilogy by Ersula K. LeGuin

—*Series:* a succession of stories or novels related in subject, format, and often theme. The separate works are sometimes numbered. Good examples include:

> The Nancy Drew series by Carolyn Keene
>
> The Hardy Boys series by Franklin W. Dixon
>
> The Sweet Valley High series, created by Francine Pascal
>
> The 18 Pine Street series by Walter Dean Myers
>
> The Chronicles of Narnia by C. S. Lewis

Sue Grafton's mystery series that follows the letters of the alphabet, beginning with *"A" Is for Alibi*

Activities:

1. This activity is designed for students working in groups. Instruct group members to select an anthology, or books that make up a sequel, trilogy, or series, and read and discuss some of the works of their selection.

   Students should explore how the works they read satisfy the definition of an anthology, sequel, trilogy, or series. What are the unifying themes, if any? Are there similarities between the stories? Differences? Distribute copies of Worksheet 40–1, "Stories in Many Categories," to help your students with their ideas. After discussing their material, each group should organize and present an oral report to the class.

   To help ensure that this activity is fair to everyone, consider providing these guidelines: If students select an anthology, group members should each read several stories; however, if the group picks a sequel, trilogy, or series, different group members should read different books.

2. Obtain some examples of anthologies, sequels, trilogies, and series. Have students meet in their groups and examine the books, noting why each fits its particular category.

Writing Activity:

• Many students have read books in a series by the time they reach middle school. Ask them to briefly write about a series they read, explaining how and why they got hooked with the series. Was it the type of story, the characters, author's writing style, or a combination of factors that caught their interest? What kept them interested? What makes this series different from others they may have read? Upon completion of the activity, display the writing of your students or conduct a class discussion about various series.

Name _____ Date _____ Section _____

Stories in Many Categories

Directions: Answer the questions below about the stories you read. Use another sheet of paper if you need more space.

1. Were the stories you read part of an anthology, sequel, trilogy, or series? _____

Who was the author, or authors? _____

_____

2. Describe how the stories were similar. _____

_____

_____

_____

_____

3. Describe how the stories were different. _____

_____

_____

_____

_____

4. Would you like to read other stories by this author, or authors? _____ Explain.

_____

_____

_____

_____

_____

_____

_____

_____

_____

_____

MINI-LESSON 41:
PSEUDONYMS—WHY AUTHORS USE THEM

Instead of their real names, some authors use fictitious names, called pseudonyms, on their works. Writers assume pseudonyms for a variety of reasons.

Procedure:

- Explain that some authors use pseudonyms, or pen names, for their books, articles, stories, or poems.
- Explain that authors use pseudonyms for many reasons, including:
  —The material may be controversial and the author does not want his or her real name associated with it. Elvira Potter who lives in a small midwestern town may not want her prim and proper neighbors to know she writes steamy romances.
  —The author may have earned recognition in another field or type of writing, and wishes his or her new material to appear under a new name. The doctor who has several medical books to his credit may feel that he should publish his new fantasy series under a pen name.
  —The author may feel that his or her name may not be catchy enough. A pen name might be easier to remember, sound more distinguished, or have special significance. Samuel Clemens is okay, but most people would agree that Mark Twain is better. The name Mark Twain also has special meaning. For a time Clemens was a steamboat pilot on the Mississippi River. The phrase "mark twain" meant two fathoms deep, and was important to pilots who wished not to run aground.
- If you wish, distribute copies of Worksheet 41–1, "Authors' Pseudonyms," to your students. The list offers several well-known authors and their pen names.

Activity:

- For this activity students may work individually, in pairs, or groups of three. Instruct your students to research various authors and their pseudonyms. You may wish to hand out copies of Worksheet 41–1 to help students with the activity. After compiling the names of various authors and their pseudonyms, students are to create a puzzle that utilizes authors' real and pen names. Some types of puzzles they might consider include a puzzle that matches the names, a crossword puzzle, or a wordsearch. Note that some puzzles—matching and crossword puzzles, for example—will require clues. Students should also create answer keys for their puzzles.

  Encourage students to plan their puzzle carefully in advance, designing and completing rough copies before attempting their finals. Careful planning will help to reduce errors on final copies.

  If students have access to personal computers and software that supports the creation of puzzles, encourage them to produce their puzzles using computers. Otherwise, suggest that students produce their puzzles on white paper using dark ink. Graph paper is particularly useful for the creation of crossword puzzles and wordsearches. Photocopy examples of the finished puzzles and distribute them to the class for a culminating exercise.

Writing Activity:

• Ask your students to pick a pseudonym for their writing. What name would they pick? Why would they pick this name? Ask them to write a short essay about this.

Name _____ Date _____ Section _____

Authors' Pseudonyms

Charlotte Brontë

Pseudonym	*True Name*
Richard Bachman	Stephen King
Imamu Amiri Baraka	LeRoi Jones
Currer Bell; C.B.; Marquis of Douro; Genius; Lord Charles Wellesley	Charlotte Brontë
Ellis Bell; R. Alcon	Emily Brontë
Edgar Box	Gore Vidal
Nancy Boyd	Edna St. Vincent Millay
Peter Collinson	Dashiell Hammett
Edith Van Dyne	L. Frank Baum
Tom Esterbrook; Elron; Rene La Fayette; Capt. B. A. Northrop; Kurt von Rachen	L. Ron Hubbard
A. A. Fair; Charles M. Green; Carleton Kendrake; Charles J. Kenny	Erle Stanley Gardner
Guy Fawkes	Robert Benchley
Paul French; Dr. A.	Isaac Asimov
Sirak Goryan	William Saroyan
Dod Grile	Ambrose Bierce
O. Henry	William Sydney Porter
Louis L'Amour; Tex Burns	Louis LaMoore
William Lee	William S. Burroughs
Anson MacDonald	Robert A. Heinlein
Agatha Christie Mallowen; Mary Westmacott	Agatha Christie
Barbara Hamilton McCorquodale	Barbara Cortland
George Orwell	Eric Arthur Blair
Constant Reader	Dorothy Parker
Dr. Seuss; Theo Lesieg	Theodor Seuss Geisel
Mark Twain	Samuel Langhorne Clemens
Villiam Christian Walter	Hans Christian Andersen

Note: Some authors publish their works under pseudonyms and their real names.

MINI-LESSON 42:
BOOK TITLES

Many authors anguish over the selection of a title for their book. These authors realize that a well-conceived title can be an important factor in winning readers.

Procedure:

- Explain that titles, especially for books, are sometimes not decided until the book is ready for publication. Until that time the book may only have a tentative title.

- Point out that great titles are easier for readers to remember. Sometimes the title of a book captures the true essence of the book and may be more memorable than the book itself.

- Explain that many titles may be considered for a book. Authors and editors often share ideas, brainstorming several titles until the right one is found.

- Note that good titles draw readers into books. Good titles will often "hook" readers by promising danger, suspense, action, mystery, or love.

- Offer this example of possible titles for *Gone with the Wind*. These were actually potential titles for Margaret Mitchell's marvelous story about the Civil War. Fortunately, as you'll see from the titles below, *Gone with the Wind* was chosen:

  —Tomorrow Is Another Day   —Milestones

  —Ba! Ba! Black Sheep   —Bugles Sang True

  —Tote the Weary Load   —Jettison

  —Not in Our Stars

  It's obvious that *Gone with the Wind* uniquely fits the underlying reality of the story that the traditions and customs of the Old South were swept away with the winds of the Civil War.

Activity:

- This activity is designed for students working in groups. While in their groups, students should select some popular novels they have read, pretend they are editors at a publishing house, and brainstorm possible new titles. Are any of the new titles potentially better than the original? Why? You may wish to distribute several copies of Worksheet 42–1, "Brainstorming Titles," to each group to help students with their ideas. Permit time for groups to report their results to the class.

Writing Activity:

- Encourage students to select one of their previous pieces of writing—a story, article, or poem—and write five alternate titles. Students should then meet in their groups, share their writing, and ask the group to select what it feels is the best title from the original and alternatives. Perhaps the group will find that the original title is best.

Name _____ Date _____ Section _____

Brainstorming Titles

Directions: Write the title of a novel on the left and possible alternative titles on the right. Then answer the question on the bottom of this page. Use another sheet of paper if you need more space.

Original Title	*Possible New Titles*
_____	_____
_____	_____
_____	_____
_____	_____
_____	_____
_____	_____
_____	_____
_____	_____
_____	_____
_____	_____

Which title is the best? Why? _____

_____

_____

_____

_____

_____

_____

_____

_____

_____

_____

MINI-LESSON 43:
THE PUBLISHING PROCESS

To most students the publishing process is a mystery. They have little understanding of the steps that take a book from its writing to publication. A mini-lesson that explains how a book is produced can not only be interesting to students, but provide them with information that makes them feel they are a part of the "reading" public that truly understands the world of books.

Procedure:

- Explain that the publication of a book is frequently a lengthy, multistep process that might take anywhere from several months to two years after a book has been written. There are exceptions, of course. The time necessary for publication of books that are very timely, and are expected to be blockbusters, may be rushed up to weeks.

- Explain that there are several thousand book publishers in the U.S. It is difficult to say precisely how many because some are very small, producing only one or two books each year. Others are companies set up by authors who self-publish their own books. A good source of book publishers in the U.S. is *Literary Market Place,* a reference available at most libraries.

- Explain the usual steps in the publication of a book.

  —The author completes a book and contacts a literary agent to represent him, or the author may contact a publisher directly. If the author signs an agreement with an agent, the agent markets the book to potential publishers. Should the agent sell the book, he or she earns a commission, usually 15% of any money the author earns from the sale of copies of the book. If the author chooses to market the book him- or herself, the author may send the whole manuscript, or, in some cases, sample chapters, to potential publishers. Most publishers will send authors information regarding their requirements for the submission of books. Publishers' requirements for submission are also listed in references such as *Writer's Market,* which can be found at most libraries and bookstores.

  —At the publishing house, if the manuscript is addressed to a particular editor, it will go to that editor. Otherwise, it will go to what is called the "slush" pile. The slush pile contains manuscripts that come to the publishing house without being addressed to a specific editor. Eventually all of the manuscripts get read, but those in the slush pile take longer.

  —After the manuscript is read, if the editor decides it does not fit the publisher's needs, it is returned to the author with a rejection form. However, if the manuscript is found to be well written and interesting, it will usually be passed to other editors for their opinion. Some publishing houses have editorial committees that meet and decide which books will be accepted for publication.

  —In making their decision whether to accept a book, editors often consider questions such as:

Does the book fit the publisher's line?

Is it well written? How much editing and revision will be necessary? (If it requires too much, it might not be worth the editor's time or the publisher's investment.)

Is the author qualified to write this book? A doctor who specializes in diets probably has the experience to write about nutrition. A person who simply likes food probably does not.

What is the competition for this book? Are there many other books about the same subject available? If there are many, perhaps this book won't be able to attract much attention.

Will the book satisfy the publisher's readers?

- After a book is accepted, the author is offered a contract. The contract may provide for an advance, which may be minimal to a few thousand to several thousand dollars, depending on the book and how much money the publisher expects to earn. The advance will be deducted from any royalties the author eventually earns. Royalties are a percentage of the book's overall profits. While some books sell hundreds of thousands of copies, most don't. Many sell only a few thousand; some sell less than that.

- Once the book has been scheduled for production, it is edited. The author may be asked to make some revisions. After the book has been revised, it is typeset. Most books are produced directly from computer disks these days. The typeset form is the print that appears on the pages of the published book. After typesetting, but before printing, the book is proofread and any final errors are corrected.

- Illustrations, photos, charts, graphs, and similar additions may be provided by the author or the publisher.

- Published books are copyrighted. This means that they are registered with the Copyright Office, usually in the author's name, but sometimes in the publisher's name. Copyright protects the author from plagiarism, the taking of the author's words by someone else and using them as his or her own. In most cases, copyright protection lasts for the author's lifetime plus 50 years.

- Published books also have an ISBN—International Standard Book Number. This number, located on the copyright page, facilitates ordering by computer.

- Books are produced in print runs. A print run may be 5,000, 10,000, or more copies. When the front matter of a book notes that it is in its second, third, fourth, or more printing, it means that the previous runs have sold out. Obviously, books that have undergone several printings are the popular ones.

- After publication, the publisher often provides advertising and promotion. Sometimes authors will help with promotion through tours, speeches, and book signings.

Activities:

1. Using the same book—preferably a novel but a text will do—review the book with your students. Note how the cover is designed with the title and/or illustrations and photographs. Point out the back jacket. Most contain a brief

description of the book. Go through the front matter with your students, noting the inside title page, publisher, place of publication, and copyright date. Explain that these comprise the bibliographical data. You might also wish to point out the contents. Most students have never been guided through a book in this manner, and the activity will give them a better understanding of the publishing process.

2. Working individually, instruct students to select a book of their choice and complete Worksheet 43–1, "Book Information." This worksheet requires students to go through their books and find essential information. After students are done, go over the worksheets orally.

3. Working in pairs or groups of three, students are to create a poster advertising a book of their choice. Suggest that they sketch out their poster on scrap paper first. Provide oaktag or poster paper for their final copies, and display the posters upon completion of the activity.

Writing Activity:

- Instruct students to imagine they are a sales representative for the publisher of a book of their choice. They are to write a sales letter to your school's librarian explaining why he or she should purchase the book for your school's library. Display the letters at the end of the activity.

Name _____ Date _____ Section _____

Book Information

Directions: Answer the following questions about the book you are examining.

1. What is the full title of your book? _____

   _____

2. Who is the author? _____

3. Who is the illustrator (if any)? _____

4. Who is the publisher? _____

5. Where was this book published? _____

6. When was it published? _____

7. In whose name is the copyright? _____

8. What is the book's ISBN? _____

9. Has this book been through more than one printing? _____

   If yes, what printing is this? _____

10. Is any other information provided in the front matter of this book? _____

    If yes, what is it? _____

    _____

    _____

    _____

    _____

    _____

MINI-LESSON 44:
FILM ADAPTATIONS AND NOVELIZATIONS

Most students consider novels and movies to be vastly different creative works. Many are unaware that stories, whether produced for TV, the movies, or as novels, follow the same basic plot formats. Many students are also unaware that popular novels are often made into movies, and some movies are rewritten and published as novels.

Procedure:

- Explain that stories created as novels and stories developed as movies have much in common. The plots are developed around lead characters who have a problem that must be solved. As the characters try to solve the problem, they encounter obstacles, which lead to conflict. Invariably, the problem becomes bigger. The problem is finally solved (making a happy ending) or not solved (an unhappy ending) in the climax.

- Explain that many screenplays have been developed from popular novels. *Gone with the Wind* by Margaret Mitchell, *Something Wicked This Way Comes* by Ray Bradbury, *Where the Red Fern Grows* by Wilson Rawls, and *Lonesome Dove* by Larry McMurtry are some examples. There are countless others.

- Note that when a novel is adapted as a screenplay, sometimes the story is changed to accommodate the visual effects of the screen. Stories may also be changed because of length. Long novels—*Gone with the Wind,* for example—are too lengthy to be shown in their entirety and are changed to satisfy time constraints. Conversely, scenes may be added to short stories. Titles may be changed, too.

- Explain that some movies that originated as screenplays are later turned into novels. This is called a novelization and entails that the screenplay be rewritten in novel form. Examples here include Steven Spielberg's *Star Wars* trilogy and the Indiana Jones movies. Originally developed as movies, the stories were later rewritten as novels.

Activity:

- Not all popular novels can be turned into successful movies. While working in their groups, students should brainstorm what they feel are the elements of successful movies. They should focus on character, plot, action, special effects, terror, and suspense. They are to then take a novel or story they recently read, and discuss whether it has the potential to be made into a successful movie. Distribute copies of Worksheet 44–1, "Novels and Movies," to help your students with their ideas. The worksheet provides space on the left for students to list what they feel are the elements of successful movies. On the right they may write notes whether the novel they are considering would be successful as a movie. They may explore each element in turn. For example, they may feel that the story has interesting characters but not enough action to sustain interest in a movie. Provide time for groups to share their conclusions with the class.

Writing Activity:

- Students are to select a movie they recently watched— one that is not based on a novel—and write an essay explaining whether, in their opinion, the movie would be successful if it were written in the form of a novel. They should examine elements such as plot, characterization, action, special effects, and suspense in their essays.

Name _____ Date _____ Section _____

Novels and Movies

Directions: Use this worksheet to help you decide if the novel you read could be produced as a successful movie. First list story elements that you feel are necessary to successful movies. Some elements you might include are plot, characterization, action, special effects, and suspense. Then decide if your novel has the material to satisfy these elements. You may write notes and opinions on the right side of this sheet. Use another sheet of paper if you need more space.

Story Element   *Notes*

MINI-LESSON 45:
HELPING STUDENTS SELECT BOOKS FOR READING

When they are young, many students are given books to read. In many cases, the books they read are selected for them. Unfortunately, some students don't receive much of an opportunity to choose their own books and, by the time they reach the upper grades, don't really know how to do so. This mini-lesson is designed to offer students tips on how they might wisely pick books that will interest them.

Procedure:

- Explain that sometimes people lack experience in selecting books that they will enjoy. As a result, these people may obtain books to read, but quickly find that the books they chose don't interest them.
- Note that most people who enjoy reading use various strategies for picking books, from browsing to suggestions from friends to information they find about books through book reviews and articles.
- Mention that many people will read several books by authors they enjoy.

Activities:

1. Distribute copies of Worksheet 45–1, "Book Selection Tips." Review and discuss the information with your students. Then conduct a class discussion of how people select books. You'll likely find that many students have their own strategies that others might find helpful.

2. This activity is designed for groups. Each group is to create a poster listing several steps for selecting books. Suggest that students brainstorm their list first, then plan their poster on scrap paper. Provide oaktag or poster paper for the final copies, and encourage students to use markers to highlight their work. Display the posters upon completion of the activity.

Writing Activity:

- Students are to write a how-to article, offering suggestions on how a person might select interesting books. Either display the articles, or have students share their finished articles with the members of their groups.

Name _____ Date _____ Section _____

Book Selection Tips

Following are suggestions for selecting books.

1. Think about your interests. What do you like to do? What types of stories do you like? What types of movies do you like to watch? Your interests are a key to the types of books you will enjoy.

2. If you read and enjoyed a particular type of book, look for books similar to it. Often in the back of the book, especially paperbacks, the titles of similar books are listed. You might find these interesting.

3. If an author whose book you enjoyed has written other books, you might like these titles as well.

4. Check book reviews in newspapers and magazines. *The Sunday New York Times Book Review* section is an excellent source. Most major newspapers contain book review sections. Online services may also offer book reviews under the keyword "Literature."

5. Browse for books in bookstores and in the library.

6. Ask librarians, English and reading teachers, and bookstore managers about books. Such people often have a wealth of knowledge about books that they are willing to share.

7. If you've seen a movie you really like, watch the closing credits. Some movies are based on books and you may discover an author whose writing will interest you.

8. When considering a book, look at its cover and title. These can give you clues about the book's content. Also, read the back cover. Although the back flap seldom provides a complete summary of the book, it usually offers details of what you will find inside. Open the book, look through the table of contents, and read a few samples from different sections. After all this, you should have a good idea whether you'd like to read this book.

MINI-LESSON 46:
BUILDING A PERSONAL LIBRARY

Many students start to acquire books at an early age. While very young children acquire storybooks, as students mature many begin to value having reference books handy. These students are beginning to see the value of a personal library.

Procedure:

- Explain that many people have a personal library. A personal library may be extensive with hundreds or thousands of books, ranging from references to classics to current fiction and nonfiction, or it may be rather small, consisting mostly of reference books.

- Emphasize that a personal library should serve the needs of its owner. Someone who makes regular use of the public library to borrow books to read may have mostly reference books in a personal library, while a person who enjoys reading and collecting books may have various titles.

- Note that personal computers have added to the flexibility of building a personal library. Compact discs can contain entire sets of encyclopedias, dictionaries, thesauruses, and references on language, science, history, and geography. The cost for an encyclopedia on compact disc may range from $30 to $100. Many online computer services also provide access to various references, which are regularly updated. Thus, if you own a personal computer, you may opt to purchase some reference sources in the form of compact discs, or access online references as needed.

- Mention that a well-rounded personal library would contain the following:
  —Unabridged dictionary
  —Encyclopedia
  —Thesaurus
  —Writer's style book that contains information on grammar
  —Atlas
  —References on various subjects such as history, economics, general science, astronomy, physics, philosophy, religion, etc.
  —Favorite books
  —Classics
  —The books of some great authors

- Mention that some personal libraries take years to build.

Activities:

1. This activity is designed for students working in groups. Instruct students to brainstorm the types of books they feel would be an asset to a personal library. Distribute copies of Worksheet 46–1, "Planning a Personal Library," which will help them to organize their ideas. Permit time for students to share their results with the class. You might then wish to sum up the activity with a class discussion.

2. While working in their groups, students should discuss some of their favorite authors and why those authors should be included in a personal library. Each group should pick three to five authors they would include in a personal library. Provide time for groups to share their selections with the class.

Writing Activity:

• Instruct your students to write an opinion essay on this question: "Will personal computers make books obsolete someday?" After students have completed their essays, have them discuss the topic in groups; or you may wish to conduct a class discussion on the topic.

Name _____ Date _____ Section _____

Planning a Personal Library

Directions: Use this sheet to determine books that would be valuable to a personal library. Note any references that might be obtained in compact disc format by the letters CD. Use another sheet of paper if you need more space.

| *Type of Book* | *Possible Alternatives (Titles)* |

Language References

_____

_____

_____

Other References

_____

_____

_____

Books for Enjoyment

_____

_____

_____

Other Books

_____

_____

_____

_____

_____

MINI-LESSON 47:
BUILDING GOOD READING HABITS

Good readers share many of the same reading habits. It is important that students understand reading is a skill, which can be practiced and improved. That is the purpose of this mini-lesson. (Mini-lesson 48 discusses poor reading habits to avoid.)

Procedure:

- Explain that reading is not an ability a person is born with; it is a process that is learned. The more a person reads, the better reader he or she will become.
- Note that most competent readers develop techniques and strategies that improve their reading ability.

Activities:

1. Distribute copies of Worksheet 47–1, "Good Reading Habits." Review and discuss the information with your students. Suggest that your students keep the handout for reference.

2. While working in their groups, students are to create a poster listing several good reading habits. Suggest that students make a rough copy of their poster first, then make the final using oaktag or poster paper. Also suggest that students illustrate their posters if they wish. To help students with their posters, distribute copies of Worksheet 47–1. Encourage them to use as many of the ideas as possible. Conduct a discussion upon completion of the activity and display the posters.

Writing Activity:

- Instruct students to write a personal account of the good reading habits they possess, and how they might improve any poor habits.

Name _____ Date _____ Section _____

Good Reading Habits

Following are several reading habits that many good readers share.

1. Good readers read a variety of materials. Most good readers have particular types of materials they enjoy.

2. Good readers tend to read material that is at their ability level or higher.

3. Good readers use context cues to understand the meaning of unfamiliar words. They seldom take the time to sound unfamiliar words out.

4. Good readers seldom focus on one word at a time, but instead see several words at once. This increases their reading speed.

5. Good readers use techniques such as scanning when they must find information fast.

6. Good readers stop reading self-selected books that don't hold their interest. They will choose another.

7. Good readers try to avoid rereading material unless absolutely necessary. They would rather press ahead.

8. Good readers talk about books with their friends. They share the titles of good books.

9. Good readers consult book reviews for suggestions of books to read.

10. Good readers seek out popular authors.

11. Good readers have favorite authors. They usually read several books by their favorite writers.

12. Good readers become engaged in what they are reading. They ask themselves questions and try to guess what may happen next. They seek the answers to their questions.

MINI-LESSON 48:
AVOIDING POOR READING HABITS

Reading is a process of many parts. At its most simple, the eyes see words and send the images of those words to the brain, which interprets them. How efficiently this happens determines whether an individual is a good reader. Research has found that specific habits, or practices, increase the efficiency of the reading process while some others slow the process. Good readers almost always share good reading habits; poor readers often share bad habits. In this mini-lesson you will describe some poor reading habits that should be avoided. (Mini-lesson 47 discusses good reading habits.)

Procedure:

- Explain that reading is a process dependent upon various skills and techniques. Just like a batter in baseball can slip into bad habits with his swing, decreasing his chances of hitting the ball, poor reading habits reduce a person's reading efficiency.

- Mention that like most things in life, reading improves with repetition. In other words, the more a person reads, the better his or her reading ability will become.

Activities:

1. Distribute copies of Worksheet 48–1, "Overcoming Poor Reading Habits." Review and discuss the information with your students, and encourage them to try to overcome any poor reading habits they might have.

2. This activity is designed for students working in groups. Instruct your groups to research why so many Americans are reported to have deficient reading skills. (Some estimates put the number as high as 40 million adults.) They should prepare an oral presentation to the class, supporting their findings with graphs and tables if possible. Provide time for sharing.

3. Set up a tutoring group in which some of your good readers help other students develop good reading habits. This may work particularly well with younger students. Your tutors should create a list of poor reading habits to avoid, which they will strive to help others understand. Perhaps this activity can be expanded into an ongoing tutoring program.

Writing Activity:

- Instruct your students to write a short article for younger students, describing how they might avoid poor reading habits.

Name _____ Date _____ Section _____

Overcoming Poor Reading Habits

Try to avoid the following habits that will undermine your reading ability.

1. Avoid placing a finger beneath the words being read. This slows down the reading rate and makes reading tedious. Also avoid using a card or other placeholder beneath the words you are reading.

2. Avoid moving your lips as you read. This slows down your reading, making it tiresome.

3. Avoid allowing your eyes to focus individually on each word. Good readers read by seeing sections of a sentence at once. They may see and comprehend three, four, or five words at the same time.

4. Avoid trying to sound out unfamiliar words. Instead, try to understand the word from the context.

5. Avoid rereading material unless necessary for understanding. Going back slows you down and disrupts your involvement with the flow of ideas.

6. Don't feel guilty if you don't like a book. It is not necessary to read a book you've selected but find that you don't like. If you don't like it after several pages, or a chapter, put it back and get another. Good reading habits are fostered when people read something they enjoy.

7. Never believe that competent readers are born, that good readers have some mysterious gift or talent. Most good readers have simply learned to read with good habits.

MINI-LESSON 49:
READING FOR DIFFERENT PURPOSES

Many students are unaware that good readers "read" differently, depending on their purpose. Adjusting their reading strategies as necessary results in efficient reading.

Procedure:

- Explain that good readers vary the way they read, based on their purpose and what they are reading.
- Note four different ways to read: (1) skimming, (2) scanning, (3) light reading, and (4) serious reading. Offer the following details of each:
  —*Skimming* is a quick way to gain a general overview of material. To skim effectively, readers should read titles and subtitles, and look at illustrations, photos, and charts for key words. They should also read the introductions and conclusions to sections, and the opening and concluding sentences of paragraphs.
  —*Scanning* is useful when the reader is looking for a name, fact, or detail, but is not concerned with an overview, relationships, or extended information. When scanning, people who have good peripheral vision move their eyes down the center of the page and pick out key words they are looking for. They will seek a name, date, or phrase while ignoring other information.
  —*Light reading* is common when a person is reading a newspaper, story, or article on a topic of interest. While the mind is engaged with the material, and the reader may ask questions, seek answers, and even make some predictions about the material, concentration may not be at its peak.
  —*Serious reading* refers to those situations when the mind is entirely engaged with the material being read. The reader concentrates fully on the material, looks for relationships, is open to insights, asks questions, and seeks answers. A good example of serious reading is the reading of an article on which a quiz will be given the next day.

Activities:

1. This activity will help to give students an understanding of skimming. Prior to the class meeting, instruct your students to bring either their science or social studies texts to class. Students should work in pairs or groups of three. They are to pick a textbook and turn to a section the class hasn't studied yet. The first student is to skim a few pages without taking any notes. This student is to then offer his or her partner(s) an overview of the material. After the first student is done, the next student skims another section of the text and offers an overview of it. Conduct a class discussion in which students volunteer to share their impressions of the activity.

2. This activity is designed for students working in pairs or groups of three. You might refer to it as the scanning game. Students are to select a book to work with. It might be a novel or text. One student looks through the book and picks a name, place, or phrase on a specific page. He then tells his partner (the scanner) the key word(s) and gives his partner a range of three or four pages, perhaps pages 21 to 24. The scanner then tries to find the key word(s). Of course, the scanner is timed, which promotes speed. After the scanner finds the key word(s), she selects information for her partner to find. Upon conclusion of the activity, you might wish to conduct a class discussion about scanning for information. Ask volunteers to describe how they found information quickly. What techniques or strategies did they use in skimming?

Writing Activity:

- Instruct students to write a short how-to article describing a reading method that works well for them. Upon conclusion of the writing, conduct a class discussion about reading methods.

MINI-LESSON 50:
CENSORSHIP

Anyone who reads, writes, is open to the sharing of ideas, and cherishes free speech must be aware of censorship. Indeed, a cornerstone of democracy is the free flow of ideas. While most people will agree with that statement, the issue of censorship has nonetheless divided more than one community, often pitting neighbors and friends against each other.

Procedure:

- Explain that censorship, in its broadest definition, is the attempt by an individual or group to prevent people from reading, writing, speaking, seeing, or hearing ideas that the censors feel are dangerous in some way. Censorship may result in the banning of books, movies, TV shows, works of art, or speeches.

- Emphasize that censors usually feel that through the act of censorship they are protecting others from ideas or information that they believe may cause harm.

- Explain that virtually all societies have groups that would censor ideas. In dictatorships, the government often censors the press and media, restricting information—particularly information the government considers damaging to itself—from the population.

- Point out that most democracies limit the powers of individuals and groups that would censor information. In the U.S., for example, the First Amendment to the Constitution guarantees freedom of speech. Some people, however, interpret the Constitution differently from others, often disputing how the Amendment applies to individual cases.

- You might wish to mention the ways censorship of books might occur, including:

  —Outright banning, which is rather rare because of potential court challenges.

  —Pressure put on publishers to eliminate certain information. Some textbook publishers treat sensitive subjects carefully because they don't want to anger powerful groups.

  —Pressure to stop schools and libraries from buying certain books.

  —The attempt to remove certain books from the shelves of libraries.

  —Limiting access to certain books by requiring parental permission for students to read a book.

- You might mention that over the years attempts have been made to ban and censor numerous books—many of which today are held in high regard. Just some of these books include:

  —*Leaves of Grass* by Walt Whitman

  —*The Adventures of Tom Sawyer* and *The Adventures of Huckleberry Finn* by Mark Twain

  —*The Grapes of Wrath* by John Steinbeck

—*The Catcher in the Rye* by J.D. Salinger

—*Forever Amber* by Kathleen Winson

—*From Here to Eternity* by James Jones

—*Slaughter-House Five* by Kurt Vonnegut, Jr.

—*Catch 22* by Joseph Heller

Activities:

1. This activity is designed for students working in groups. Instruct your groups to research censorship and be prepared to debate the question: "Is censorship ever justified? For example, during war, does the government have the right to censor information it considers harmful to the nation?"

2. Working in groups, students are to research cases of censorship (such cases are included in most books about censorship), select at least one case they find particularly interesting, and provide an oral report to the class. You might wish to monitor the groups closely and make sure that groups don't select the same cases. Having each group report on a different case will broaden the activity.

3. This activity is designed for students working individually. Assign the reading of Ray Bradbury's *Fahrenheit 451,* a novel whose theme is censorship. Distribute copies of Worksheet 50–1, "Book Burning!" to help your students explore the topic of censorship. Upon completion of the reading and worksheet, conduct a class discussion about censorship and the novel.

Writing Activity:

• Instruct students to research the topic of censorship and write a personal opinion essay, describing their feelings about this often-controversial subject.

Name _____ Date _____ Section _____

Book Burning!

Directions: Answer the questions below about *Fahr-enheit 451*. Use another sheet of paper if you need more space.

1. Why did Beatty believe it was necessary to burn

books? _____

_____

Do you agree? _____ Explain. _____

_____

2. How did Montag feel about burning books in the

beginning of the story? _____

_____

How did he feel about book burning at the end? _____

_____

Explain why his feelings changed. _____

_____

3. Explain what you think Faber meant when he said, "Those who don't build burn." _____

_____

_____

4. Do you think people like Faber and Montag can help to bring about change in their

world so that books are no longer burned? _____ Explain. _____

_____

_____

5. Explain what you think Ray Bradbury's purpose was in writing this story. _____

_____

_____

_____

_____

Mini-lessons
51 through 76
STORY ELEMENTS

MINI-LESSON 51:
BEGINNINGS: PREFACES, FOREWORDS, PROLOGUES, AND INTRODUCTIONS

The words *preface, foreword, prologue,* and *introduction* may be found at the beginning of a book. While some students will be familiar with them, others won't. Since these terms have slightly different meanings, a mini-lesson discussing them is practical.

Procedure:

• Explain that authors often use prefaces, forewords, prologues, and introductions to start their books. Define each for your students.

—*Foreword:* A foreword provides information or background about a book. Often it is written by someone other than the author. In the paperback edition of *The Secret Garden* by Frances Hodgson Burnett (Tor Books, 1990), a foreword is written by Jane Yolen.

—*Preface:* A preface is a statement or essay, usually written by the author, to introduce a book or explain its scope or intention. Many books begin with prefaces.

—*Prologue:* Originally prologues were used to introduce a play. They have since been used with stories, offering prior action or background that is helpful to understanding the story but is not actually a part of the story. Prologues may also serve as hooks, through which the author attempts to seize the reader's interest. A good example is Ray Bradbury's collection of stories in *The Illustrated Man.* Bradbury uses a prologue as a framework for the stories that follow.

—*Introduction:* "Introduction" is a generic term that often is used to describe a preface, foreword, or prologue. Sometimes, the word itself is used in the beginning of a book.

• Note that the length of a foreword, preface, prologue, or introduction depends on the material that follows it. These "beginnings" are only as long as they need to be.

• Explain that students (and adults) should always read the introductory material of books. Such material often provides information that can help readers better understand the material that is to come.

• Mention that sometimes introductory material may appear under titles such as "A Word to the Reader," "Before You Start," or "Read This First."

Activities:

1. This activity is designed for students working individually. You may use either a book the entire class is reading, or have students select a book of their choice. The book should have either a foreword, preface, prologue, or introduction. Distribute copies of Worksheet 51–1, "Beginnings," and instruct your students to answer the questions on the worksheet, applying the questions to the book they are reading. Conduct a class discussion about

the topic after completion of the activity. If students have used different books to answer the questions on the worksheet, ask volunteers to briefly describe the introductory material of their book.

2. Using some of the books they've read, or will be reading, show students examples of forewords, prefaces, prologues, and introductions.

Writing Activities:

1. Encourage students to use a foreword, preface, prologue, or introduction in a piece of their own writing. Display the finished writings at the end of the activity.

2. If students are keeping portfolios, suggest that they write an introduction for the portfolio. This makes the writing of an introduction a truly practical activity.

Name _____ Date _____ Section _____

Beginnings

Directions: Answer the questions below about the beginning of the book you are reading. Use another sheet of paper if you need more space.

1. What is the title of your book? _____

_____

Who is the author? _____

2. Does this book have a foreword, preface, prologue, or introduction? _____

   Does the book's introductory material have another title? _____ If yes, what? _____

_____

3. Briefly summarize the introductory material. _____

_____

_____

_____

_____

4. What is the purpose of the introductory material? _____

_____

_____

5. Is the introductory material helpful to the reader? _____ Explain. _____

_____

_____

_____

_____

_____

_____

MINI-LESSON 52:
ENDINGS: EPILOGUES, AFTERWORDS, AND CONCLUSIONS

Although *epilogues, afterwords,* and *conclusions* are all endings and have much in common, they also have slight differences. A short mini-lesson will help students to recognize these words when they encounter them in their reading.

Procedure:

- Explain each of the terms.

  —*Epilogue:* In the past, an epilogue referred to a short poem or speech spoken directly to the audience at the conclusion of a play. Nowadays, it may also be a short addition or concluding section at the end of a story, often dealing with the future of the characters after the story has ended. Note that some stories contain both prologues and epilogues, some contain either one or the other, and most contain neither.

  —*Afterword:* An afterword is sometimes used as an epilogue, although it might also be a final comment on a story, offer information about the author, or explain how the book was written.

  —*Conclusion:* This is the ending of a story or book. It may or may not be labeled. In fiction, the conclusion ties together any loose ends after the climax. For example, the characters are shown to live happily ever after. In nonfiction, the conclusion might contain a summary of the material, offer the author's opinions, or leave the reader with a final idea to consider.

Activities:

1. This activity is designed for students working individually. Students may use the same book or different books. You may wish to have students use books that contain epilogues or afterwords, or simply have them concentrate their efforts on their book's conclusion. Distribute copies of Worksheet 52–1, "Endings," and instruct students to answer the questions about their book's epilogue, afterword, or conclusion. Conduct a class discussion upon completion of the activity. If students use different books for the activity, have volunteers briefly describe the epilogue, afterword, or conclusion their book contained.

2. If your students—either the whole class or groups— are reading a book that contains an epilogue or afterword, have your students meet in their groups and discuss whether the epilogue or afterword is essential to the book. What did this "ending" add to the book? Would the impact of the book be lessened if the epilogue or afterword was eliminated? Did they find the epilogue or afterword interesting? Groups should present their conclusions orally to the class.

3. Point out examples of epilogues, afterwords, and conclusions in books the class is reading or has read.

Writing Activity:

- Encourage students to include an epilogue or afterword, or concentrate on their conclusion, in a piece of their own writing. Display the writings when students are done.

Name _____ Date _____ Section _____

Endings

Directions: Answer the questions below about the ending of the book you are reading. Use another sheet of paper if you need more space.

1. What is the title of your book? _____

_____

Who is the author? _____

2. Does your book contain an epilogue or afterword? _____

3. Briefly describe the epilogue or afterword. (If your book does

not have an epilogue or afterword, describe its conclusion.) _____

_____

_____

_____

_____

_____

4. What is the purpose of the epilogue, afterword, or conclusion of this book? _____

_____

_____

5. In your opinion, is the epilogue, afterword, or conclusion necessary to this book? _____

Explain. _____

_____

_____

_____

_____

MINI-LESSON 53:
WHAT MAKES A GOOD LEAD?

The lead is the beginning of a story or article. Since authors know that if their lead is weak, readers may not continue reading, most authors strive to make their leads as effective as possible. The best leads are those that "hook" the reader immediately and pull him or her into the rest of the work.

Procedure:

- Explain that the most important purpose of a lead is to grab the interest of the reader. From there the lead introduces the subject (in nonfiction) or the problem (in fiction), and draws the reader into the rest of the material.
- Note that although leads vary in length, depending on the material, the best ones are tight and compelling.

Activities:

1. You might wish to distribute copies of Worksheet 53–1, "Leads in Fiction and Nonfiction," and discuss the examples of the different kinds of leads with your students.

2. Select a favorite lead of a story you enjoy and read the lead to your class. You might consider reading the lead for Charles Dickens's *A Tale of Two Cities*—"It was the best of times, it was the worst of times . . . " Many consider this lead to be one of the best in literature.

3. This activity may be used with the whole class or with groups, provided students are reading the same material. Instruct students to consider the lead of the book, article, or story they are currently reading. They should focus on the question: What makes this lead effective? Or perhaps some students might not feel the lead is so effective as it might be. If so, how might the lead be improved? Hand out copies of Worksheet 53–2, "Leads," to help your students analyze the lead with which they are working. At the end of the activity, either conduct a class discussion or have students meet in groups to discuss the topic.

4. Have students meet in groups. Each member is to share the lead of a story or article he or she has read, but the other members didn't. (Before beginning this activity, give students a few days to review a story or article they'd like to share with their group. Make sure that students of the same group don't use the same material.) Remind students to be specific in describing the lead they are sharing, and tell if they feel it is strong or weak and why. If you wish, you may hand out copies of Worksheet 53–2 to help students with this activity.

Writing Activity:

- Students should use the information they have learned about leads to write a strong lead for a piece they are currently working on. Display the writings upon completion.

Name _____ Date _____ Section _____

Leads in Fiction and Nonfiction

The lead of a *story or article* has three important goals:

- Grab the reader's attention and interest.
- Reveal a problem or conflict (fiction), or introduce the subject (nonfiction).
- Carry the reader easily into the body of the story or article.

Leads for *fiction* often reveal a problem or conflict, or hint at a problem to come. The author may:

- Open the story with action, showing characters trying to solve a problem.
- Offer clues that a problem is about to happen.
- Show conflict or hostility.
- Open the story in a setting of fear, doom, terror, or impending tragedy.
- Offer a humorous scene.
- Begin the story with dialogue, showing the characters having a conversation about a problem.

Leads for *nonfiction* introduce the subject. The author may:

- State a problem.
- Ask the reader a question that is tied to a problem.
- Share a brief story or interesting situation.
- Put the reader in a familiar situation.
- Share an interesting or compelling quotation from someone, usually an authority on a subject.
- Begin the piece with a description of tragedy.
- State an unusual, frightening, or surprising statistic.
- Tell a joke.
- Exaggerate an ordinary situation, usually in a humorous manner.

Note: Authors will often combine some of the above elements to create strong leads.

Name _____ Date _____ Section _____

Leads

Directions: Answer the following questions about the lead of the material you are reading. Use another sheet of paper if you need more space.

Oh! Here's a Bite!

1. What is the title of your material? _____

_____

Who is the author? _____

2. Briefly describe the lead. _____

_____

_____

_____

_____

_____

_____

_____

3. How does this lead attempt to grab the attention of the reader? _____

_____

_____

_____

4. In your opinion, might this lead be improved? _____ Explain. _____

_____

_____

_____

_____

MINI-LESSON 54:
PLOT

Plot is essential to every story. If a plot is weak, the best ideas will not hold together and the story will be unsatisfying to readers. A strong plot with interesting characters engages the imagination of readers and keeps their interest.

Procedure:

- Explain that plot is the backbone of a story; it provides the structure from which the action arises. A solid plot is the essence of great stories.
- Note that in the typical plot the lead characters are faced with a problem they try to solve. Trying to solve it, though, leads to conflict. As they try to solve the problem, they encounter complications (or setbacks) that worsen the problem. The complications, conflict, and problem grow until the story reaches the climax. At this point the lead characters either solve the problem or they fail.
- Emphasize that in many novels the major problem often results in other problems. Plots can become quite involved, especially in long novels with many characters. In short stories, plots usually focus around one problem and a few complications.
- You might mention that some short stories don't have a standard plot. These stories focus on unresolved problems or simply a situation, and are frequently referred to as a "slice of life."

Activities:

1. This activity may be used with the entire class or with groups, provided students are reading the same novel. You may work with the class or have students meet in their groups to discuss the plot of a story they are reading. Distribute copies of Worksheet 54–1, "Plot—The Action Plan of a Story," to help students with their ideas.
2. This activity is designed for groups and works best when each group is reading a different story. Instruct group members to identify the major problem of the story, then list resulting complications and problems. Have students write their lists on poster paper or oaktag with markers, and then present a summary of the plot of their book to the class.

Writing Activity:

- Instruct students to write a story in which they focus their attention on the plot. Suggest that they write out the major problem of their story and its complications before starting the story. This type of prewriting can provide them with a general direction for their writing. Display the stories upon conclusion of the activity.

Name _____ Date _____ Section _____

Plot—The Action Plan of a Story

Directions: Answer the questions below about the plot of the story you are reading. Use another sheet of paper if you need more space.

1. Who are the lead characters of this story? _____

_____

2. What problem do the lead characters face? _____

_____

_____

_____

3. Describe the conflict that arises from the problem.

_____

_____

_____

_____

4. Describe some complications that arise during the

story. _____

_____

_____

_____

5. What actions do the lead characters take to solve the problem? _____

_____

_____

_____

_____

6. Do the lead characters solve the problem? _____ Explain. _____

_____

_____

_____

MINI-LESSON 55:
THEME

All typical stories have a theme in which the author, through the action of the story, shares a perception of life with the reader. Some stories have multiple themes.

Procedure:

- Explain that, at its simplest, the theme of a story is the author's message to his or her readers. This message usually centers around some aspect of life. The author shares his or her impression of life with the reader.

- Note that the theme of many stories portrays the fight of good against evil.

- Emphasize that theme arises out of the action of a story; thus, the reader draws conclusions about life from what he or she reads.

- You might wish to share the themes of the following novels as examples:

  —One of the themes of *A Separate Peace* by John Knowles is that people must confront their own fears and hatreds—their own wars—and make their own "separate" peace.

  —A major theme of *The Adventures of Huckleberry Finn* by Mark Twain is that goodness is an inner quality.

  —A theme of *Slaughterhouse-Five* by Kurt Vonnegut is that war is destructive to all of its participants. There is no winner in war.

- Mention that complex stories often have multiple themes, sometimes centering around individual characters. *Gone with the Wind* by Margaret Mitchell is a good example. Readers can easily identify the following themes:

  —War brings destruction to the innocent as well as the military.

  —Nobility can be found even in the rogue.

  —Despite their best efforts, schemers often find their best plans undone.

Activities:

1. This activity may be used with the entire class or with groups, provided students are reading the same story. Focus your students' attention on the theme of the story. You might wish to distribute copies of Worksheet 55–1, "Action and Theme," to help your students identify and explore the theme of the story. Conduct a class discussion or have students meet in groups to discuss the theme (or themes), noting in particular how it arises out of action.

2. Students may work individually or meet in groups for this activity. They are to consider the theme of the story they are reading and answer the questions on Worksheet 55–2, "Themes—An Author's Message." Conduct a class discussion or allow students to meet in groups to discuss the topic after they have completed the worksheet.

Writing Activity:

- Students should select a story they have previously written, or are currently writing, and write an essay explaining their theme. In their essay they should attempt to answer the following questions: What is the theme? Why did they select this theme for this story? Why do they feel this theme is important?

Name _____ Date _____ Section _____

Action and Theme

Directions: Answer the questions below about the theme of the story you are reading. Use another sheet of paper if you need more space.

1. Briefly describe the theme of this story. _____

_____

_____

_____

_____

2. Describe at least three actions in the story that support the theme. _____

_____

_____

_____

_____

_____

Name _____ Date _____ Section _____

Themes—An Author's Message

Directions: Answer the questions below about the theme of the story you are reading. Use another sheet of paper if you need more space.

1. What is the major theme of this story? _____

_____

_____

2. Does this story have other themes? _____ If yes, what are they? _____

_____

_____

_____

_____

3. Do you think the theme(s) is important? _____ Explain. _____

_____

_____

_____

_____

4. Do you agree or disagree with this theme(s)? _____

Explain. _____

_____

_____

_____

_____

_____

_____

_____

MINI-LESSON 56:
THE CLIMAX

In many stories, the climax is the emotional highpoint for readers when they become most engaged with the characters and action. Satisfying climaxes are the result of many factors that authors carefully construct for the best effects.

Procedure:

- Explain that the climax of a story is that moment when the lead characters either solve the problem facing them, or they fail. It is the event that all of the previous action leads to.
- Point out that great climaxes are often the most dramatic, suspenseful, and interesting parts of stories. They are a time when the problem confronting the lead characters is the greatest, when hope is almost lost.
- You might wish to mention some examples of climaxes:
  —In *The Sword in the Stone* by T.H. White, the climax occurs when Wart (the future King Arthur), in desperation to find Kay a sword, pulls the sword that is stuck in the anvil at a church. It is the sword that can be pulled out only by the new king of England.
  —In *A Wrinkle in Time* by Madeleine L'Engle, the climax occurs when Meg confronts IT and saves her brother by professing her love for him.
  —In *The Pearl* by John Steinbeck, the climax occurs when Kino and his wife, Juana, take their infant son and leave their village because Kino has killed a man who tried to steal Kino's great pearl. As they are trying to get away, three men follow them. Kino attacks them, but one of the men fires a bullet and kills Kino's son.
  —In *A Little Love* by Virginia Hamilton, the climax occurs when Sheema finally finds her father, but realizes he is not the man she hoped to meet.
- Note that some long, complex novels may contain many climaxes that lead up to the final one. Two good examples are:
  —*Gone with the Wind* by Margaret Mitchell. Many climaxes occur until the final one when Rhett at last leaves Scarlett.
  —*Dune* by Frank Herbert. Many climaxes lead up to the final battle in which Paul Atreides, leader of the Freemen, defeats the Harkonnens and the forces of the Emperor.

Activities:

1. This activity may be used with the entire class or with students working in groups, provided students are reading the same story. Instruct your students to consider the climax of the story. Distributing copies of Worksheet 56–1, "The Climax—A Story's Great Event," will help your students with their ideas. Either conduct a class discussion or have students meet in groups to discuss the climax of the story.
2. While working in groups, have students share the climaxes of some of their favorite stories. Students should then discuss what makes a strong climax.

Writing Activities:

1. Encourage students to write a story on a topic of their choice, focusing on the climax. Remind them that the climax should arise from the action of the story.

2. Instruct students to choose a climax from a favorite story and rewrite it so that the opposite happens. They should then consider how the new climax would necessitate changes in the previous action. What other types of changes would they have to make in the story to support the new climax? Provide time for students to orally share their new climax, and discuss the changes that would be needed in the rest of the story.

Name _____ Date _____ Section _____

The Climax—A Story's Great Event

Directions: Answer the following questions about the climax of the story you are reading. Use another sheet of paper if you need more space.

1. Describe the climax of the story. _____

_____

_____

_____

_____

_____

_____

_____

2. Describe at least three events that lead up to the climax. _____

_____

_____

_____

_____

_____

_____

3. Do the lead characters solve the problem they face, or do they fail? _____ Explain.

_____

_____

4. Were you satisfied with this climax? _____ Explain. _____

_____

_____

_____

MINI-LESSON 57:
UNDERSTANDING CHARACTER

Characterization is the way a writer distinguishes his or her characters from one another. When authors share the personalities and physical attributes of their characters with readers, making the characters seem like real people, they are revealing character.

Procedure:

- Explain that authors create characters who may be based in part on real people the author knows, or the characters may be invented entirely in the author's imagination.
- Note that the best stories have characters who seem like real people, who the reader comes to care deeply about. Suggest that students think of a favorite story. Most likely they'll quickly recall the lead characters of that story.
- Explain that authors show, or reveal, the traits of their characters through action, description, and dialogue. Skillful use of these techniques reveals the natures of characters and paints a clear picture of individual characters in the minds of readers.
- Although motivation is covered separately in Mini-lesson 58, you may wish to mention that the actions of characters in stories are always motivated. Real people always have reasons for doing things and so do the characters in stories.
- You might mention that most authors carefully select names to "fit" their characters. Billy is good for a young boy; Bill is better for a father. Aunt Jenny fits an older woman, but Jen is better for a young woman. Bateman sounds tough; maybe he's a cop, while Marty Lowe sounds like the crook he's after. Suggest that students think about the characters in some of the stories they've read and note how names often match the character's personality.

Activities:

1. Distribute copies of Worksheet 57–1, "Character Revealed," and review the information with your students.
2. This activity is designed for students working in groups. Instruct students to meet in their groups and consider the main characters in a story they are reading. They should explore how the author has revealed the traits of these characters. Hand out copies of Worksheet 57–1 to help your students with this activity. Suggest that, on a sheet of paper, students write the characters' names; then below the names list their traits and how they were revealed. Allow time for students to share their findings with the class at the end of the activity.
3. This activity is also designed for groups. Instruct students to consider the characters of a story they are reading. Each member of the group is to decide on a character he or she most likes and dislikes. Students should formulate

reasons for their opinions. Group members should then share the characters they chose with the rest of the group. To help your students get to "know" their characters, pass out several copies of Worksheet 57–2, "A Character Chart," and suggest that students fill in a sheet for each character they are considering.

4. TV shows and movies offer an excellent opportunity for students to learn about characterization. Suggest that your students watch a movie or a favorite show on TV. Instruct them to note (on paper or they will forget) the ways in which character is revealed throughout the show. In class, have your students meet in their groups and discuss their findings.

Writing Activities:

1. Instruct students to select a character from a story they are reading, or have read, and write a short biography of that character, based upon the traits revealed in the story. Allow time for students to share their biographies, either by reading them or orally presenting them.

2. Instruct students to write a story on a topic of their choice, and pay close attention to the development of their characters. Suggest that they use Worksheet 57–2 to help them create believable characters. Display the stories upon completion of the writing.

Name _____ Date _____ Section _____

Character Revealed

Authors reveal, or show, the traits of their characters in several ways.

Revealing Character Through Action

- What a character does tells readers a lot about him or her. The author may not say that a character is honest, but when the character finds and returns a lost wallet— even though the character desperately needs the money that was in it—the reader knows that the character is honest. If a character runs from a fight, leaving his friends behind, readers know the character is a coward.

- What a character says often shows what type of person he or she is. A person who always talks about the negative things in life is quite different from someone who only talks about the positive.

- What other characters say about a character can reveal a character's true nature. Do other characters speak highly of the character? Do the character's enemies speak highly of him or her, even if grudgingly? Do other characters, who are good people, dislike a character? Authors often use the words of characters to describe each other.

Revealing Character Through Thoughts and Emotions

- A character's thoughts and desires can tell much about the character. A character who desires wealth at any cost will be ruthless. A character who thinks he or she is a failure will act like one.

- A character who struggles with his or her emotions can reveal his or her basic traits to readers. The young woman who feels sympathy for a sparrow with a broken wing impresses the reader differently than does the teenager who wickedly threw the stone that broke the sparrow's wing.

- A character thinking about another character may be used to show traits of both characters. For example, when Joe plans to murder Bob, because Joe knows Bob won't let him cheat investors of their life-savings, readers learn much about both men.

Revealing Character Through Description

- Virtually all authors physically describe their characters. Physical descriptions help readers to form mental images of characters in their minds. The authors of novels usually provide more details of characters than do the authors of short stories. In short stories, authors may only show a few physical traits.

- Attention to physical details can help bring a character to life for readers. Typical physical details include:

  —Height, weight, strength (or lack of), body type

  —Shape of face; facial expressions

  —Color of eyes, hair, skin

  —Sound of voice

  —Gestures, unique mannerisms, such as clicking the tongue or snapping the fingers

- Clothing reflects the way the characters live. A farmer works in the field in overalls; a business tycoon wears thousand-dollar suits. Depending on the scene, characters may be dressed casually in jeans or shorts, or they may be wearing winter coats and heavy sweatshirts.

Name _____ Date _____ Section _____

A Character Chart

Character's Name: _____ Age _____

Positive Traits: _____

_____

_____

_____

Negative Traits: _____

_____

_____

_____

Goals: _____

_____

_____

_____

Background: _____

_____

_____

_____

Color Eyes: _____ Color Hair: _____

Hairstyle: _____

Height: _____ Weight: _____

Body Type: _____

Special Traits: _____

A one-sentence description of this character: _____

_____

_____

_____

MINI-LESSON 58:
MOTIVATION

In life, people do things for reasons. In stories, characters do things for reasons, too. These reasons, or motivations, reveal much about them. When students understand the motivations of characters in a story, they are more likely to understand the characters and the story.

Procedure:

- Explain that motivation refers to the reasons why people do things. People always have reasons for their actions. Even the madman has reasons for the things he does. He acts because of forces resulting from his madness.
- Emphasize that in stories the actions of characters are always motivated. When readers understand the motivations of characters, they not only gain insight to the characters but to the story as well.
- Point out that motivation is linked to a character's goals. All characters have goals they wish to achieve. Their actions arise from their attempts to realize their goals.
- Note that, sometimes, the motivations of characters may not be easily apparent and the reader may have to analyze characters carefully to understand them.
- Also note that, sometimes, a character's motivations may be clear to the reader but not to the character.

Activities:

1. Working individually, students are to select a major character from a story the class or their group is reading and explore this character's goals and motivation. Distribute copies of Worksheet 58–1, "Motivation and Action," and instruct students to answer the questions on the sheet. This will help them understand the motivations of their character. Students should then meet in their groups and discuss the characters they selected, describing the motivations of the character's major actions. You may also conduct a class discussion on the topic.
2. This activity is designed for students working in groups. Groups should select three or four characters of a story they are reading. They should identify the goals of these characters and list the actions the characters take to achieve their goals. Allow time for groups to share their conclusions with the class.

Writing Activity:

- Tell your students to think of a time they had an important goal. What did they do to achieve this goal? The goal, of course, becomes motivation which in turn leads to action. Instruct your students to write a personal account of the way they tried to achieve their goal. Either display the accounts or have students orally share their accounts with the class.

Name _____ Date _____ Section _____

Motivation and Action

Directions: Select a character from the story you are reading and answer the following questions. Use another sheet of paper if you need more space.

1. What is the name of your character? _____

_____

2. Briefly describe this character. _____

_____

_____

_____

3. What is this character's goals? _____

_____

_____

4. How does the character attempt to achieve his or her goals? _____

_____

_____

5. Does he or she achieve the goals? _____ Explain. _____

_____

_____

6. What do the actions of this character tell you about him or her? _____

_____

_____

MINI-LESSON 59:
DIALOGUE

Dialogue makes up a significant part of the action in most stories. Not only does dialogue reveal much about character, it also moves the plot forward and provides the author with an opportunity to share information with the reader.

Procedure:

- Explain that dialogue refers to the conversations of characters. Without dialogue most stories would be flat and uninteresting.

- Note that dialogue is an important part of action. Readers want to hear what characters have to say as well as see what they do.

- Note that dialogue reveals much about character. Social status, education, and attitudes are reflected in the way a person speaks.

- Emphasize that authors try very hard to have their characters speak realistically in terms of their background, the places they live, their education, and their professions. People of Colonial America spoke differently from Americans today. An old cowpoke speaks quite differently from a university professor; an English governess' words are different from the words of the children she is caring for. Realistic dialogue adds believability to stories.

- Point out that authors may use dialogue to share information with the reader. When two characters are planning a bank robbery, the reader gains insight to plot. Dialogue can also reveal the motivations, thoughts, and emotions of characters.

Activities:

1. This activity works well with the entire class or with groups, provided that students are reading the same story. Instruct students to select a scene that has significant dialogue. Students are to analyze the dialogue, and try to determine if the dialogue reveals information about the plot or the motivations, thoughts, or emotions of the characters. Distributing copies of Worksheet 59–1, "Analyzing Dialogue," can help students clarify their ideas. Either conduct a class discussion or have students meet in their groups to discuss the importance of dialogue in the story.

2. For this activity, students are to work in groups. They are to select three or four major characters of the story they are currently reading, and explore the voices of these characters. They should look at such factors as accent, slang, tone, and speech patterns. Are the voices of these characters realistic? Does each character speak with his or her "own" voice? How does the author achieve this? Students should share their findings with the class at the conclusion of the activity.

3. For this activity, students should work in groups of three or four. (More than that might become somewhat unwieldy.) Also, each group will need a tape recorder and blank tape. You might ask your media specialist if he or

she can supply you with tape recorders, or you might ask students to work on this activity at home.

Instruct students to write a script—a few pages will do—that contains dialogue they might use in the lunch room, walking home from school, or simply hanging out with friends. Topics may vary, but should be interesting enough to sustain a conversation. The content is not so important as the activity. (You might wish to remind students that this is a school activity and that their scripts should reflect appropriate language.) After students have written the script, in which each group member has a part, they are to read the dialogue as if they were actually speaking it. They should record this dialogue. When they are finished, students are to play back the tape and analyze the dialogue. In particular, they should try to note differences in tone and speech patterns. Does each person speak with his or her own voice? Most students are surprised at how they sound on tape. Conduct a class discussion at the end of the activity and share students' experiences.

Writing Activity:

- Instruct students to select a scene from a story they are reading, in which dialogue plays a major role. Students are to rewrite this scene in exposition, without dialogue. Many students will likely find this to be difficult. Upon completion of the writing, discuss whether the rewritten scenes had so much impact as the originals. From there, continue with a discussion of the overall importance of dialogue to stories.

Name _____ Date _____ Section _____

Analyzing Dialogue

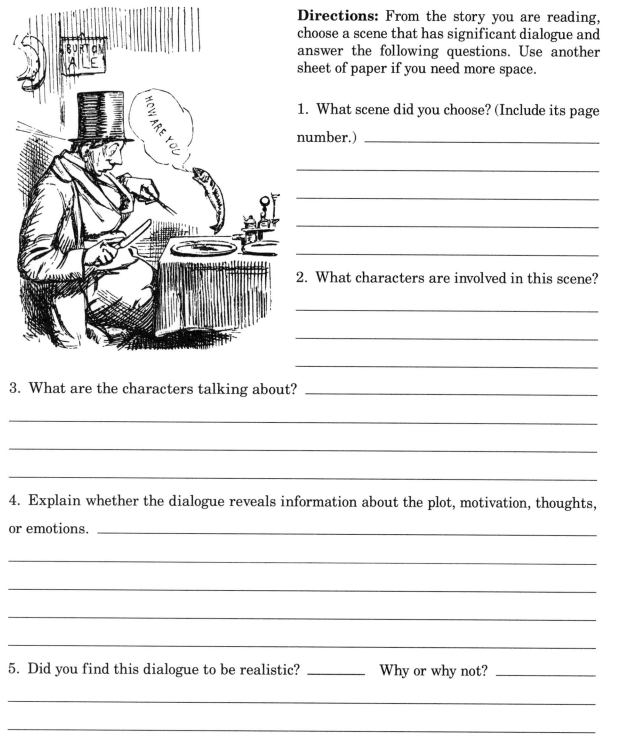

Directions: From the story you are reading, choose a scene that has significant dialogue and answer the following questions. Use another sheet of paper if you need more space.

1. What scene did you choose? (Include its page number.) _____

_____

_____

_____

_____

2. What characters are involved in this scene?

_____

_____

_____

3. What are the characters talking about? _____

_____

_____

_____

4. Explain whether the dialogue reveals information about the plot, motivation, thoughts, or emotions. _____

_____

_____

_____

_____

5. Did you find this dialogue to be realistic? _____ Why or why not? _____

_____

_____

MINI-LESSON 60:
CONFLICT

Conflict is essential to every story. As the lead characters find themselves in conflict, the story is propelled forward.

Procedure:

- Explain that every story has conflict, which may be physical or emotional.

- Note that conflict is important to plot. As the lead characters try to solve the problem confronting them, they encounter obstacles that result in conflict.

- Emphasize that stories without conflict would be quite boring. Conflict gives rise to action, suspense, and drama.

- Explain that conflict may have many forms. It may take place between characters, between characters and their environment, or within characters. In many stories, conflict takes several forms. Following are some examples:

  —In *Julie of the Wolves* by Jean Craighead George, conflict arises between Julie and nature, Julie and her husband, and Julie and her father.

  —In *I Will Call It Georgie's Blues* by Suzanne Newton, conflict arises between Neal and his father, Neal's family and the father, and within Neal himself over his secretly immersing himself in playing jazz to escape the problems with his family.

  —In *Fahrenheit 451* by Ray Bradbury, conflict arises between Montag and his wife, Montag and those who would burn books, and within Montag himself over his changing feelings regarding book burning.

Activities:

1. This activity works well with the whole class or with groups, provided students are reading the same story. Instruct your students to consider a scene in the story in which conflict plays a major part. Who, or what, is the conflict between? How does it arise? What are its results? How does it effect the characters? Distribute copies of Worksheet 60–1, "The Causes and Effects of Conflict," to help your students focus their efforts. Either conduct a class discussion or have students meet in their groups to discuss the role of conflict in their story.

2. While working in their groups, instruct students to trace the conflict through the story they are reading. Suggest that they identify at least five scenes in which conflict plays a major role. They should note the type of conflict, how it arose, and its effects. Encourage students to construct simple charts to record their information. Allow time for students to share their findings with the class.

3. Have students meet in their groups and discuss a time they were in a situation that can be characterized as conflict. (Remind students that they need not discuss an event that is too personal. Each of us has plenty of situations where we find ourselves in relatively harmless conflict.) Ask

students to relate the cause of this conflict, who was involved, and what resulted. Explain that these are the ways authors view conflict and include it in their stories.

Writing Activity:

• Instruct students to select a scene from the book they are reading in which conflict plays a major part. Students are to rewrite the scene with a different resolution. They should then consider how this would change the story. Provide time for students to orally share their rewritten scenes.

Name _____ Date _____ Section _____

The Causes and Effects of Conflict

Directions: Select a scene in which conflict plays a major part in the story you are reading, then answer the questions below. Use another sheet of paper if you need more space.

1. Briefly describe the scene you have selected. (Include the characters who are involved

and the page numbers.) _____

_____

_____

_____

_____

_____

_____

_____

_____

_____

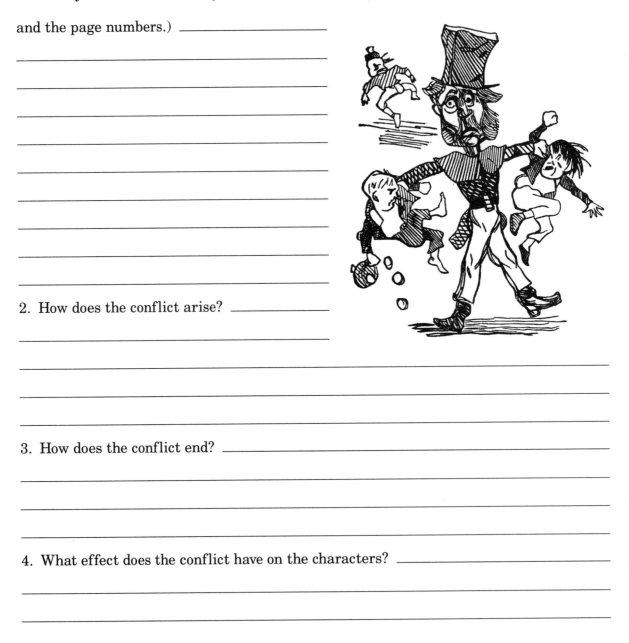

2. How does the conflict arise? _____

_____

_____

_____

_____

3. How does the conflict end? _____

_____

_____

_____

4. What effect does the conflict have on the characters? _____

_____

_____

_____

MINI-LESSON 61:
SETTING

The setting of a story is where and when the story takes place. Fully understanding and appreciating settings can enhance stories for readers, as well as aid in overall comprehension.

Procedure:

- Explain that settings are the "stage" on which the action of a story occurs. Time and place are the ingredients of a setting.
- Explain that settings may be in a city, small town, a future colony on the moon, or the days of King Arthur in England. Stories may be set in a forest, a church, a palace, or anywhere else.
- Point out that many stories, especially novels, may have numerous settings, which change as the story develops.
- Explain that authors strive to make settings realistic. They use vivid descriptive words that appeal to the senses to help readers visualize the setting. Remind students that the five senses are sight, hearing, touch, smell, and taste.
- Note that settings can help to create mood. Old mansions are often the setting for mysteries and stories with supernatural elements. Harsh, rugged settings provide an excellent environment for survival stories.
- You might wish to mention that modern authors usually weave descriptive details of the setting in with action. In the past, authors often provided large chunks of descriptive information between action. This slowed the action, but was the "style" of the day. Weaving description in with action keeps the story moving faster. (Perhaps this is in response to a reading public greatly influenced by the fast action of TV and movies.)

Activities:

1. This activity will work well with either the whole class or groups, as long as students are reading the same story. Instruct students to select a setting of the story and examine how the author describes it. They should especially focus on how the author makes settings realistic. Hand out copies of Worksheet 61–1, "Settings—The Background of Stories," which will help your students investigate the settings of their story. At the end of the activity conduct a class discussion, or have your students meet in groups to discuss the settings and their importance to the story.

2. Review examples of settings in the story your students are reading. Point out how settings are developed, how they support the action, and how authors employ sensory words to help readers "see" the setting in their imaginations. Discuss the importance of settings to stories.

Writing Activity:

- Instruct students to write a description of a familiar setting. This may be their room at home, their house, the classroom, a park, a playground, a shopping mall, or other place they know well. As they write about this place, students should concentrate on using descriptive words and details that will help to make this place vivid for the reader. Encourage students to use sensory words to enliven their descriptions. Upon conclusion of the activity display the finished writings.

Name _____ Date _____ Section _____

Settings—The Background of Stories

Directions: Pick a setting of the story you are reading, then answer the questions below. Use another sheet of paper if you need more space.

1. Describe this setting (include its page numbers). _____

_____

_____

_____

_____

_____

_____

_____

_____

_____

2. List any sensory words the author used to describe this setting. _____

_____

_____

_____

_____

_____

_____

3. Could the author have chosen another setting for this story? _____ Explain.

_____

_____

_____

_____

_____

_____

MINI-LESSON 62:
IMAGERY AND FIGURATIVE LANGUAGE

When people read, they see images, or pictures, in their minds. Writers know that strong, powerful images are made by using specific details that appeal to the senses and experiences of readers. Powerful imagery may result in figurative language, which goes beyond the literal meaning of words.

Procedure:

- Explain that *imagery* refers to the pictures people see in their imaginations as they read. Read this sentence to your students: "Watching the playful puppy, the little girl smiled." Ask your students how many of them have an image of that scene. Most probably will. This is a simple example of how we "see" images in our minds.

- Emphasize that images in stories are the result of authors using specific descriptive words that appeal to the reader's senses and experiences. The purpose of the image is to arouse interest and emotion—perhaps sympathy, fear, anticipation, horror, etc.

- Mention that vivid images make memorable settings, characters, and action.

- Explain that *figurative language* is phrases and sentences that express more than mere literal meaning. Figurative language is the result of strong imagery. Offer this example:

  The great slow-moving convoy of trucks was like a line of elephants plodding along the road.

  Obviously, trucks are not elephants, but the image—the pictures, or figures, conceived in the reader's mind—helps the reader to visualize the scene clearly.

- You might wish to note the following examples of strong images:

  —In *A Wrinkle in Time* by Madeleine L'Engle, IT is described as a "living, pulsating brain." This is a clear image that most readers can easily picture.

  —In *A Separate Peace* by John Knowles, Gene, upon returning to the Devon School at the beginning of the novel, describes the tree that caused Phineas's tragedy: "The tree was not only stripped by the cold season, it seemed weary from age, enfeebled, dry."

  —In *The Illustrated Man* by Ray Bradbury, the flesh of the man covered with illustrations is described as " . . . a riot of rockets and fountains and people, in such intricate detail and color that you could hear the voices murmuring small and muted, from the crowds that inhabited his body."

Activities:

1. This activity is designed for the entire class or students working in groups, provided they are reading the same story. Instruct your students to select a scene they feel is memorable because it contains a powerful image. They are

to analyze this scene and try to determine what makes the image so powerful. Distribute copies of Worksheet 62–1, "Pictures Painted with Words," to help your students with their ideas. At the end of the activity, conduct a class discussion or permit students to meet in groups to discuss imagery.

2. While working in groups, instruct your students to consider some of their favorite stories, movies, or TV shows. Ask them to select a few scenes they feel contain powerful images. Suggest that they write notes why the imagery of these scenes is powerful. Students should then share these scenes with the members of their group and discuss what makes strong imagery. Instruct groups to identify what they feel are the elements of powerful imagery; allow time for groups to report their conclusions to the class.

3. Review examples of imagery in stories and novels the class has read.

Writing Activity:

- Students are to select an object, and, without naming it, write a descriptive paragraph. They should be as accurate as possible and try to create a clear image of the object in the minds of their readers. After completion of the writing, have students read their paragraphs to the class and let the class try to guess what the object is.

Name _____ Date _____ Section _____

Pictures Painted with Words

Directions: From the story you are reading, select a scene that has a powerful image. Then answer the questions below. Use another sheet of paper if you need more space.

1. Describe the scene you selected (include its

page numbers). _____

_____

_____

_____

_____

_____

_____

2. What emotion(s) does the author try to arouse in the reader with this scene? _____

_____

_____

3. How does he or she do this? _____

_____

_____

_____

_____

4. What makes the imagery in this scene so powerful? _____

_____

_____

_____

MINI-LESSON 63:
STYLE AND TONE

Every author develops his or her own writing style, which may become recognizable to that author's regular readers. Style embodies tone—an elusive element to be sure—but one that often has the power to affect a reader's comprehension and conclusions.

Procedure:

- Explain that style refers to the flow of an author's writing. Most authors have their own style, which astute readers will recognize. Style is affected by many factors, including sentence construction, use of descriptive details, use of similes and metaphors, and use of author's devices such as comparison and contrast. The styles of some authors display distinct rhythm and patterns.

- Explain that tone, which is best described as an author's manner of expression, is imbedded in style. Tone may be serious in an editorial, light in a comedy, or tense in a mystery. Tone can affect the mood and atmosphere the material creates.

- Offer these examples of style and tone.
  —In *The Scarlet Letter* by Nathaniel Hawthorne, the style and tone create a mood that is serious and somber, reflecting the atmosphere of a Puritan setting.
  —In *I Know Why the Caged Bird Sings* by Maya Angelou, the author's style is often an interplay of prose and poetry.
  —In the stories and poems of Edgar Allan Poe, style and tone often create an atmosphere of suspense, melancholy, and foreboding with a promise of terror.

Activities:

1. This activity is designed for the entire class or students working in groups. Students must be reading the same material. For this activity, students should concentrate their attention on how the author's style and tone affect the mood of the piece. Distributing copies of Worksheet 63–1, "Reflections on Style," will help your students analyze these elements. At the end of the activity, conduct a class discussion or have students meet in groups to evaluate the author's style, tone, and the resulting mood of the material.

2. Working in groups, instruct your students to share with the members of their group a story, or an excerpt of a story, they previously read in which they found the author's style and tone to be particularly impressive. Suggest that students write down notes why they find this material impressive, and encourage them to read some excerpts to the group. Perhaps each group can select an example of what they feel is superior style and the student who brought this example to the group can read it to the class.

3. Working with the class, point out examples of style and tone in books, stories, or articles your students have read. Discuss how these elements enhance the author's message and material.

Writing Activity:

• Instruct students to select a composition they have previously completed. They are to revise this piece, concentrating on improving their style and tone so that they foster the mood the piece is designed to arouse. Display the writings—before and after—upon completion of the activity.

Name _____ Date _____ Section _____

Reflections on Style

Directions: Answer the following questions on the style, tone, and mood of the material you are reading. Use another sheet of paper if you need more space.

1. Describe the style of this material. _____

_____

_____

_____

2. What is the tone? (light, serious, informative, scary, etc.) _____ Explain

why you feel this way. _____

_____

_____

_____

3. What kind of mood do the style and tone support in the story? _____

_____

_____

_____

4. In your opinion, do the style, tone, and mood fit this story? _____ Explain.

_____

MINI-LESSON 64:
REALISM

All novels are a mixture of reality and fiction. This blend of the real with imagination can make wonderful stories that enthrall readers.

Procedure:

- Explain that all stories are a unique combination of reality and fiction. It is *realism,* however, that helps make stories believable.

- Note that realism depends on accurate descriptions and the author's careful use of facts. To achieve realism, many writers conduct extensive research and visit the places they are writing about.

- Mention that even stories that take place in the far past or distant future are based on facts as we understand them today. Science fiction and fantasy are based on what we know, with the author's imagination taking over from there.

- Emphasize that authors often exaggerate real facts, especially events that affect characters. They do this to achieve dramatic results. Without exaggeration, most stories would be boring.

- You may wish to point out realistic elements in the stories your students have read. An excellent example of realism is *All Quiet on the Western Front* by Erich Maria Remarque. The author served in World War I and the descriptions of trench warfare are vivid and chilling.

Activities:

1. This activity may be used with the entire class or with groups, provided students are reading the same stories. Instruct your students to find examples of realism in the story they are reading. They should try to determine how important realism is to the story. Could the story be as interesting without it? Distribute copies of Worksheet 64–1, "The Real Facts," which will help your students with their work. Upon conclusion of the activity, conduct a class discussion or have students meet in groups to discuss realism and its importance to stories.

2. This activity is designed for students working in groups. In some stories today—whether in the form of novels, movies, or TV shows—realism is unchecked. Violence may be graphic; sex may be explicit; pain and suffering may leave little to the imagination. Students are to research the topic "Unchecked Realism" and try to decide if some stories may have too much realism. Their arguments should be supported with facts. After students have completed their research, you might wish to organize a debate, with groups taking different sides of the issue.

Writing Activity:

- For this activity students are to write a story on a topic of their choice. Encourage them to focus their attention on using realistic details to make the story believable to readers. Display the stories upon conclusion of the activity.

Name _____ Date _____ Section _____

The Real Facts

Directions: From the story you are reading, select a scene that is a good example of realism. Then answer the questions below. Use another sheet of paper if you need more space.

1. Describe this scene (include its page numbers). _____

_____

_____

_____

_____

2. How does the author use realistic details to make this scene believable? _____

_____

_____

_____

3. In your opinion, did the author use too much realism in this scene? Not enough? Or just the right amount? _____ Explain. _____

_____

_____

_____

_____

_____

_____

_____

_____

_____

_____

MINI-LESSON 65:
SYMBOLISM

Symbolism in stories is the author's giving a character, object, or place a meaning more than just itself. Although symbolism is an important element of many stories, many students find symbols confusing.

Procedure:

- Define symbolism. Simply put, a symbol is something that has meaning beyond itself in a story.
- Note that the symbol gains importance through the author's comparing it or linking it to another idea. Symbols are frequently tied to a story's theme.
- Mention that stories may have multiple symbols.
- Point out that symbolism is a part of everyday life. The fox is a symbol for slyness, a flag is a symbol of its country, and a blindfolded woman is a symbol for equal justice.
- You might wish to mention the following examples of symbols in stories:
  —In *The Contender* by Robert Lipsyte, "contending" in the boxing ring symbolizes contending in the arena of life.
  —In *The Pearl* by John Steinbeck, the pearl Kino finds represents material wealth and the tragedy wealth often brings.
  —In *The Lord of the Flies* by William Golding, the fire represents hope and rescue, the beastie symbolizes the bestiality that Golding believes is found in all people, and the conch is a symbol of authority.
  —In *Wuthering Heights* by Emily Brontë, the wind in Lockwood's dream symbolizes the passion of human beings and the power of nature.

Activities:

1. This activity may be used with the class or with groups, as long as students are reading the same story. Students should examine the story for examples of symbolism, noting how the author uses symbols and what they represent. Handing out copies of Worksheet 65–1, "Symbols," will help your students to focus their ideas. At the end of the activity, conduct a class discussion or have students meet in groups to discuss the symbolism in the story.

2. While working in a group, students are to select a symbol of some aspect of life. They are to discuss this symbol and how it might be represented. Next, they are to create a model or drawing of this symbol that shows what it represents. Upon completion permit groups to show and describe their symbol to the class. You might also like to display their finished work. *Note:* You will probably need a variety of materials for this activity, and you may wish to collaborate with your students' art teacher.

3. Organize a debate on a well-known symbol in our society; for example, the American flag. Suggest that students research the symbol and try to answer questions such as the following: How important is this symbol? Do people,

who truly believe in a cause, or an idea, need a symbol? What is the purpose of symbols? Are symbols worthy of protection by law (as in the case of flag burning)?

Writing Activity:

- Instruct your students to select a symbol from a story they have read, or a symbol from life, and write an essay about it. They should seek to answer the following questions in their essays: Why is this object or idea a symbol? What meaning does it provide to people? How important is it? Display the essays upon completion. You might also wish to publish them in a class anthology about symbolism.

Name _____ Date _____ Section _____

Symbols

Directions: Answer the following questions about symbolism in the story you are reading. Use another sheet of paper if you need more space.

1. Describe an example of symbolism in the story. _____

_____

_____

_____

_____

_____

_____

2. To what does the author link this symbol? _____

_____

_____

_____

3. Does this symbol appear often in the story? _____ Why do you think it appears more than once? (If it appears only once, why do you think it doesn't appear more often?)

_____

_____

_____

_____

_____

4. In your opinion, is this symbol important to the story? _____ Explain. _____

_____

_____

_____

_____

MINI-LESSON 66:
FLASHBACKS

Flashbacks appear in stories when current action needs to be explained by events that happened in the past. Rather than starting at that event, which may be long before the current action, the author "flashes" back to it, then returns to the present. Readers who don't understand flashbacks may have trouble following the chronology of a story.

Procedure:

- Explain that a flashback is a return to an event that happened before the current action of the story. The information provided by the flashback is necessary to understand the current action. For example, a character's intense fear of water might be the result of witnessing her young brother drown several years earlier.

- Note that flashbacks may be a few sentences, a paragraph or two, a scene, a chapter, or sometimes several chapters, depending on the story.

- Mention that while many stories use flashbacks, most flashbacks are brief. Some stories, however, such as, Anne Tyler's *Dinner at the Homesick Restaurant,* rely on flashbacks to share past information about the characters. In *Flowers for Algernon* by Daniel Keyes, Charlie recalls many experiences of his youth through flashbacks.

Activities:

1. This activity may be used with the whole class or with students working in groups. Students must be reading the same story, which contains examples of flashbacks. Instruct your students to identify and analyze examples of flashbacks. Distribute copies of Worksheet 66–1, "Back to the Past," which will help your students with their understanding of flashbacks. At the end of the activity, conduct a class discussion or have students meet in groups to discuss the use and purpose of flashbacks in the story.

2. While working with the class, point out examples of flashbacks in stories and novels students are reading or have read. Discuss how the information the flashbacks reveal is necessary to the current action.

Writing Activity:

- Instruct students to write a story in which they use at least one flashback. After they write their drafts, have students share their stories with an editing partner, who should read the story and offer suggestions for improvement, particularly in regard to the flashback. Display the stories at the end of the activity.

Name _____ Date _____ Section _____

Back to the Past

Directions: Answer the following questions about flashbacks in the story you are reading. Use another sheet of paper if you need more space.

1. Describe a scene in which a flashback takes place (include its page numbers). _____

_____

_____

_____

2. What information does the flashback provide? _____

_____

_____

3. How is this information important to the current action? _____

_____

_____

4. Is this flashback effective? _____ Explain. _____

_____

_____

5. Is there any other way the author might
have provided this information?_____

Explain. _____

_____

_____

_____

_____

_____

_____

_____

_____

_____

MINI-LESSON 67:
FORESHADOWING

Foreshadowing is an author's technique by which clues of coming events are given to the reader. Good readers key on foreshadowing to help them predict what is going to happen in a story.

Procedure:

- Explain that authors use foreshadowing as hints, or clues, of coming action in a story.

- Note that effective foreshadowing can heighten suspense and anticipation for readers. Many readers use foreshadowing to predict what will happen in a story. Understanding foreshadowing aids comprehension.

- Mention that foreshadowing supports the plot of a story by providing a logical sequence of events. Instead of events merely happening in a random manner, readers can see a clear progression. This enhances believability.

- You might wish to mention the following novels, which contain examples of foreshadowing:

  —In *Of Mice and Men* by John Steinbeck, Lenny's accidental killing of the mouse and the puppy foreshadows his killing of Curley's wife.

  —In *Jane Eyre* by Charlotte Brontë, much of the mystery in Thornfield Hall foreshadows the tragedy of Mr. Rochester's mad wife.

  —In *Where the Red Fern Grows* by Wilson Rawls, the Pritchard boys' ganging up on Billy when hunting for the ghost coon is foreshadowed by the Pritchards' earlier unsavory behavior and reputation.

  —In *I Will Call It Georgie's Blues* by Suzanne Newton, Georgie's running away from the family is foreshadowed through his earlier fantasies that his real parents had been abducted.

Activities:

1. You may use this activity with the class or with groups, provided students are reading the same story and the story has examples of foreshadowing. Instruct your students to concentrate on examples of the foreshadowing of the climax or a major event in the story. Hand out copies of Worksheet 67–1, "Things to Come," to help your students with their ideas. After students have completed the worksheet, conduct a class discussion or have students meet in their groups to review instances of foreshadowing in the story.

2. This activity is designed for students working individually. Students are to select a novel or story they have read and identify examples of foreshadowing. If you wish, distribute copies of Worksheet 67–1 which students may find helpful for this activity. At the end of the activity, conduct a class discussion and ask for volunteers to share examples of foreshadowing they identified in their stories.

3. While working with the class, review examples of foreshadowing in some of the stories the class has read.

Writing Activity:

- Students should select a story of their choice—it may be one they have already read or are currently reading—and write a short essay on the author's use of foreshadowing. What events has the author foreshadowed? How did he or she foreshadow them? Did his or her use of foreshadowing make the action stronger? Display the essays upon completion of the writing.

Name _____ Date _____ Section _____

Things to Come

Directions: Answer the following questions about foreshadowing in the story you are reading. Use another sheet of paper if you need more space.

1. Title of story: _____

_____

Author: _____

2. Describe a major event of this story that has

been foreshadowed. _____

_____

_____

_____

_____

_____

_____

_____

3. How did the author foreshadow the event? What clues or hints did he or she provide?

_____

_____

_____

_____

4. Was the foreshadowing necessary? _____ Explain. _____

_____

_____

_____

_____

MINI-LESSON 68:
IRONY

Irony is an author's technique of using words or ideas to convey the opposite of their literal meaning. Irony requires alert readers and should always be pointed out to students, who may miss its subtleties.

Procedure:

- Explain that irony is an idea or situation that is opposite to its literal, or obvious, meaning. Authors use irony for humor or emphasis. Ironic statements can be arresting in their power.

- Note that irony may be humorous or serious, depending on the story and the point the author hopes to make.

- You might wish to mention the following stories which are recognized for their irony:

  —*Farewell to Manzanar* by Jeanne Wakatsuki Houston and James Houston. In this story about Japanese internment during World War II, it is ironic that many Japanese children, who were very young at the beginning of their internment, are afraid to leave the internment camp at the end of the war.

  —*Animal Farm* by George Orwell. In this political satire, animals rebel from their human master only to gain a new master in Napoleon, the pig. Ironically, their lives are much harder now, but because of Napoleon's skillful use of propaganda, they don't realize it.

  —*The Scarlet Letter* by Nathaniel Hawthorne. As Dimmesdale struggles with his guilt over his secret affair with Hester, his reputation as a minister grows.

  —*All Quiet on the Western Front* by Erich Maria Remarque. In one of the most tragic and ironic moments of literature, the lead character, Paul, after having survived months of horrific trench warfare, is killed on a "quiet" day at the front.

Activities:

1. This activity is designed for the whole class or for groups, as long as students are reading the same story and the story has clear examples of irony. Instruct your students to identify ironic situations in the story. Hand out copies of Worksheet 68–1 to help your students with the activity. Upon completion of the worksheet, conduct a class discussion or have students meet in groups to discuss irony in the story.

2. While working individually, students are to identify examples of irony in a story they are currently reading or one they read previously. If you wish, you may distribute copies of "Understanding Irony" to help them. Conduct a class discussion about irony and ask for volunteers to share some examples of irony they have found in stories they read.

3. Point out examples of irony in stories the class has read. Discuss why authors use irony, and why irony can be a powerful literary device.

Writing Activity:

- Start this activity by brainstorming with the class instances of irony in real life. List ideas on the board or an overhead projector as students volunteer them. Some examples include:

  —Farmers are praying for rain because a drought is killing their crops, but then they get so much rain that their land is beset by floods.

  —A family is going on vacation and hoping for nice, sunny weather. When they arrive, it is so sunny and hot that they don't feel like leaving the air-conditioning of their hotel room.

  —Because of a bet in which he brags that he can outscore the best student in class, an underachieving student studies hours and hours for a science test. He is ready! He is prepared! He is convinced he will win the bet . . . until he finds that he studied the wrong chapter.

  After listing several examples of irony, instruct students to select an ironic situation they experienced or heard about and write an account of it. Provide time for students to read their ironic episodes to the class, or be sure to display them.

Name _____ Date _____ Section _____

Understanding Irony

Directions: Answer the following questions about irony in the story you are reading. Use another sheet of paper if you need more space.

1. Title of story: _____

_____

Author: _____

2. Describe an example of irony in the story

(include its page numbers). _____

_____

_____

_____

_____

_____

_____

3. How did the author develop the irony? _____

_____

_____

4. Was the irony humorous or serious? _____ What effect does it have on the reader?

_____

_____

_____

5. Explain why you think the author used irony in this story. _____

_____

_____

_____

MINI-LESSON 69:
SATIRE

Satire is an author's technique that reveals human weakness through irony, wit, or outright mockery. Frequently, satire is subtle and may be overlooked by readers, who then miss an important aspect of the material they are reading.

Procedure:

- Explain that satire is a method, or author's technique, through which the author exposes human weaknesses with irony, humor, or derision.

- Note that satire may be very subtle, interwoven with action and description, or it may be rather obvious.

- Mention that throughout history authors have employed satire to expose the failings in people. Political satire is one of the most common forms.

- You might wish to mention that *Animal Farm* by George Orwell is considered to be one of the greatest political satires ever written. Throughout the novel Orwell satirizes communism and how the system claims, through propaganda, that it elevates the lot of people when in fact it subjugates people and reduces their freedom. In the story, animals who have rebelled from their human master are told that they now enjoy greater freedom under their new leader, the pig, Napoleon. They accept this, even though their lives are now more difficult.

- You might also wish to share these other examples of satire in literature:
  —*Gulliver's Travels* by Jonathan Swift, which is a marvelous satire on human nature.
  —*Catch-22* by Joseph Heller, which satirizes the horrors of war and the power of modern society.
  —Much of Jane Austen's works satirize English domestic and social life.
  —Much of Mark Twain's works satirize human nature.

Activities:

1. You may use this activity with the entire class or have students work in groups. They should be reading the same material, which should have clear examples of satire. Instruct students to review the story and identify examples of satire and the author's purpose for using them. Distribute copies of Worksheet 69–1, "Satire in Stories," to help your students focus their ideas. After completion of the worksheet, conduct a class discussion or have students meet in groups to discuss satire and its effects.

2. While working with the class, review and discuss examples of satire in stories the class has read.

Writing Activity:

- Discuss satire and how its purpose is to expose human weakness. Ask your students to consider a weakness they find in people, and then write a brief satirical story exposing it. Display the stories upon completion.

Name _____ Date _____ Section _____

Satire in Stories

Directions: Answer the following questions about satire in the story you are reading. Use another sheet of paper if you need more space.

1. Describe a satirical scene or situation in the story

(include its page numbers). _____

_____

_____

_____

_____

_____

_____

_____

_____

2. How does the author develop the satire? _____

_____

_____

_____

_____

3. Explain what you think the author's purpose was in using satire. _____

_____

_____

_____

4. Was this satire effective? _____ Explain. _____

_____

_____

MINI-LESSON 70:
POINT OF VIEW (OVERVIEW)

By far the greatest number of stories are written in either the first-person or the third-person point of view. Within the scope of these two points of view are many variations. This mini-lesson offers some basics about point of view. Mini-lesson 71, "First-Person Point of View," and Mini-lesson 72, "Third-Person Point of View," address the topics in greater depth.

Procedure:

- Explain that point of view refers to the narrator of a story. It is the person from whose perspective the story is being told.
- Explain the two basic forms of point of view: first person and third person. Offer these details.
  - —The "first person" refers to the pronoun "I." In stories written in the first-person point of view, the author is not only the narrator of the story but a participant. The author tells the story to the reader and refers to him- or herself as "I."
  - —The "third person" refers to the third person pronouns "he," "she," and "it." In stories written in the third-person point of view, the author refers to the lead characters as "he" or "she." The author is not a participant in the story. It is assumed that the author is outside of the story.
- Explain that authors select the point of view they feel will work best for the story. The first-person point of view, for example, is very personal. The author/narrator speaks directly to the reader, and can share his or her most intimate thoughts and emotions. However, the first-person point of view is limited. The author can only share what the author/narrator knows from the action of the story. The third-person point of view is more removed, less personal, but allows the author more flexibility in writing the story.

Activity:

- This activity may be used with the entire class or with students working in groups, provided students are reading the same story. Instruct your students to focus their attention on the point of view of the story they are currently reading. Distribute copies of Worksheet 70–1, "What's the Point of View?" to help your students organize their ideas. At the end of the activity, conduct a class discussion or have students meet in groups to discuss the point of view of the story.

Writing Activity:

- Instruct students to write an account of an incident that happened to them. Remind them that their account must be written in the first-person point of view. After they have completed their account, they are to rewrite it, but from the third-person point of view. Encourage them to note how they had to change their account. Upon completion of the activity, display both versions of their accounts.

Name _____ Date _____ Section _____

What's the Point of View?

Directions: Answer the following questions about point of view for the story you are reading. Use another sheet of paper if you need more space.

1. Did the author use the first-person point of view or the third-person point of view in this story? _____

2. How do you know which point of view this is? _____

_____

_____

_____

_____

3. Why do you think the author chose this point of view?

_____

_____

_____

_____

_____

_____

4. In your opinion, would another point of view have been as effective? _____ Explain.

_____

_____

_____

_____

_____

_____

_____

MINI-LESSON 71:
FIRST-PERSON POINT OF VIEW

Many novels and short stories are told in the first-person point of view, especially stories in which the authors feel the narrator must be a part of the action. Stories based on the personal experiences of authors are frequently written in the first person.

Procedure:

- Explain that a story written in the first-person point of view has the author as the narrator and a participant in the story. Usually the narrator is the lead character, although he or she may take a secondary role.

- Emphasize that the first-person point of view requires the author to use "I" and "me" in referring to him- or herself.

- You might wish to explain some of the *advantages* authors gain by using the first-person point of view, including:

  —Writing in the first person is natural, arising from the way we speak. Many authors find it easier to write in this point of view.

  —The reader participates in everything the author/narrator does. The reader feels close to the action.

  —The reader shares the author/narrator's innermost thoughts, feelings, emotions, and attitudes. Because of this, the reader has the chance to identify with and truly come to care about the author/narrator.

  —The story assumes a tone of personal experience with heightened realism.

- You might also wish to mention these *disadvantages* of the first-person point of view, including:

  —The powers of the author/narrator to relate the story are restricted to only what he or she knows, experiences, or hears about in the story. For example, the author/narrator can't give detailed background about each character, unless he or she has learned about the background in some way. It is for this reason that long, complex novels are usually written in the third person from multiple points of view (see Mini-lesson 72).

  —The description of the author/narrator as a character in the story is limited. He or she can't constantly describe him- or herself without sounding vain.

  —When a story is told from only one point of view, readers aren't able to see inside the minds of other characters or experience their feelings.

  —If the reader doesn't like the point-of-view character, he or she may lose interest in the story.

- You might like to mention the following examples of stories written in the first person:

  —*The Adventures of Huckleberry Finn* by Mark Twain

  —*The House on Mango Street* by Sandra Cisneros

  —*A Separate Peace* by John Knowles

—Flowers for Algernon by Daniel Keyes

—To Kill a Mockingbird by Harper Lee

Activities:

1. This activity is designed for the entire class or for groups, provided students are reading the same story which is written in the first-person point of view. Instruct your students to analyze the point of view of the story, focusing their attention on why the author selected this point of view and how it enhances the story. Distribute copies of Worksheet 71–1, "Analyzing the First-person Point of View," to help your students with their ideas. Upon completion of the worksheets, conduct a class discussion or have students meet in groups to discuss the point of view of the story.

2. While working in groups, students are to discuss the author/narrator of a story they are currently reading. They should explore the point of view and try to determine how—if at all—the story would change if the point of view was changed from the first person to the third person. They should also try to decide if the story would be as effective. Allow time for groups to report their conclusions to the class.

Writing Activities:

1. Instruct students to write a story on a topic of their choice, using the first-person point of view. Upon completion of their writing, display the stories.

2. Instruct students to select an excerpt from a story written in the first-person point of view and rewrite the material in the third person. They should note how the story must be changed.

Name _____ Date _____ Section _____

Analyzing the First-person Point of View

Directions: Answer the questions below about the point of view of the story you are reading. Use another sheet of paper if you need more space.

1. Describe the narrator of this story. _____

_____

_____

_____

_____

_____

_____

_____

2. Why do you think the author chose this character to

be the narrator of the story? _____

_____

_____

3. Could this story have been written from the point of view of another character? _____

Explain. _____

_____

_____

_____

4. Could this story have been written as effectively in the third-person point of view?

_____ Explain. _____

_____

_____

_____

_____

MINI-LESSON 72:
THIRD-PERSON POINT OF VIEW

Most stories are written in the third-person point of view. This point of view permits authors more scope in developing their stories, and, especially in the third-person, multiple point of view, gives the reader the chance to experience the story from the perspectives of different characters.

Procedure:

- Explain that a story written in the third-person point of view is written from a perspective outside the story. The narrator is not a participant of the story as he or she is in a story written in the first-person point of view. In the third-person point of view, the author refers to all the characters as "he" or "she."

- Note that in a story written from the third-person point of view, the author may write the story from the point of view of one character or several. Long, complex stories are usually written from multiple points of view. Selection of the point of view depends on the story and how the author decides to tell it.

- Explain that when using the third-person point of view, the author may choose to restrict the powers of narration—that is, limit the amount of information he or she tells from the point-of-view characters—or the author may use omniscient powers, acting as a god in telling the story. When using third-person omniscient powers, the author is free to reveal as much information as he or she feels is necessary to the telling of the story.

- You may wish to mention some *advantages* the author gains when using the third-person point of view:
  - —The author can share the thoughts, feelings, emotions, and attitudes of several characters.
  - —The author can reveal action from the perspectives of different characters; the reader then sees the action through the eyes of different characters, resulting in variety.
  - —The author can provide background information that characters may not know about.

- You may also wish to mention that the major disadvantage of the third-person point of view is the potential loss of a personal tone that can be achieved with the first-person point of view.

- Mention that most novels and short stories are told in the third-person point of view. Note examples of this point of view in some of the stories your students have read.

Activities:

1. This activity may be used with the whole class or with groups, provided students are reading the same story, written in the third-person point of view. Instruct your students to explore the use of the third-person point of view in this story, focusing their attention on how this point of view is the "right"

one for the story. Distribute copies of Worksheet 72–1, "Analyzing the Third-person Point of View," which can help your students with this activity. Upon completion of the worksheets, conduct a class discussion or have students meet in groups to discuss the story's point of view.

2. This activity is designed for students working in groups, whose members are reading the same multi-point-of-view novel. Instruct your students to go through the novel and note the different points of view and where they change. They should discuss the author's use of point of view and focus on how the changes in viewpoint enhance the novel. Who, for example, is the dominant point-of-view character? Why did the author choose to tell this story from multiple points of view? Could the point-of-view characters of any scenes be changed? How would this affect the story? Each group should then prepare a brief summary of their conclusions regarding the author's use of point of view and share their conclusions with the class.

3. Students are to select a story—in the third-person point of view—that they previously read. They are to bring the story to their group, briefly summarize the story, and share their feelings with the group's members how the third-person point of view enhances the story. (Of course, if they feel that the story would have been better had it been written in the first person, they may offer their opinions about that.) At the beginning of this activity, monitor the groups closely so that group members bring a variety of stories to the meeting. This will broaden the scope of the activity.

Writing Activities:

1. Instruct students to write a story on a topic of their choice, using the third-person point of view. Display the stories upon completion.

2. Instruct students to select an excerpt from a story written in the third-person point of view and rewrite it in the first person. Students should note how the change in point of view affects the story.

Name _____ Date _____ Section _____

Analyzing the Third-person Point of View

Directions: Answer the questions below about the point of view of the story you are reading. Use an extra sheet of paper if you need more space.

1. Who is the point-of-view character(s) in this story? _____

_____

_____

2. Why do you think the author selected this character(s) as the point-of-view character(s)?

_____

_____

_____

_____

3. Why do you think the author chose to tell this story in the third-person point of view?

_____

_____

_____

4. Could this story have been told as well in the first-person point of view? _____

Explain. _____

_____

_____

_____

_____

_____

_____

_____

_____

MINI-LESSON 73:
FIGURES OF SPEECH

Authors use figures of speech to enhance imagery and style. The most common figures of speech are *similes, metaphors, personification,* and *hyperboles.* When readers understand figures of speech, they are more likely to understand and enjoy what they are reading. (Depending on your class and curriculum, you might wish to cover this topic with more detail and divide this mini-lesson into two or three parts. I'd suggest doing similes and metaphors one day, and personification and hyperboles on two additional days.)

Procedure:

- Explain each of these figures of speech: similes, metaphors, personification, and hyperboles. (Before you do, you may wish to hand out Worksheet 73–1, "Examples of Figures of Speech," so that students will have samples of each.)

  —Similes are comparisons that use the words *like, as,* or *than.* The purpose of similes is to help the reader understand something better by telling how it is *similar* to something else that is usually very different. This creates a strong image by broadening the reader's perception.

  —Metaphors make comparisons *without* using the words *like, as,* or *than.* Unlike a simile, a metaphor tells that a thing *is* something else. This, too, creates a powerful image.

  —Personification is the giving of human qualities to nonhuman things such as animals, plants, objects, and ideas. By giving humanlike attributes to other things, personification stimulates the imaginations of readers.

  —Hyperboles are figures of speech that rely on overstatement or exaggeration. Because of their obvious exaggeration, hyperboles can add emphasis and imagery to reading.

Activities:

1. Distribute copies of "Examples of Figures of Speech" to your students and review and discuss the examples.

2. This activity is designed for students to first work individually and then meet in their groups. Students should be reading the same material, which contains examples of figures of speech. Instruct your students that they are to find examples of figures of speech in the story they are currently reading. Hand out copies of Worksheet 73–2, "Finding Figures of Speech," which will guide students in their efforts. You might also wish to distribute copies of "Examples of Figures of Speech" which students may use for reference. After students have individually completed the worksheet, they are to meet in their groups and share examples of figures of speech. Group members should then try to pick what they feel are the best examples. Allow time for groups to share their results with the class.

Writing Activities:

1. Working individually, students are to select a topic, write a story, article, or poem, and use at least three figures of speech. Encourage your students to use strong, clear images. Display the writings, or have students read their work to the class.

2. This activity is a group story. The group is to select a topic to write about, and in the course of the writing each member is to contribute at least one figure of speech. You may wish to allow students to make their stories silly and amusing—the real focus here is using figures of speech. Permit each group to read its story to the class upon completion.

Name _____ Date _____ Section _____

Examples of Figures of Speech

The most common figures of speech in the English language are similes, metaphors, personification, and hyperboles. Authors use figures of speech to compare ideas and create strong images for their readers.

Similes

Similes use the words *like, as,* or *than* to make comparisons.

- The ice crystals glistened like diamonds in the sun.
- His fury was hot as fire.
- The old scout's eyesight was keener than an eagle's.

Metaphors

Metaphors make comparisons *without* using *like, as,* or *than.*

- The river, swollen from the spring rains, was a sea preventing their crossing.
- The puck was lightning blazing into the goal.

Personification

Personification gives human traits or emotions to nonhuman things or ideas.

- The sky's tears were fitting for the mournful day.
- They awoke to the songs of the birds.
- The dark forest dared them to enter.

Hyperboles

Hyperboles create strong images through exaggeration.

- He was so tired he could *sleep for a year.*
- The exploding thunder made her *jump ten feet high.*

Name _____ Date _____ Section _____

Finding Figures of Speech

Directions: In the story you are currently reading, find at least one example of each figure of speech listed below. Include its page number. Use another sheet of paper if you need more space.

1. An example of a simile: _____

_____

_____

_____

_____

_____

2. An example of a metaphor: _____

_____

3. An example of personification: _____

_____

4. An example of hyperbole: _____

_____

5. Which figure of speech do you like the best? _____

Why? _____

_____

_____

_____

MINI-LESSON 74:
IDIOMS

Idioms are common expressions used in written and spoken language. Since idioms are figurative phrases that cannot be taken literally, students may find unfamiliar idioms confusing.

Procedure:

- Explain that idioms are figurative expressions that should not be taken literally. Offer this example:

  > Knowing their parents would be home soon, the children hurried *to straighten up the house.*

  Obviously, they couldn't "straighten" up the house—it's unlikely the house was crooked. However, most students will understand this idiom to mean that the children had to clean the house or put things in their proper places.

- Point out that many idioms have evolved to have special meanings. The expression "He put his foot in his mouth" doesn't mean this person actually put his foot in his mouth, but rather he said the wrong thing.

- Emphasize that idioms that appear in reading material must be understood, or the reader may not fully comprehend the material.

Activities:

1. Distribute copies of Worksheet 74–1, "Common Idioms." Review and discuss the idioms and their meanings with your students. Then encourage students to write down idioms they know but that are not on the list.

2. This activity is designed for students working in pairs or groups of three. Distribute copies of Worksheet 74–2, "Idioms and Meanings," and instruct your students to work together and write the meanings for the given idioms. After students have completed the worksheets, discuss their answers.

3. This activity is designed for groups. Many idioms we use today—that have no apparent literal meaning—were once used very literally. Instruct your groups to research the origins of common idioms. (Books about idioms are available in most libraries.) Students should compile the origins of idioms and share their findings with the class.

Writing Activity:

- Although idioms are common in language, appearing in speech and written material, they are generally considered to be examples of weak writing. Because they are familiar to most people, idioms detract from style and should be avoided in writing unless necessary to the author's purpose. With this in mind, instruct your students to review several pieces of their previous writing, read through them, and identify idioms. Suggest that they think of ways they might revise the idioms to make their writing fresher. You might wish to hand out copies of Worksheet 74–1 to help your students identify idioms in their writing.

Name _____ Date _____ Section _____

Common Idioms

Idioms are expressions that have special meanings and should never be taken literally. Many of the idioms below will probably be familiar to you. Note that these are only some of the most common idioms. On the back of this sheet, write down any other idioms you can think of.

Raining cats and dogs . . .

By the skin of your teeth . . .

A rat race . . .

In hot water . . .

All in the same boat . . .

Got the ax . . .

Stopped on a dime . . .

That's the way the cookie crumbles . . .

Cat got your tongue . . .

Keep a stiff upper lip . . .

Made it by the seat of his pants . . .

Went all out . . .

Threw in the towel . . .

Over the hill . . .

Blew his stack . . .

On the spur of the moment . . .

Grinning from ear to ear . . .

Bury the hatchet . . .

Over the barrel . . .

Straight from the horse's mouth . . .

Hold your horses . . .

Bull session . . .

Name _____ Date _____ Section _____

Idioms and Meanings

Directions: Write the meanings of the idioms below.

1. He's always *a ball of fire.* _____

_____

_____

_____

2. After you arrive, *drop me a line.* _____

_____

_____

3. Getting an A in reading is *in the bag.* _____

_____

4. The little girl was always *bugging* her older brother. _____

_____

5. They were *shooting the breeze* after school. _____

_____

6. His mother has a *green thumb.* _____

_____

7. He's *out in left field.* _____

_____

8. She told him to *go fly a kite.* _____

_____

9. Although they were best friends, they never *saw eye to eye.* _____

_____

10. He knew he was *up the creek.* _____

_____

_____

MINI-LESSON 75:
ALLITERATION

Alliteration refers to a phrase or sentence in which two or more words have the same beginning sounds. Authors use alliteration to enhance their writing, add rhythm to their words, or emphasize their ideas. Alliteration can add beauty and power to language.

Procedure:

- Explain that alliteration is a phrase or sentence in which two or more words have the same beginning sounds. Offer this example:

     The rays of the golden sun sparkled across the sea.

  The "s" sounds of "sun," "sparkled," and "sea" are certainly striking. Additional "s" sounds in "rays" and "across" further enhance the alliterative effect.

- Note that alliteration may be used for emphasis, as well as help written material flow easily and provide rhythm.

- Point out that alliteration, when used with figurative language, can paint clear, powerful images in the minds of readers.

- Mention that while poets are well known for using alliteration, authors of prose use it, too.

- You might wish to mention that Edgar Allan Poe used much alliteration in his poetry. Perhaps you'd like to point out some examples, which can easily be found in any anthology of Poe's works.

Activities:

1. Students should work individually for this activity. Distribute copies of Worksheet 75–1, "Finding Examples of Alliteration," and instruct your students to circle the alliterative words in the sentences. Encourage them to write examples of their own. After students have completed the worksheets, go over them orally and discuss alliteration.

     Answer key:

     1. sunset, splashed, sky
     2. wintry, wind; forest, floor
     3. wolf's, wail; lonely, long
     4. day, dawned
     5. rocket, roared; streaked, sky
     6. damp, dark, downward
     7. night, never; fell, feared, find, forest; would, way
     8. playful, puppy; blue, ball
     9. time, turtles, tardy
     10. covered, cheerful, color

2. This activity is designed for students working in groups, provided students are reading the same story. While working together, each group is to find several examples of alliteration in the story they are reading. Remind students to write down the page numbers of their examples. Each group should then pick three examples that it feels are particularly good and share them with the class.

3. Study the work of poets—Edgar Allan Poe is a good choice here—and note how they use alliteration to embellish their poems.

Writing Activity:

* Instruct students to write a poem on a topic of their choice and encourage them to use alliteration.

Name _____ Date _____ Section _____

Finding Examples of Alliteration

Directions: Find examples of alliteration in the sentences below. Then write some of your own. Use another sheet of paper if you need more space.

1. The sunset splashed red and gold across the sky.
2. The wintry wind stirred the leaves on the forest floor.
3. The wolf's lonely wail was long and mournful.
4. The day dawned gray and cold.
5. The rocket roared as it streaked through the sky.
6. Damp and dark, the cave angled sharply downward.
7. Night fell and the lost hikers feared they would never find their way out of the forest.
8. The playful puppy loved chasing his blue ball.
9. Following their own time, turtles don't worry about being tardy.
10. Wildflowers covered the hillside with cheerful color.

Write some sentences of your own that have alliteration.

_____

_____

_____

_____

_____

_____

_____

_____

_____

MINI-LESSON 76:
ONOMATOPOEIA

Some words in English "sound" like the sounds they describe. This is called onomatopoeia.

Procedure:

- Explain that onomatopoeia is the use of words that sound like the things they describe. For example, bees *buzz*. The verb "buzz" reminds the reader of the sound bees make when they fly. Here are two others:
  —Cows *moo*. If you have ever heard a mooing cow, you know that "moo" is the perfect word here.
  —Steaks *sizzle* on a hot grill. Most readers can hear that "sizzling" steak as they read that sentence. (Some can even smell it!)
- Note that onomatopoeia is used to create strong, clear images.

Activity:

- Distribute copies of Worksheet 76–1, "Words That Describe Sounds," and review the list with your students. See how many other "sound" words your students can come up with.

Writing Activity:

- For this activity, permit students to work in pairs or groups of three. Instruct your students that they are to write a poem or short article about "Sound Words." Their material may be silly or serious (most will probably be silly), but they should use their creativity to illustrate the use of onomatopoeia. At the end of the activity, permit students to read their material to the class. Distributing copies of Worksheet 76–1 will give students examples of "sound" words.

Name _____ Date _____ Section _____

Words That Describe Sounds

Words that suggest the sounds they describe are examples of *onomatopoeia*. These words appeal to the sense of hearing and can add interest and style to written expression. Following are several examples.

bang	hiss	sizzle
boom	honk	slurp
bow-wow	hoot	snort
buzz	howl	splash
clang	hum	squish
clink	meow	swish
coo	moo	tick-tock
crack	neigh	thud
crackle	puff	thump
cuckoo	purr	tinkle
fizz	raspy	twang
growl	rev	whirl
grunt	roar	whiz

Mini-lessons
77 through 100
SPECIFIC
READING SKILLS

MINI-LESSON 77:
COMPREHENSION

Comprehension is fundamental to reading competence. Many students are unaware that there are different types of comprehension, and that understanding them can be valuable in the overall process of reading.

Procedure:

- Define comprehension as the understanding of what has been read.
- Explain that there are three important types of comprehension: *literal, interpretative,* and *applied.* Offer explanations about each.
  - Literal comprehension is basic understanding, such as the names of characters and places, events, and descriptions.
  - Interpretative comprehension includes processes on the part of the reader such as analyzing, drawing conclusions, and making decisions about facts and events.
  - Applied comprehension includes processes on the part of the reader such as speculating over what has been read, making predictions, extrapolating information, or applying the information learned to another subject.

Activities:

1. This activity is designed for the whole class or students working in groups, provided they are reading the same story. Distribute copies of Worksheet 77–1, "Understanding the Types of Comprehension," and instruct your students to individually answer the questions. (Note that this activity will work best if it is focused on a specific chapter or scene.) Upon completion of the worksheet, correct the worksheets orally with the class or have students meet in groups to correct the worksheets and discuss the three major types of comprehension. In your discussion, point out that question one is literal comprehension, question two is interpretative, and question three is applied.

2. This activity requires students to first work alone and then meet in their groups. Working individually, students are to find examples of literal, interpretative, and applied comprehension in books or articles they are reading. They are then to meet in their groups and share and discuss the examples they found.

3. For this activity, students should work in pairs or groups of three. The class should be reading the same material. Each pair or group is to write at least one example of a literal, interpretative, and applied comprehension question for the material the class is currently reading. After composing their questions, each group should exchange questions with another group and answer each other's questions. This activity will reinforce your students' understanding of the different types of comprehension. Conduct a class discussion upon completion of the activity.

4. While working in groups, students are to create a collage that describes the three types of reading comprehension, or shows the importance of reading.

Old magazines—which you can collect in advance from colleagues and students—can provide lots of material for the collages. Since you will also need materials such as scissors, glue, markers, rulers, pencils, pens, and, of course, poster paper, you might like to collaborate with your students' art teacher for this activity. Display the posters upon completion of the activity.

Writing Activity:

• Encourage your students to write a persuasive essay, or a letter to the editor of a local newspaper in support of reading. (Perhaps you might like to forward the best letters to the editor of the newspaper.) Suggest that, in their letters, students focus on the importance of being able to read in our society. Remind them to use a standard business letter format, and, if possible, write their letters on typewriters or computers.

Name _____ Date _____ Section _____

Understanding the Types of Comprehension

Directions: Answer the comprehension questions about the story you are currently reading. Use another sheet of paper if you need more space.

1. Describe the chapter or scene you are reading. _____

_____

_____

_____

_____

2. Relate this chapter or scene to your own experiences. Explain how it is alike or different

from anything you have done, read, or heard about. _____

_____

_____

_____

_____

3. Based on the events of this chapter or scene, what prediction can you make about the

rest of the story? _____

_____

_____

_____

_____

_____

_____

_____

_____

_____

_____

MINI-LESSON 78:
STRATEGIES FOR IMPROVING READING COMPREHENSION

While it's true that people become good readers by reading, discovering for themselves the techniques that will make them competent and efficient readers, there are strategies you can offer your students to help them master the skills needed for effective reading. Some of the most helpful follow in this mini-lesson.

Procedure:

- Explain that good readers utilize various strategies to help them understand what they read. Many readers discover the techniques that work best for them through their reading experiences. They may use these strategies unconsciously, but they still use them.
- Emphasize that being an active reader in which your mind is engaged fully with what you are reading is the foundation of comprehension.
- Emphasize that the key to learning to read well is to read. Like any other activity, the more people read, the better readers they become.

Activities:

1. Distribute and review copies of Worksheet 78–1, "Improving Your Reading Comprehension." Point out to your students that while not all good readers use all of these strategies, most good readers use at least some of them. Encourage your students to use them, too.
2. Have your students meet in groups and discuss which of the reading strategies noted on Worksheet 78–1 they use. If some students claim they don't use any, suggest that they discuss the ones they feel might be helpful. Ask students to share any strategies they might use that are not on the list.

Writing Activity:

- An excellent strategy for improving comprehension is to summarize material. For this activity, suggest that students summarize an article or short story, or a chapter or section of a book they are reading. In their summaries they should focus on the main ideas and details. Display their summaries upon completion.

Name _____ Date _____ Section _____

Improving Your
Reading Comprehension

There are many ways to improve your reading comprehension. Following are some of the most helpful.

- Preview the material. For *books,* before beginning to read, look at the cover, back page, contents, and introductory material. Such parts of a book frequently give important information of what the book is about, which can help prepare your mind for the material to come. For *articles or stories,* look at any subtitles, illustrations, or pictures.

- Read in a place without distractions. Interruptions break your concentration and undermine your understanding.

- Visualize what you are reading. Try to see detailed pictures in your mind. Not only will this help you to understand better, but it will also help you to remember what you read.

- Focus your attention on key words and events. Ask yourself who and what are involved, as well as where, when, and why the event happened.

- Be aware of cause and effect. Make mental notes of what happens first, what happens next, and so on.

- Analyze what you read and compare the information to your own experiences. Ask yourself how this new information compares with what you know about the world.

- Draw inferences and conclusions, then see if your ideas were right.

- As you read, make predictions of what you believe will happen next. This keeps your mind engaged.

- Study illustrations, photographs, diagrams, graphs, and charts. These can provide vital information that can be easily seen.

- Group things and events into categories. Ask yourself what ideas are related. Look for similarities and differences. Look for connections, and ask yourself why and how.

- Be aware of signal words, such as the following:

  —*Sequence:* first, second, third, etc.; now, next, in addition, afterward, then, finally, last . . .

  —*Change of direction:* although, however, despite, rather, while, but, on the contrary, even though, on the other hand, yet . . .

—*Illustration:* for example, for instance, such as, similar to, like . . .

—*Cause:* because, for, while, so that, resulting from, then, until, therefore, so, in order that . . .

- Use context cues to help you understand new words.

- Reread if necessary. If you don't understand something, go back and read it again. Good readers do this all the time.

- When reading difficult material, take notes. Writing down important facts (and their page numbers) can help keep you focused and also serve as reference points.

- Highlight material with a bright marker. (Don't do this to textbooks or library books, however. Also, be careful not to *overuse* this technique, because you may have so much highlighted that you won't know where to focus your attention.)

- Summarize material you've read, focusing on the main ideas and supporting details. This can boost your comprehension.

MINI-LESSON 79:
THE IMPORTANCE OF USING CONTEXT CUES

When good readers encounter unfamiliar words, most attempt to find their meaning from context. This is perhaps the most efficient method of learning new words, because it is least disruptive to the reading process. Point out the importance of using context cues to your students.

Procedure:

- Explain that while there are many ways to learn new words, one of the most efficient is through context cues, which enable a reader to guess at the meaning of a new word from the way it is used in a sentence.
- Note that unfamiliar words are often defined in another part of the sentence. On the board or an overhead projector, offer this example:

  —Many people find arachnids, the group to which spiders belong, frightening.

  Point out how the definition of "arachnids" follows the word. Now offer this example:

  —In ancient Greek myths, ambrosia was thought to be the food of the gods.

  Explain that the meaning of "ambrosia" is given as "the food of the gods." Offer this next example:

  —The scintillating lights filled the downtown street with brilliant colors.

  Note how the meaning of the word "scintillating" is hinted at in "brilliant colors."

- Explain that even if the definition of an unfamiliar word is not given in the sentence, its meaning can often be inferred from its usage. Offer this example:

  —Ferdinand Magellan led an expedition that was the first to circumnavigate the earth, leaving from Spain and sailing westward around the tip of South America, across the Pacific, through the Philippines, around Africa, and finally back to Spain.

  Note how the meaning of "circumnavigate" becomes clear by the end of the sentence.

Activities:

1. This activity is designed for students working individually. Instruct your students to find examples of words they don't know in their reading. They should try to determine the meanings of these words through their context. Each student is to write what he or she thinks the word means, then look the words up in a dictionary. Suggest that each student try to find three to five unfamiliar words. When students are done, conduct a class discussion about context cues, and ask volunteers to share some of the new words they discovered. Perhaps add these words to your students' vocabulary lists.

2. Read a passage of new material to your students and model how they can use context cues to understand the meanings of unfamiliar words.

Writing Activity:

- Everyone has his or her own methods for coping with unfamiliar words during reading. Ask your students to share the methods they use in a brief essay. They should explain why they use these methods, and how the methods might be helpful to others. If a student claims that he or she doesn't use any method, suggest that this student write about some ways he or she might find useful. Display the writings upon completion of the activity.

MINI-LESSON 80:
BUILDING A READING VOCABULARY

For most people, the better their vocabulary, the better their reading ability. There are several steps your students can take to build their reading vocabularies.

Procedure:

- Explain that most good readers have good vocabularies. The more words they know, the less chance they have of encountering unfamiliar ones that can weaken their comprehension. This is especially important during test-taking.

- Note that when people improve their vocabularies, they also improve their abilities in speaking and writing.

- Point out that improving vocabulary results not only in improving comprehension but reading rate as well.

- Emphasize that while improving your vocabulary does require some effort, it can be done and the rewards are significant.

- Explain these basics for improving vocabulary:
  —Develop a positive attitude regarding your vocabulary. Make a firm decision that you will work to improve it.
  —Develop the habit of focusing your attention on new words and trying to understand their meanings. Use context cues, and, if necessary, dictionaries to learn the meanings of new words.
  —Work to expand your vocabulary outside of school as well as in school.

Activities:

1. Distribute and review Worksheet 80–1, "Steps for Building a Reading Vocabulary." Discuss and emphasize the importance of the various steps. (Depending on the needs and abilities of your students, you might prefer to expand some of these steps—for example, learning key prefixes and suffixes—and design a separate mini-lesson for them.)

2. Suggest that students keep a vocabulary notebook in which they record new words and their definitions. A simple way to do this is to use a spiral notebook and on the top of the first page write "A," then "B" on the next page, etc. Suggest that students try to enter their words in rough alphabetical order. Thus "ache" would be written near the top of the page, while "apple" would be written in the middle. Over the year students who enter new words regularly will build rather impressive vocabulary lists. You might wish to implement quizzes on these words, allowing students to select 10 or 20 that they want to be quizzed on. Having partners quiz each other eliminates the problem of you having to administer so many different quizzes.

3. This activity works well for students working in pairs or groups of three. Have students create flash cards of new words. Flash cards can be easily made with markers and three-inch by five-inch index cards. When students encounter new words, they simply write the word on an index card. On the

back of the card they should write the definition of the word. After they have accumulated several cards, they can quiz each other orally. Once students have learned the new words, you might wish to administer formal quizzes on them. Having students administer the quizzes to each other reduces your workload.

Writing Activity:

• This activity is a good follow-up to Activities 2 and 3 above. After students have built lists of new words, instruct them to write a story on a topic of their choice, incorporating some of the new words they learned. Display the stories upon completion of the writing.

Name _____ Date _____ Section _____

Steps for Building a Reading Vocabulary

Following are some steps you can take to build your vocabulary.

- Try to find the meaning of unfamiliar words through context cues. This is often the most efficient way to learn new words without disrupting your reading.

- Learn key prefixes and suffixes, and also the roots of words. If you don't know the meaning of an unfamiliar, multisyllable word, you may know a part of it that can help you figure out the rest from context cues. Although there are many prefixes and suffixes, here are some common examples.

  —*Prefixes for greatness or bigness, number, size, or scope:* mega, hyper, ultra, extra, macro, multi, super. *Examples:* extraordinary, multinational, supernatural, hyperinflation.

  —*Prefixes for the opposite or negative:* a, an, counter, de, dis, il, im, in, ir, neg, non, un. *Examples:* dishonest, illegal, irrational, nonsense, uncomfortable.

  —*Suffixes for small:* ette, ling, let, et, cule, kin. *Examples:* dinette, duckling, owlet, midget.

  —*Suffixes for full of:* ful, ose, ous, ulent. *Examples*: thoughtful, joyful, comatose, joyous, fraudulent.

  —*Suffixes for female:* ine, ess. *Examples:* actress, heroine, lioness, princess.

- Break apart compound words, which often makes their meanings clear. Some examples: airmail, buttermilk, leftover, loudspeaker, sunflower, wildcat.

- Get in the habit of classifying or grouping words. This will help you to remember their meanings. For example, *proton, neutron,* and *electron* are all parts of atoms. *Numerator* and *denominator* are parts of fractions. *Hurricane* and *typhoon* are tropical storms of the Atlantic and Pacific.

- Associate words that are synonyms or antonyms. For instance, small, tiny, minuscule, and little are all synonyms. Antonyms of these words include big, great, huge, enormous, and large. By associating words in this manner you increase your chances for finding the meanings of unfamiliar words through context cues.

- Look up the meanings of new words in a dictionary.

- Finally, but perhaps most importantly, read often.

MINI-LESSON 81:
FINDING MAIN IDEAS

When students understand the main ideas of paragraphs, they are more likely to comprehend the material they are reading. Being able to identify main ideas is an essential reading skill.

Procedure:

- Explain that every well-written paragraph contains a main idea. Understanding the main idea of a paragraph helps comprehension, because details that relate to the main idea become more clear and the "whole" makes more sense.
- Note that all of the other sentences and details in a paragraph attempt to develop the main idea.
- Emphasize that the topic sentence of a paragraph frequently contains the main idea of the paragraph.
- Explain that in many paragraphs the first sentence is the topic sentence and contains the main idea. Sometimes, however, the topic sentence may be in the middle or near the end of the paragraph. It may even be the last sentence.
- Tell your students that the topic sentence usually contains information about the most important person, place, or thing in the sentence.
- Offer these suggestions for finding the topic sentence of a paragraph:
  —Assume that the first sentence is the topic sentence. Check to see that the rest of the sentences of the paragraph explain or add details to the information contained in the first sentence. If they do, it is likely to be the topic sentence.
  —If the first sentence is not the topic sentence, look at the last sentence of the paragraph. That is the next most likely place for the topic sentence to be.
  —If the first or last sentence of the paragraph is not the topic sentence, look for it throughout the rest of the paragraph.

Activity:

- This activity may be used with the whole class or with groups, as long as students are reading the same material. Select three paragraphs from material students are currently reading and instruct them to work individually to identify the main ideas and details of each paragraph. (It is best to choose descriptive paragraphs that contain several details.) Distribute copies of Worksheet 81–1, "Finding Main Ideas and Details," which will help students with their efforts. Upon completion of the worksheet, go over the answers orally or have students meet in groups to discuss their answers. (If you feel it is necessary, have students find the main idea and details of more paragraphs.)

Writing Activity:

- Instruct your students to write an essay on a topic related to their current reading. You might suggest that they compare characters, analyze the plot, or examine the author's use of imagery. While writing their essays, students should focus their attention on composing sound paragraphs with good topic sentences and details that support their main ideas. Display the essays upon completion of the activity.

Name _____ Date _____ Section _____

Finding Main Ideas and Details

Directions: Find the main ideas and details in the selected paragraphs of your reading. Use another sheet of paper if you need more space.

Main idea of paragraph 1: _____

_____

Details that support the main idea: _____

_____

_____

_____

_____

_____

Main idea of paragraph 2: _____

_____

Details that support the main idea: _____

_____

_____

_____

_____

Main idea of paragraph 3: _____

_____

Details that support the main idea: _____

_____

_____

_____

_____

_____

MINI-LESSON 82:
RECALLING DETAILS

While understanding main ideas is vital to comprehension, remembering details that support them is equally significant. This is particularly true when students are reading textbooks or studying for tests.

Procedure:

- Explain that reading for details is an important life skill. Whether reading for details in studying for a test, reading to find information for a job, or reading about places to go on a vacation, understanding and recalling details is essential.
- Explain that the easiest way to recall details is to relate them to the main idea. All details support the main idea in a paragraph. Relating details to the main idea results in building a whole that is easier to remember.
- Note that writing down details can help a reader recall them. This may be done by writing the main idea and listing its details below it, forming a simple outline. Such "idea" lists can be especially useful when studying for tests.
- Mention that, in material students own, underlining and highlighting details can be helpful. Writing notes in margins is another technique that can aid in remembering details. (Remind students not to do this in their textbooks.)

Activities:

1. This activity may be used with the whole class or with groups, provided students are reading the same material. Select a chapter, or a section, of the material students are currently reading and instruct them to compose an outline of it. They should focus their attention on main ideas and details. Hand out copies of Worksheet 82–1, "A Simple Outline for Ideas and Details," which students will likely find helpful. (You may wish to use this only as a guide to show students how they might organize their outlines, then have them do their outlines on a separate sheet of paper.) When students are done, either discuss the outlines with the entire class or have them meet in groups to compare their work.

2. This activity may be used with the whole class or with groups. For the activity students will need to bring their science or social studies text to class; remind them the day before which text to bring. You might wish to consult with your students' science or social studies teacher to find out what topic he or she is covering in that class and use that material. For the activity, select a section of the text—perhaps three or four pages—and instruct your students to list the main ideas and details of the section, creating a simple outline of the material. At the end of the activity, either discuss the lists as a class or have students meet in groups to compare their lists. Did most students list many of the same details? If not, why not?

Writing Activity:

- Instruct students to write an article or story on a topic of their choice. Suggest that they compose a simple outline, or list their main ideas and details as a prewriting exercise to help them organize their material before writing. Display the work of your students.

Name _____ Date _____ Section _____

A Simple Outline for
Ideas and Details

Directions: Use this form as a guide for outlining the assigned material. Use another sheet of paper to continue your outline if you need more space.

Main Idea: I. _____

Details: A. _____

   B. _____

   C. _____

   D. _____

Main Idea: II. _____

Details: A. _____

   B. _____

   C. _____

   D. _____

Main Idea: III. _____

Details: A. _____

   B. _____

   C. _____

   D. _____

MINI-LESSON 83:
MAKING INFERENCES AND DRAWING CONCLUSIONS

Sometimes authors share their conclusions with readers, making it easy for readers to draw conclusions. Some authors don't do this, however, and readers must make inferences and draw their own conclusions.

Procedure:

- Explain that readers are often required to infer ideas and draw conclusions about the material they are reading. This is especially true when authors present a situation, but leave it to readers to analyze information and decide what it means. Readers must arrive at their own conclusions, based on inferences.
- Define inference and conclusion.
   —An *inference* is the process of deriving a conclusion from facts of premises.
   —A *conclusion* is a judgment, decision, or a prediction.
- Offer this example. "It is a hot humid day in August. Dark clouds are gathering in the western sky." From these facts one might infer that a storm is coming. The conclusion is the belief (or judgment, based upon the facts) that a storm indeed will arrive soon.
- Explain that the best way to draw conclusions is to pay close attention to the facts that are available.

Activities:

1. This activity is designed for the whole class or for students working in groups, provided they are reading the same material. Select a chapter or scene of the material students are reading that lends itself to students drawing conclusions or making a prediction of what will happen next. Distribute copies of Worksheet 83–1, "Inferences and Conclusions," and instruct your students to complete the worksheet individually. When students are done, conduct a class discussion or have students meet in groups to discuss the inferences and conclusions they made.

2. This activity is designed for groups. Have each group select a major event for which conclusions or predictions of the outcome may be made. Some suggestions for topics include a major sports event, an election, an awards show (for example, the Academy Awards or MTV Awards), or an event at school. Instruct your students to discuss what factors they would find helpful in drawing conclusions or making predictions about how the event or situation might turn out. Try to have each group choose a different topic, for this will broaden any culminating discussion. Each group should prepare a brief summary of what they discussed and present it to the class.

Writing Activity:

- Students are to write a paragraph that describes—but doesn't name—an event, such as an approaching storm, a place or situation at school, or another occurrence or setting that will be familiar to most of the class. The descriptions should provide enough details so that students may infer and conclude what is being described. Photocopy the descriptions and have others try to conclude what the author is describing.

Name _____ Date _____ Section _____

Inferences and Conclusions

Directions: Answer the following questions about the material you read. Use another sheet of paper if you need more space.

1. Briefly summarize this material. _____

_____

_____

_____

_____

_____

2. What conclusion can you make from this material? _____

_____

_____

_____

3. Why did you infer, or make, this conclusion? _____

_____

_____

_____

_____

_____

_____

_____

_____

MINI-LESSON 84:
IDENTIFYING FACT AND OPINION

Good readers are able to distinguish between fact and opinion. While most authors are careful to keep facts and their opinions separate, not all do. Thus, it remains for the reader to be able to tell the difference.

Procedure:

- Explain that knowing the difference between facts and opinions is a critical reading skill. This is not always easy.

- Define a *fact* as information that can be proven. For example, water freezes at 32 degrees F. This can be proven with water, a temperature of 32 degrees F, and a thermometer.

- Define an *opinion* as an author's belief about something. Here's a good example: "A temperature of 32 degrees F is very cold." This is an opinion, because some people, especially those who live in the far north, might find such a temperature to be relatively mild.

- Offer these clues for identifying opinions:

    —Opinion statements often contain words like "I think," "I believe," or "I feel." Here's an example.

    > *I think* Stephen King is the best author of horror.

    —Opinion statements may contain strong descriptive words such as best, worst, wonderful, fantastic, awful, etc. Here's an example.

    > New York City is the *greatest* baseball city in the country.

Activities:

1. For this activity, students should work individually. Instruct them to review the material they are currently reading and try to find examples of facts and opinions. Finding facts will likely be easier, particularly if students are reading a novel or short story. If they are reading a story, suggest that, along with opinions stated by the author, they look for opinions stated or held by characters. Hand out copies of Worksheet 84–1, "Facts and Opinions in Reading," which students may use to record their findings. After students have completed the worksheet, conduct a class discussion. Ask volunteers to share some examples of the facts and opinions they found.

2. This activity is designed for students working individually, with a class discussion upon conclusion. Distribute copies of Worksheet 84–2, "Facts or Opinions?" Instruct your students to identify the statements on the worksheet as either being a fact or an opinion, explaining why an opinion statement is indeed an opinion. When students are done with the worksheet, go over the sheet orally and discuss the differences between facts and opinions.

    Answer key: (1) O (It may be one of the world's most magnificent, but it's questionable if it is *the* most magnificent.) (2) F. (3) F. (4) O (The speaker *believes* Florida contains more exciting activities than other states.) (5) F.

(6) O (For some people there might be many things more distressing than rainy days.) (7) F. (8) O (The speaker *thinks* there will be a human colony on Mars within 30 years. Even though that is a likely possibility, it is still his opinion.) (9) O (Cold weather may not be tougher to endure for some people.) (10) F.

3. This activity is designed for students working in groups. A few days before you assign this activity, ask students (and your colleagues) to bring in old newspapers and magazines. While working in their groups, students are to search the articles in newspapers and magazines for examples of facts and opinions. They should share and discuss these examples, noting what types of articles contained mostly facts and what kinds included opinions. In articles in which the authors offered opinions, students should discuss the author's purpose in writing the article. Was it primarily to inform readers or state his or her opinion on a topic or problem? Conclude the activity with a discussion summarizing the differences between facts and opinions.

Writing Activity:

• This activity contains two parts. First, instruct students to select a favorite place and write a description of it. (Because the activity has two parts, you might suggest that students limit the length of their descriptions.) They might write about a park, a playground, mall, park, a place they have visited while on vacation, or a similar spot with which they are familiar. They are to write this description using only facts, and not offer their opinions.

After completing their descriptions, students should write another description, but this time they should include their opinions and feelings. They should then examine the two pieces. How are the two pieces alike? How are they different? Display both descriptions at the end of the activity.

Name _____ Date _____ Section _____

Facts and Opinions in Reading

Directions: Review the material you have read and find two examples of facts and two examples of opinions. Write the examples down (including their page numbers), and explain why the statement is a fact or an opinion.

Fact Number 1: _____

_____

Why is this a fact? _____

_____

Fact Number 2: _____

_____

_____

Why is this a fact? _____

_____

_____

_____

* * *

Opinion Number 1: _____

_____

_____

Why is this an opinion? _____

_____

_____

Opinion Number 2: _____

_____

Why is this an opinion? _____

_____

Name _____ Date _____ Section _____

Facts or Opinions?

Directions: Mark F for the statements that are facts and O for the statements that are opinions on the lines in front of the statements. For the opinion statements, explain why they are opinions on the lines that follow.

_____ 1. The Golden Gate Bridge in San Francisco is the world's most magnificent bridge.

_____

_____ 2. Owls are nocturnal creatures. They are most active at night.

_____

_____ 3. Because of their increase in numbers in recent years, alligators are no longer an endangered species.

_____

_____ 4. I believe there are more exciting things to do in Florida than in any other state.

_____

_____ 5. The sun is approximately 93 million miles from Earth.

_____

_____ 6. Nothing is more distressing than a rainy day.

_____

_____ 7. Computers are an important part of the success of many businesses.

_____

_____ 8. I think there will be a human colony on Mars within 30 years.

_____

_____

_____ 9. Cold weather is tougher to endure than hot weather.

_____

_____

_____ 10. Two times two is always four.

_____

_____

MINI-LESSON 85:
CAUSE AND EFFECT

Understanding cause and effect is basic to comprehension. When students are able to perceive relationships between actions and events, they are more likely to gain an overall understanding of their reading.

Procedure:

- Explain that every cause has an effect, or result. Likewise, every effect is the consequence of a cause.

- Note that understanding the relationship between causes and effects is not only essential to understanding factual material, but also in comprehending the plots of stories.

- Point out that major effects are often the result of many causes linked together in a sequence. Also, major causes can lead to several effects. Sometimes a cause leads to an effect, which then becomes the cause of another effect.

- Emphasize that cause-and-effect relationships are not always easy to see in reading. Sometimes readers must concentrate to find them.

- Offer these suggestions for finding causes and effects.

  —Find the cause of an action and follow the steps that lead to the effect.

  —Find the effect and follow the sequence of actions back to the cause.

  —Be aware of signal words for causes and effects. Signal words for causes include *because, since,* and *as a result of.* Signal words for effects include *consequently, therefore,* and also *as a result of.*

  —If you can't find clue words and are having trouble identifying cause and effect, arrange the events in the order in which they occurred. Look for any connections between the events; this should help you find the causes and effects.

Activities:

1. This activity will work well with the whole class or with students working in groups, as long as they are reading the same story. Select a major event in the story and instruct your students to find the causes that lead to an effect, or result, that occurred during or right after the event. Hand out copies of Worksheet 85–1, "Understanding Cause-and-effect Relationships," which will help your students with their ideas. Upon completion of the worksheet, conduct a class discussion about the answers or have students meet in groups to discuss the causes and effects they identified on the worksheet.

2. This activity is designed for students working in pairs or groups of three. Instruct your students to work together and generate a list of causes and effects. They should try to create at least ten, as in the next example. Perhaps show the following examples on an overhead projector or the board to give students an idea of what they will be doing. Note that causes and effects should be mixed up so that students may match them later.

<u>Cause</u>   <u>Effect</u>

Twisted ankle   Being late for school
School bus broke down   Unable to play in big game

The student who twisted his or her ankle wouldn't be able to play in the big game, and because the bus broke down students were late for school. These are obvious causes and effects. Your students should generate more causes and effects like these. When students are done composing their lists, you might like to photocopy them and distribute them to the class, allowing students to match the causes and their effects by drawing lines between them. This is an enjoyable activity that gives students practice in recognizing the relationships between causes and effects.

Writing Activity:

• Mystery stories are an excellent showcase for cause and effect. Ask your students to write a mystery. You may offer these topics to help them generate ideas:

     The Case of the Disappearing Kitten
     The Lost Computer Files
     Strange Sounds in the Night
     The Phantom Dog
     Blinking Lights in the Abandoned House

Encourage students to focus their attention on cause and effect as they are writing their stories. Display the stories upon completion.

Name _____ Date _____ Section _____

Understanding Cause-and-effect Relationships

Directions: Identify the cause(s) and effect(s) for the selected event of the story you are reading. Use another sheet of paper if you need more space.

1. Briefly describe this event. _____

_____

_____

_____

_____

2. Describe the effect or result of this event. What impact did it have on the characters or

the plot? _____

_____

_____

_____

_____

3. List the cause(s) of this effect. _____

_____

_____

_____

_____

_____

_____

_____

_____

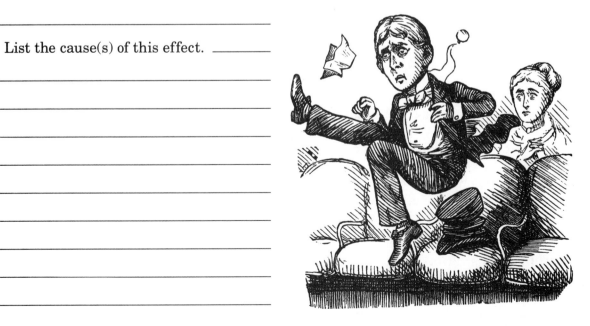

MINI-LESSON 86:
COMPARISON AND CONTRAST

Good readers are always comparing and contrasting the information they encounter in their reading. Competence in comparing and contrasting improves understanding.

Procedure:

- Explain that competent readers are always finding similarities and differences in the people, places, things, actions, events, and ideas in their reading. When they do this, they are using the skills of comparison and contrast.
- Define each term.
  —*Comparison* is the process of examining similarities.
  —*Contrast* is the process of finding differences.
- Note that through comparison and contrast, clear details of characters, places, and events may be discovered.
- Emphasize that sometimes authors will clearly present comparisons and contrasts for their readers, but sometimes they don't. When they don't, the reader must identify similarities and differences.

Activities:

1. This activity may be used with the whole class or with students working in groups, provided they are reading the same material. Select one pair of the following from the material your students are currently reading: two major events, two ideas, two characters, or two settings, and instruct your students to compare and contrast them. If your students are working in groups, you may wish to give each group different subjects to compare and contrast. This will add variety and scope to the activity. Hand out copies of Worksheet 86–1, "Finding Similarities and Differences," to help your students with their ideas. Upon completion of the worksheet, conduct a class discussion or have students meet in groups to discuss the similarities and differences they identified.

2. For this activity students are to work individually and then meet in groups. Students are to choose a favorite book and consider its characters. They are to select two characters—a hero (or heroine) and a villain, or a young character and an old one, or characters from different backgrounds. Students are to compare and contrast these two characters, listing similarities and differences in physical details, attitudes, goals, likes, and dislikes. They should especially note how the author brings out the traits and details of the characters. Distribute copies of Worksheet 86–2, "Comparing and Contrasting Characters," which will help students organize their ideas. After your students have completed the worksheets, they should meet in groups and discuss the characters they selected, comparing and contrasting them.

Writing Activity:

- Instruct students to choose two places, people, or ideas, and write an essay comparing and contrasting them. Encourage them to pick subjects that are related, but that also have similarities and differences. Display the essays upon completion of the activity.

Name _____ Date _____ Section _____

Finding Similarities and Differences

Directions: Compare and contrast the subjects your teacher assigned to you. First list details about each subject, then identify the details that are similar and different. Use another sheet of paper if you need more space.

Subjects for comparison and contrast:

_____

_____

_____

_____

1. Details of subject one: _____

_____

_____

_____

_____

2. Details of subject two: _____

_____

_____

_____

3. Similarities of the subjects: _____

_____

_____

_____

4. Differences between the subjects: _____

_____

_____

_____

Name _____ Date _____ Section _____

Comparing and Contrasting Characters

Directions: Select one of your favorite stories and choose two characters to compare and contrast. List the traits of the characters for the
categories below. Use another sheet of paper if you need more space.

Character One

Name: _____ Age: _____

Physical details: _____

_____

Attitudes: _____

_____

Goals: _____

_____

Things this character likes: _____

_____

Things this character dislikes: _____

_____

Character Two

Name: _____ Age: _____

Physical details: _____

_____

Attitudes: _____

_____

Goals: _____

_____

Things this character likes: _____

_____

Things this character dislikes: _____

_____

MINI-LESSON 87:
USING A DICTIONARY

Most students know that dictionaries are books in which they can look up the spellings, syllabication, and meanings of words. Many, unfortunately, are unaware of the many other kinds of information dictionaries provide.

Procedure:

- Explain that dictionaries are reference books that, at their most simplest level, provide an alphabetical list of words and their meanings.
- Note that there are many kinds of dictionaries, including medical dictionaries, dictionaries of science words, biographical dictionaries, geographical dictionaries, and, of course, dictionaries of various languages.
- Emphasize that, depending on their size, dictionaries usually offer much information. You might wish to mention some, or all, of these features:
  —An alphabetical list of words and their definitions. The words are usually divided into syllables.
  —Pronunciation keys and accent marks, which help readers pronounce words correctly. Although not all Americans speak alike—because of regional accents and colloquial phrases—dictionaries provide accepted standards for pronunciation and usage of English.
  —Inflected forms of words, such as the principal parts of verbs, irregular forms of plurals, and the comparative and superlative forms of adjectives and adverbs.
  —Various forms of words. Words spelled the same but which have different meanings are entered separately. The different forms are accompanied by little numbers called superscript numbers.
  —Explanatory notes on usage, often including sample phrases or sentences showing how specific words are used.
  —Labels for a word's part of speech.
  —Synonyms and antonyms.
  —Idioms.
  —The etymology of words. A word's etymology traces its origin. Although English is a Teutonic (German) language, many of its words have their origins in Latin and Greek. English has also absorbed words from many other languages around the world.
- Explain that guide words, which appear at the top of a dictionary page, are also the first and last entry on that page. Guide words make it easier to find words in a dictionary.
- Emphasize that large dictionaries are important reference tools that often contain additional sections of information, including:
  —Geographical entries
  —Biographical entries
  —Lists of abbreviations

—Writer's style book, including rules for grammar and punctuation
—Maps
—Tables of weights and measures

Activities:

1. Distribute copies of dictionaries and review their parts and uses with your students. If you don't have enough dictionaries, let students work in pairs, or conduct this class in the library where you will have greater access to dictionaries. Many students truly have little idea of the immense wealth of information contained in the typical dictionary.

2. For this activity, students are to work individually. Pick five words from your students' current reading, with which they are likely to be unfamiliar. Students are to write the syllabication, meanings (as pertains to the story), inflected forms, any special usage or examples of the words, and the etymologies of these words. If you wish, make a copy of Worksheet 87–1, "The Many Uses of the Dictionary," write the five words on the spaces, then photocopy enough worksheets for the class. (Of course, you might simply hand out copies of the worksheet and have students write in the words you have selected. An option is to permit students to choose words of their own to work with.) After students are done with the worksheets, go over them orally, reviewing the many uses of the dictionary.

Writing Activity:

*   Instruct students to write an article describing the value and uses of a dictionary. Display the articles upon completion.

Name _____ Date _____ Section _____

The Many Uses of the Dictionary

Directions: Use your dictionary to do the following for each word your teacher has assigned. (1) Divide it into syllables, (2) define it (the way it is used in your reading), (3) write any inflected forms of the word, (4) write any examples of its usage, and (5) include its etymology. Feel free to include any other interesting information you may find about the word. Use another sheet of paper if you need more space.

1. _____

_____

_____

2. _____

_____

_____

3. _____

_____

_____

_____

_____

4. _____

_____

_____

_____

_____

_____

_____

5. _____

_____

_____

_____

_____

_____

MINI-LESSON 88:
USING THE CARD CATALOG (TRADITIONAL AND COMPUTERIZED)

Card catalogs make finding books in a library easy. In recent years, more and more traditional card catalogs—that actually contained cards—have been replaced by computerized catalogs, or databases. These "new" card catalogs, which serve the same function as their predecessors, are "electronically" searchable and more efficient. Although most students are introduced to card catalogs in the early grades, periodic reviews of the use and value of card catalogs are helpful.

Procedure:

- Explain that the purpose of any card catalog—whether traditional or computerized—is to help people find books and reference materials.

- Note that virtually all libraries classify their materials according to one of two classification systems: the Dewey Decimal System, which uses numbers for identifying ten major subject categories, and the Library of Congress System, which uses letters for identifying 21 major categories. The Library of Congress system tends to be preferred by most large city and university libraries.

- Mention the system your school library uses. (Check with the librarian if you are not sure.)

- Point out that whichever classification system is used, books and other materials are divided into categories and shelved according to their call number. Materials of the same category are shelved together.

- Explain that the call number of a book corresponds to its card in the card catalog. Card catalogs contain alphabetically arranged cards listing the call number of each book in a library. Each book is usually listed on three cards: an author card, title card, and subject card. Cards include additional information such as the publisher, place of publication, publication date, number of pages, and whether the book contains any illustrations.

- Explain that many libraries are converting their traditional card catalogs to computerized systems. These systems, which typically consist of a keyboard, monitor, and processing unit, contain the same information as traditional card catalogs. Because they are searchable—and computers do the work—they are easier and faster to use. For example, a person can type in an author's name and quickly have appear on the monitor's screen a list of the author's books that the library owns. In most cases, the availability of the book is also provided. Subjects are searchable, too. Thus, if a person wanted to find books about the American Revolution, a simple search would provide numerous potential sources.

Activity:

1. Reserve time in your school library, meet with your class there, and review the uses and value of the card catalog. Perhaps your librarian could give your students a short lesson on the use of the card catalog.

2. Distribute copies of Worksheet 88–1, "Card Catalogs by the Numbers," and review the information with your students. This handout contains the categories of the Dewey Decimal and Library of Congress card catalog systems. Explain which system your library uses, and point out to students the various categories.

Writing Activity:

- Ask your students to write a brief article entitled "How to Use the Card Catalog." Display the articles upon completion of the activity.

Name _____ Date _____ Section _____

Card Catalogs by the Numbers

In most public and school libraries, books are divided into two broad categories: fiction and nonfiction. In the fiction section, books are arranged alphabetically according to the author's last name. Nonfiction books are classified in one of two main systems: the Dewey Decimal System and the Library of Congress System. While it is not necessary to memorize the different categories of each, you should be aware of them.

Dewey Decimal Classification Scheme (Abbreviated)

000–099 — General Works
100–199 — Philosophy and Psychology
200–299 — Religion
300–399 — Social Sciences
400–499 — Language
500–599 — Pure Sciences
600–699 — Technology
700–799 — The Arts
800–899 — Literature
900–999 — History

Library of Congress Classification Scheme (Abbreviated)

A — General Works
B — Philosophy, Psychology, Religion
C — History: Auxiliary Sciences (Archaeology, Numismatics, Genealogy, etc.)
D — History: General and Old World
E — History: American and U.S., general
F — History: American and U.S., local
G — Geography, Anthropology, Folklore, Dance, Sports
H — Social Sciences: Sociology, Business, and Economics
J — Political Science
K — Law
L — Education
M — Music
N — Fine Arts: Art and Architecture
P — Literature
Q — Science
R — Medicine
S — Agriculture
T — Technology
U — Military Science
V — Naval Science
Z — Bibliography and Library Science

MINI-LESSON 89:
REFERENCE SOURCES IN THE LIBRARY

Modern libraries are centers of information where the public not only may borrow books, but can find information from various reference sources, including electronic and online databases. Being familiar with the many references and resources of your library will be immensely helpful to students.

Procedure:

- Explain that libraries are storehouses of information. Along with books that may be borrowed, libraries contain newspapers, magazines, dictionaries, atlases, encyclopedias, almanacs, and numerous other references. Many libraries have entire rooms or sections devoted to reference.

- Encourage students to become proficient at the library, using the library's many resources. When they have a question or have trouble finding information, they should ask librarians for assistance. Librarians are some of the most helpful people in the world.

- Remind students of library courtesy. Loud talking, joking, or making noise are unacceptable and disturbing to others.

Activities:

1. Distribute copies of Worksheet 89–1, "Important Library References," and review and discuss the listed references with your students. Unfortunately, many students view libraries only as places from which to borrow books and conduct research using encyclopedias. This handout shows them some of the many other reference sources in libraries.

2. Schedule a period for your class to visit the library and ask the librarian to show and explain the various reference sources available. When students know which references are available, what they might be used for, and where they are stocked, they are more likely to use them.

Writing Activity:

- Instruct students to select a topic with which they are interested, but with which they are largely unfamiliar. You might wish to brainstorm potential topics with the class to generate ideas and excitement. Use the opening "I wish I knew . . ." and list the ideas your students suggest on an overhead projector or the board. Some example topics include:

    Why Is the Sky Blue?
    What Happens to Insects During the Winter?
    What Causes Spring Flowers to Grow?
    Are Bears the Only Animals That Hibernate?
    Why Are There Twelve Months in a Year?

Encourage your students to use the sources of the library to conduct research and then write a brief report about their topic. You might wish to have students list their sources in standard bibliographical format. Display the reports upon completion of their writing.

Name _____ Date _____ Section _____

Important Library References

Even small libraries contain numerous reference sources. Following are some of the most important ones.

Reader's Guide to Periodical Literature—This reference is an index of articles published in popular magazines. It is alphabetically arranged according to subject, making it easy to find articles on specific subjects and topics. Many libraries contain past issues of magazines on microfilm or microfiche.

Facts on File—This reference is a weekly summary of important events, trends, and newsworthy facts.

The New York Times Index—This index provides a short summary of the articles published by *The New York Times,* according to topic or subject.

Marquis Who's Who Series—Each volume of this series offers biographical details of well-known and important individuals.

Biography Index—This provides sources of information on important people in numerous periodicals, books, and other bibliographical sources.

Guinness Book of World Records—This reference contains old and new world records in numerous categories.

Encyclopedia of Associations—This guide offers information about associations and how they may be contacted. Associations are often excellent sources of information.

Various Literary Reference Books—Most libraries contain several references that cover topics in literature, including *Subject Guide to Books in Print, Bartlett's Familiar Quotations,* and *The Oxford Companion to American Literature.* It's likely your library has several shelves filled with references about reading and writing.

Almanacs and Yearbooks—These references, which are published yearly, summarize the events of the previous year and provide information on various subjects.

Maps and Atlases—These references can be helpful in locating places, finding information about geography, climate, population, ocean currents, etc.

Periodicals—Most libraries subscribe to numerous newspapers and magazines, which they make available to the public. Periodicals can be excellent sources of information.

Online References—Online service providers, as well as institutions, companies, and individuals, provide an enormous amount of information on the World Wide Web. Encyclopedias, which are constantly being updated, a variety of dictionaries, periodicals, and other references are available from online services. Many providers offer search features that allow users to find information with relative ease. In many cases, the problem is not finding enough information, but finding too much. To avoid this problem, searches should be focused on key words as much as possible.

MINI-LESSON 90:
LOCATING INFORMATION

An essential study skill, closely linked to reading, is the ability to find information. This mini-lesson offers students some strategies in obtaining those hard-to-find facts.

Procedure:

- Explain to your students that they will encounter many occasions when they will need to find information. They might need to write a report for school, conduct a job search, find information about a company they are interested in working for, or look for information about that perfect vacation.

- Emphasize that some people are more successful at finding information than others. Also emphasize that such people haven't been born with any special abilities; they have simply learned some techniques that make it easier for them to find information.

- Explain that one of the most useful strategies in finding information is to narrow and focus the topic. Offer this obvious example to illustrate the point. If students are seeking information about the legendary baseball player Babe Ruth, looking up "Babe Ruth" would no doubt provide them with more useful information than looking up "Great Baseball Players."

- Suggest that students look for key words in their topics, and search sources using key words.

- Note that sometimes the search of a key word will lead to a topic that offers a reference to another topic or key word that might provide helpful information. Such cross-references should always be explored.

- Emphasize that locating information might include reference materials in the library—found via the card catalog—computerized databases, on-line services, or the internet. Using key words for searching such sources is essential.

- Mention that experts on subjects, local or national organizations, even the Yellow Pages can be sources of information.

Activity:

- This activity is designed for students working in groups. Each group is to select a topic in literature to research and provide an oral report. You might like to brainstorm topics with your class, listing possible topics on an overhead projector or the board. Some possible topics include:

    Black Authors
    Women Authors
    Women Poets
    The History of Science Fiction
    Epic Stories
    The Dark Themes of Edgar Allan Poe
    The Development of the Romance Story

The Development of the Mystery
The Gothic Novel
From Novel to the Big Screen
Great Characters in Literature
Comedy in Literature

Hand out copies of Worksheet 90–1, "Researching and Finding Information," which will help your students in their research efforts. Provide time for groups to share their reports with the class.

Name _____ Date _____ Section _____

Researching and Finding Information

Directions: Answer the questions below to focus your research efforts.

1. My topic is _____

_____

2. Key words I will use in searching for information include: _____

_____

_____

_____

3. References and sources to check for information include: _____

_____

_____

_____

_____

_____

_____

_____

_____

_____

_____

_____

MINI-LESSON 91:
NOTE-TAKING

Note-taking is, without doubt, a task most students would like to skip. However, when reading to obtain information, note-taking is a useful skill. This mini-lesson offers some insights and suggestions that can make it easier for your students to take notes effectively.

Procedure:

- Explain that note-taking is an important skill. When reading factual material that must be remembered—for example, studying for tests or gathering information for a report—written notes can not only help a person recall more facts, but can serve as a guide for further study.
- Mention that efficient note-takers usually develop a system that works for them. Most effective note-taking systems share many common points, some of which are offered in Worksheet 91–1, "Tips for Effective Note-taking."
- Emphasize that writing down notes helps to keep a person's mind engaged with reading, maintaining sharper concentration and focus. This in turn aids memory.
- Mention that note cards are a good choice for writing down notes, because the cards can be assorted and arranged by topic, making organization easier. It is generally best to write only one main idea per card. Separate sheets of paper may be used instead of note cards.
- Mention the importance of bibliographical information when taking notes from several sources. The source from which information was obtained should be written on each card (or sheet of paper). This makes it easier to recheck facts, return to sources for more information, as well as compile a bibliography as you go along. Bibliographical formats are included in English texts, handbooks for punctuation and grammar, and author's stylebooks.

Activities:

1. Distribute copies of Worksheet 91–1 and review and discuss the suggestions with the class. Ask students which, if any, of the tips they have used in the past.
2. This activity is designed for the whole class or for students working in groups, provided students are reading the same material. Instruct your students to take notes on a chapter or section of the material they are currently reading. Students should strive to write down the most important facts that help them to remember the material. (Having students record their notes on note cards will give them practice with note cards; however, regular paper is acceptable.) Encourage your students to use some of the suggestions from "Tips for Effective Note-taking." When your students are done, conduct a class discussion or have students meet in groups to discuss what the main ideas and details of the material were. Students should also compare their methods of note-taking.

Writing Activity:

- This activity may be incorporated as part of your students' efforts in the writing of a major report or term paper. The project may be on a topic of your choice, or you may permit students to select their own topics. After selecting topics, encourage your students to research their topics and utilize the note-taking suggestions of "Tips for Effective Note-taking." Students should include full bibliographical data with their reports. Display the reports upon completion.

Name _____ Date _____ Section _____

Tips for Effective Note-taking

Following are several suggestions that will help you to take notes efficiently.

1. To find information, identify key words, concepts, and topics.

2. Find main ideas and related details. Writing one main idea and its details on a separate note card makes it easier to organize ideas after research is finished.

3. Write phrases instead of entire sentences. Be clear and concise in taking notes.

4. Develop your own personal shorthand for taking notes. Use abbreviations and symbols whenever possible. Here are some examples:

   John = J   and = +   for = 4   number = #
   without = w/o   information = info with = w/

   Here is a phrase in personal shorthand:

   Einstein's Theory of Relativity = Ein T of Rel

5. Pay attention to signal words such as *first, second, third, next, last, in summary, therefore,* and *finally.* Such words usually precede important information.

6. Always look for relationships and connections while taking notes. Try to see how the parts relate to the whole.

7. Write down your own ideas and questions next to your notes. This will stimulate your thinking and might lead to insights later.

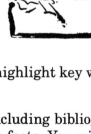

8. If you own a book and are taking notes, consider highlighting main ideas and details, and writing notes, insights, and questions that make you think in the margins. You might also highlight key words and phrases.

9. Always include full bibliographical data with your notes. By including bibliographical information with your notes, it is easier to go back and recheck facts. You will also be compiling your bibliography as you go along.

MINI-LESSON 92:
THE TABLE OF CONTENTS

Although just about all books contain a table of contents, most students glance through this opening matter or ignore it entirely. Many students don't realize that the table of contents can offer more than just a list of chapters.

Procedure:

- Explain that most books contain a table of contents. While some tables of contents only list chapter numbers and pages, others may include chapter titles, subtitles, illustrations, photographs, tables, charts, graphs, etc.
- Note that most magazines, pamphlets, and booklets also have a table of contents.
- Explain that reading a table of contents gives a person an idea of what is contained in the material.
- Note that a detailed table of contents can help a reader find information in the book quickly. This can be helpful during research, or if the reader wants to locate a specific topic. In a magazine, the contents permits readers to easily turn to the articles they are most interested in.

Activities:

1. Review the tables of contents of some of the books your students have. A social studies or science text and a novel are good choices. Review and discuss the tables of contents. In the discussion, point out that textbooks have a more detailed table of contents than novels. Why is this so?
2. This activity is designed for students working individually. Students are to use one of their textbooks (social studies or science), look through the text, and write four questions, the answers to which may be found within the text. After writing their questions, each student is to exchange his or her questions with those of another student. Looking through the contents only, the students are to identify the sections of the text where they might find the answers to the questions. At the end of the activity, permit the students who shared questions to discuss the answers. If you wish, distribute copies of Worksheet 92–1, "Using a Table of Contents to Find Information," which will help students with their work.

Writing Activity:

- Instruct students to write a summary of how the table of contents of a book is helpful to readers. Upon completion, conduct a discussion about the usefulness of a book's table of contents.

Name _____ Date _____ Section _____

Using a Table of Contents
to Find Information

Directions: Using one of your textbooks, write four questions that other students can answer by finding the appropriate section in the text through the table of contents. After you have written your questions, exchange your paper with someone else. Now try to find the answers to this person's questions while he or she tries to find the answers to yours. Use another sheet of paper if you need more space.

Question Number 1: _____

_____

Answer: _____

_____

_____

Found in chapter _____, page _____

Question Number 2: _____

_____

Answer: _____

_____

Found in chapter _____, page _____

Question Number 3: _____

_____

Answer: _____

_____

Found in chapter _____, page _____

Question Number 4: _____

_____

Answer: _____

_____

Found in chapter _____, page _____

MINI-LESSON 93:
USING A GLOSSARY

Many textbooks and other books of information contain glossaries. While glossaries can be useful in the understanding of unfamiliar words, many students fail to consult them. Part of this problem may be that some students are unaware of a glossary's value.

Procedure:

- Explain that books about specific subjects often contain glossaries at the back.
- Define a glossary as an alphabetical list of words and their definitions. The purpose of a glossary is to help readers with their understanding of the book's contents. Glossaries can save readers the time and effort needed to consult dictionaries.
- Note that some glossaries are simple, providing words and their definitions, while others may offer pronunciations and detailed explanations.
- Emphasize that—in books that include glossaries—students should consult the glossary when they encounter unfamiliar words. If the word is not contained in the glossary, they should next check a dictionary.
- Mention that some novels have glossaries. Frank Herbert's *Dune* has an extended glossary that readers find helpful.

Activities:

1. Ask your students to bring to class one of their textbooks that has a glossary. (*Note:* Students should all bring the same text.) Review the glossary with your students and discuss its features.

2. This activity may be used with the whole class or with groups, provided students are reading the same material. Instruct students to create a glossary for the book or story they are currently reading. If your students are working in groups, have the members of the group compile the glossary. Perhaps make photocopies of the glossaries and then use the words in spelling tests. If students are working in groups, members may quiz each other. You may wish to distribute copies of Worksheet 93–1, "Compiling a Glossary," which will help students in creating their glossaries.

Writing Activity:

- For a story or article your students are writing, suggest that they include a glossary of words they feel might be new or unfamiliar to their readers.

Name _____ Date _____ Section _____

Compiling a Glossary

Directions: Using the book or story you are currently reading, compile a glossary of words you feel may be new or unfamiliar to many students. First, select a list of words and alphabetize them. Then write the words and their definitions on the lines below. Use another sheet of paper if you need more space.

_____

_____

_____

_____

_____

_____

_____

_____

_____

_____

_____

_____

_____

_____

_____

_____

_____

_____

_____

_____

_____

_____

_____

_____

MINI-LESSON 94:
USING AN INDEX

When researching or looking up topics or subjects in a book, many students will check the contents or simply page through the book. Many of these students never consider checking the index, which should be their first option.

Procedure:

- Explain that many nonfiction books contain an index. An index is an alphabetical list of names, places, and topics, with the page numbers on which they may be found. Indexes appear in the back of a book.
- Note that an index can help a reader or researcher find a topic or subject quickly. When looking for specific information, the index is the best choice.
- Point out that key words in a topic or subject are the best strategy for finding information in an index.
- Mention that indexes are usually cross-referenced. If a subject appears under different topics, the various topics will be listed.

Activities:

1. Review and discuss the use of indexes with your students by using one of their textbooks as an example. Instruct your students to bring their science or social studies text to class. Show them how the topics and subjects are arranged; especially point out instances of cross-referencing.

2. Working as individuals, students are to use one of their textbooks (or another book that contains an index), and select at least ten topics or subjects. They should write their selections down, then exchange their papers with a partner. Partners should then find the page numbers of the topics. This simple activity will give students practice in using an index. You may wish to distribute copies of Worksheet 94–1, "Finding Information Through an Index," to help your students with the activity. Upon completion of the activity, summarize the value of indexes for your students.

Writing Activity:

- Suggest that students imagine they have a friend who doesn't understand the value of an index for finding topics in a book. Students are to write a dialogue with this friend, in which they try to convince their friend how useful an index can be. Display the dialogues upon completion of the activity.

Name _____ Date _____ Section _____

Finding Information Through an Index

Directions: Using a book that contains an index, select ten topics and write them below. (*Do not* write the page numbers where the topics can be found.) Exchange your list with a class-mate who has made his or her own list. You and your partner are now to find the topics in the index of the book and write their page numbers.

1. Topic: _____

    Page Number(s): _____

2. Topic: _____

    Page Number(s): _____

3. Topic: _____

    Page Number(s): _____

4. Topic: _____

    Page Number(s): _____

5. Topic: _____

    Page Number(s): _____

6. Topic: _____

    Page Number(s): _____

7. Topic: _____

    Page Number(s): _____

8. Topic: _____

    Page Number(s): _____

9. Topic: _____

    Page Number(s): _____

10. Topic: _____

    Page Number(s): _____

MINI-LESSON 95:
UNDERSTANDING TABLES

A common method for presenting large amounts of information is a table. Because tables are so common, students should be familiar with them.

Procedure:

- Explain that a table presents information in columns with headings. Tables may be simple with just a few columns and facts, or complex with several columns and numerous bits of information.

- Note that tables make it easy to comprehend information and many facts. They can be most helpful in illustrating complex data.

- Caution students that to fully understand a table, they should read its title and headings, paying close attention to how the information is presented.

Activities:

1. Distribute copies of Worksheet 95–1, "A Sample Table." Review and discuss the table with your students.

2. This activity is designed for students working individually. Hand out copies of Worksheet 95–2, "Interpreting an Information Table," along with "A Sample Table." Instruct your students to answer the questions on the worksheet, using the sample table. After they have completed the worksheets, go over the answers orally.

   Answer key: (1) 92,900,000 miles; (2) 48,700,000; (3) 9.9 hours; (4) 164.8 years; (5) 23; (6) 0; (7) Venus; (8) no; (9) Saturn; (10) Mercury, Venus, Earth

3. This activity is designed for groups. Ask students to bring to class tables they find in newspapers and magazines. (If you wish, rather than asking students to bring in examples of tables from home, you might collect magazines and newspapers from colleagues and students in advance and distribute them among your groups. Students may then use these materials to find tables.) Have students meet in their groups to share and discuss the various tables. In particular, they should note the purposes and organizational formats of the tables. Each group should select a table that a spokesperson for the group will describe to the class.

Writing Activity:

- Using Worksheet 95–1 or another example of a table, students are to write a summary of the information the table presents. Afterward discuss how the written summary and the table differ, as well as how they might be alike.

Name _____ Date _____ Section _____

A Sample Table

Study the table below. Note how it organizes information in columns.

Facts About the Planets

Planet	Average Distance from Sun in Millions of Miles	Period of Revolution	Period of Rotation	Number of Moons	Mean Density
Mercury	36,000,000	88.0 D	58.7 D	0	5.4
Venus	67,200,000	224.7 D	243.0 D	0	5.3
Earth	92,900,000	365.3 D	23.9 H	1	5.5
Mars	141,600,000	687.0 D	24.6 H	2	3.9
Jupiter	483,300,000	11.9 Y	9.9 H	16	1.3
Saturn	886,200,000	29.5 Y	10.7 H	23	0.7
Uranus	1,783,000,000	84.0 Y	17.2 H	15	1.2
Neptune	2,794,000,000	164.8 Y	17.0 H	8	1.7
Pluto	3,670,000,000	248.5 Y	6.4 D	1	1.0

Note: The periods of revolution and rotation are given in Earth time. H = Hours, D = Days, Y = Years. The *period of revolution* is how long a planet takes to circle the sun. The *period of rotation* is the length of the planet's day. The *mean density* is based on water = 1. The mean density of Pluto is an estimate because of its great distance from Earth.

Name _____ Date _____ Section _____

Interpreting an Information Table

Directions: Using the table "Facts About the Planets," answer the questions below.

1. How far is Earth from the sun? _____

2. How much farther is Mars from the sun than Earth is? _____

3. How long is a day on Jupiter (in Earth time)? _____

4. How long is Neptune's year (in Earth time)? _____

5. How many moons does Saturn have? _____

6. How many moons does Venus have? _____

7. Which planet's day is longer than its year? _____

8. Does the table note which planets have rings? _____

9. Which planet is less dense than water? _____

10. Which three planets have about the same density? _____

    _____

11. What is the purpose of information tables? _____

    _____

    _____

    _____

    _____

    _____

    _____

    _____

    _____

    _____

    _____

    _____

    _____

MINI-LESSON 96:
UNDERSTANDING BASIC GRAPHS

Readers encounter graphs frequently. They may accompany newspaper and magazine articles, or add support to an author's ideas in books. The most common graphs are *line, bar, circle,* and *pictographs.* Students should be able to interpret each. (Depending on the abilities of your students, you may prefer to break this mini-lesson down into parts, addressing each graph on a separate day. Of course, for students well acquainted with graphs, this mini-lesson might serve as a review and the material can be covered in one lesson.)

Procedure:

- Explain that your students will encounter various types of graphs in the material they read, both in school and out of school.
- Explain that graphs illustrate information, making facts easy to understand.
- Note the four main types of graphs: line, bar, circle, and pictograph. Offer the following details about each:
  - —*Line graphs* are useful for showing numerical facts that change over a specific time period.
  - —*Bar graphs* illustrate information through the use of bars. They are useful for comparing information because the differences in the bars are easy to see.
  - —*Circle* (also known as *pie*) *graphs* are used for showing percentages of a whole. Remind students that circle graphs are based on 100%. They are good for comparing a part to the whole.
  - —Pictographs illustrate information through symbols. The symbols may stand for people or objects, with each symbol representing a specific number. Because the numbers represented by symbols are often rounded off, these graphs may not be so accurate as the others, but they make a strong visual impression.
- Emphasize to your students that whenever they are reading graphs, they should pay close attention to the graph's labels, numbers, and the way the information is displayed. They should make sure that all the information needed for comparisons is provided and that the graph depicts precisely what it is supposed to.

Activities:

1. Distribute copies of Worksheet 96–1, "Sample Graphs," to your students. Review and discuss each of the graphs, being sure to point out the scales and how the information is presented. Caution students that if any information is missing on a graph, it will be difficult to draw valid conclusions from its data.
2. This activity is designed for students working individually. Hand out copies of Worksheet 96–2, "Interpreting Graphs," along with copies of Worksheet 96–1 Instruct your students to answer the questions of the worksheet by

using the sample graphs. At the end of the activity, go over the answers orally and discuss the graphs.

Answer key: (1) 38, 59, 30, Feb., probably because of colds and flu; (2) 38, 10, 18, 16, track and field, swimming, field hockey, softball, wrestling, etc.; (3) Recreation, 20%, 15%, 10%; (4) 200 CDs, alternative, accept any reasonable answer.

3. Working in pairs or groups of three, students are to select a topic, gather information about it, and create a graph to display their information. Some topics for graphs include:

> Facts or Records in Sports
> Phenomena of Weather
> Data About Rock Stars or Musical Groups
> Popular Books
> Favorite Foods of Students

To create attractive graphs, students will need various materials including markers, pencils, pens, colored pencils, drawing paper, oak tag, and rulers. Because such items may not be available in your reading class, you might wish to collaborate with your students' art teacher. Perhaps your colleague can handle the design and creation of the graphs while you ensure that students have gathered the necessary information. Display the graphs upon completion of the activity.

Writing Activity:

- Instruct students to select a graph from a newspaper or magazine (or you may simply permit them to use one of the sample graphs included in this lesson), and write a summary of it. Students should staple their graph to their summary before handing it in. Remind your students to be as accurate as possible in their summaries. Display the summaries upon completion.

Name _____ Date _____ Section _____

Sample Graphs

Line Graph

Average Number of Students Absent from Lazy River High

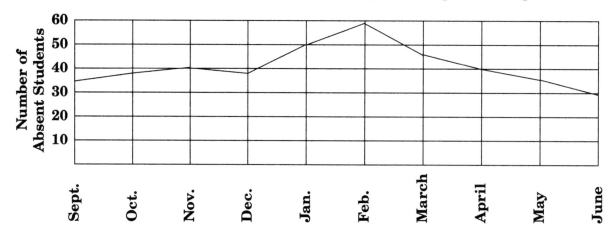

Bar Graph

Favorite Sports of Students at Jackson High

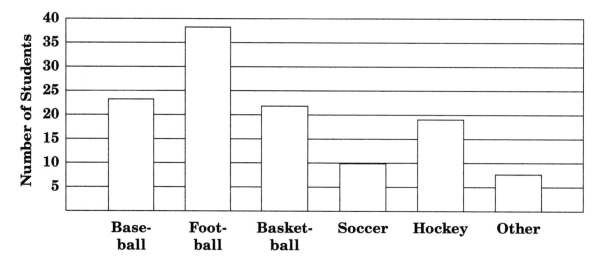

Circle Graph

Joe's Monthly Budget

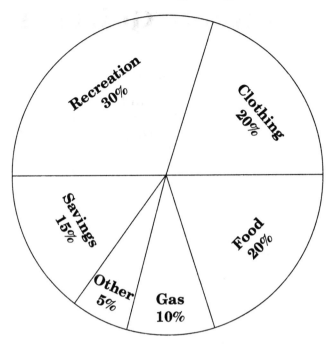

Pictograph

Sales of CDs at Got the Beat Music Center

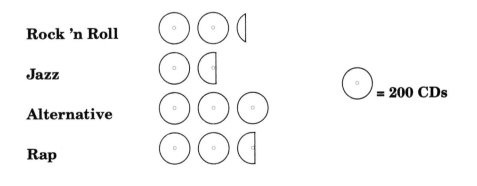

Worksheet 96–2

Name _____ Date _____ Section _____

Interpreting Graphs

Directions: Use the graphs on "Sample Graphs" to answer the questions below.

1. What was the average number of student absences from Lazy River High in October? _____ February? _____ June? _____ During which month was the average rate of absences the highest? _____ What do you think might have been the reason for this? _____

_____

2. How many students at Jackson High consider football to be their favorite sport? _____ Soccer? _____ Hockey? _____ How many like football more than basketball? _____ What might "other" sports include? _____

_____

3. On the circle graph, what does Joe spend the most money on each month? _____ What percent of his monthly budget does he spend on clothing? _____ Savings? _____ Gasoline for his car? _____

4. What does each symbol on the pictograph stand for? _____ Which type of CD had the highest sales? _____ In your opinion, is a pictograph an accurate way of presenting information? _____ Explain. _____

_____

_____
_____
_____
_____
_____
_____
_____

308

MINI-LESSON 97:
THE SQ3R SYSTEM

Many good readers develop their own methods for comprehending and remembering what they read. Many others, however, haven't discovered a method and will benefit from using the SQ3R System. Developed in 1941 by Francis Robinson, the SQ3R System has become one of the most popular and effective reading/study methods.

Procedure:

- Explain that over the years many different systems have been developed to help people with reading and studying. One of the most effective is the SQ3R System.

- Break the system down into parts for your students. The *S* stands for *survey,* the *Q* for *question,* and the *3R* for *read, recite,* and *review.* Worksheet 97–1, "Steps of the SQ3R System," details each part.

- Point out that the SQ3R System helps most people to read faster, find important information, and remember facts. The system helps people become active readers.

- Remind students that mastery of the SQ3R System takes practice. The more they use it, however, the more efficient they will become with it and their reading will improve.

Activities:

1. Distribute copies of Worksheet 97–1. Review and discuss the steps of the system with your students.

2. This activity may be used with either the whole class or with groups. Assign new reading material for your students, and instruct them to utilize the SQ3R System in reading it. Students should survey the material first, write questions, read, recite, and review the material. Upon completion, conduct a class discussion or have students meet in groups to share the questions they formulated (and their answers), along with discussing the SQ3R System.

Writing Activity:

- Instruct your students to write a letter to a friend, explaining the SQ3R System and its benefits. Display the letters upon completion of the activity.

Name _____ Date _____ Section _____

Steps of the SQ3R System

The SQ3R System is one of the most widely used methods for improving reading. Following is an explanation of its parts.

S means *survey:*

Survey, or preview, the material. Look at titles and subtitles. Read any introductions and conclusions, and also the first and last sentences of the other paragraphs. Note any illustrations, photographs, charts, tables, or graphs, and pay close attention to captions and explanations. Surveying helps you get an idea of what the material is about before you begin reading. This helps prepare your mind for the material.

Q means *question:*

Based on your survey, formulate questions about the material. What are some of the things you'd like to find out? Write these questions down. Also think about any questions your teacher has given you. Having questions in your mind while you read helps you to be an involved, active reader. You will read with a purpose, your mind seeking the answers to your questions.

The *first R* means *read actively:*

As you read the material, try to answer the questions you have formulated. You will understand and remember facts better.

The *second R* means to *recite your answers:*

When you find the answer to a question, pause and repeat it to yourself. Write it down if necessary. This will help you to remember the information.

The *third R* means to *review:*

After you are done reading and have found the answers to your questions, review the material. If you were not able to find some answers, try to find out why you couldn't. Maybe the information wasn't there (you formulated a question that couldn't be answered by the material), or maybe you missed it. Reviewing will help you to clarify any remaining questions and also help you to recall facts even better.

MINI-LESSON 98:
READING TEST-TAKING STRATEGIES

No matter how much reading students do, it's likely that part of their grade—as well as, for some, placement in particular courses and acceptance to college—will be determined through tests. For most students, their scores are a result of not only what they know, but also their understanding of how to take tests. (Three handouts accompany this mini-lesson, and, depending on your students, you might decide to cover the material in two or three separate lessons.)

Procedure:

- Explain that tests are designed to measure how much students know about a topic or subject. They are necessary for determining grades, are taken into account for placement in certain courses, and are important for admission to colleges. There is no getting away from taking tests.

- Explain that most students who do well on tests not only understand the material they are being tested on, but they also know how to take tests.

- Emphasize the importance of attitude. Students who are confident usually do better on tests than those who are anxious or worried.

- Emphasize the importance of being prepared. Confidence in test-taking is usually a result of studying. Students should study for tests in a quiet place, without the distractions of the TV, radio, or stereo. When studying, students should review the main ideas and details of the material, and concentrate on relationships. They should utilize any study guides or suggestions their teachers give them.

- Point out that students who "cram" the night before a test usually are not so familiar with the material as students who prepare in a more systematic manner. Furthermore, students who cram are more likely to be tired, nervous, and anxious when they take the test.

Activities:

1. Distribute copies of Worksheet 98–1, "How to Prepare for Reading Tests." Review and discuss the suggestions with your students.

2. Distribute copies of Worksheet 98–2, "Taking Reading Tests the Smart Way." Review and discuss the suggestions with your students.

3. Hand out copies of Worksheet 98–3, "Strategies for Answering Essay Questions." Review and discuss the suggestions with your students.

Writing Activity:

- Instruct your students to write an essay about test-taking strategies or tips that they find most useful. Upon conclusion of the writing, conduct a class discussion. Perhaps have volunteers share some of their writing and ideas with the class.

Name _____ Date _____ Section _____

How to Prepare for Reading Tests

Following are suggestions that will help you prepare for reading tests.

1. Anticipate and try to think of the types of questions that will be on the test. If your teacher gives you a study guide, be sure to review the questions or topics on it. Think of the ideas and topics that were covered in class. These will most likely appear on the test.

2. Be sure to take your book, notebook, and any other materials related to the test home so that you can study before the test.

3. Avoid cramming. Try studying for the test over two or three nights. On the first night, review the material by skimming it. The next night, you should study the material more deeply. Make sure that you understand concepts and ideas. On the following night, review the material once again. If possible, have someone ask you sample questions. Saying the answers out loud will help you to remember facts.

4. Get a good night's sleep before the test.

5. Try to wake up a few minutes earlier than usual and review the material briefly once more. This will help to keep it fresh in your mind.

6. Eat a nutritious breakfast. A good breakfast will help your body and mind perform at high efficiency.

7. Be confident. Tell yourself that you have prepared for the test and that you will do well. Students who take tests with a positive attitude usually do better than those who are anxious or nervous.

Name _____ Date _____ Section _____

Taking Reading Tests
the Smart Way

Following are several tips that will help you improve your scores on reading tests.

1. Arrive at class on time. This will give you a chance to get settled, clear your thoughts, and hear all of the directions your teacher gives.

2. Make certain that you bring the proper materials to class—pencils, pens, books, etc.

3. Listen carefully to your teacher's instructions. He or she may point out a change in format, or offer some hints that may make the test easier. If you have any questions, ask for clarification.

4. Make sure you put your name, date, and class, as well as any other necessary information, on the test.

5. Once you begin the test, budget your time. Note how long you have to take the test and estimate how long you should spend on each section.

6. If you don't know the answer to a particular question, make your best guess unless there is a penalty for guessing. When making your best guess, eliminate the answers you know aren't correct, and guess from the remaining answers. This method increases your chances for guessing right.

7. Answer objective questions before you attempt to answer essays. Sometimes you can find information in the objective part of a test that will help you to answer the essay questions.

8. Pay close attention to words such as *never, always, often, seldom, many, all, none,* etc. Such words can help you to find the correct answer.

9. If you don't understand a question, don't panic. Move on to the next one and return to it later.

10. If there is time, be sure to recheck your work. Finding a careless mistake will add a few points to your score. However, change an answer only if you are certain it is wrong.

Name _____ Date _____ Section _____

Strategies for Answering Essay Questions

Essay questions are often a part of reading tests. Following are some suggestions on how to answer essay questions.

1. Before the test, try to prepare for potential essay questions. Think about the major concepts of the material you have been studying. Which concepts has your teacher stressed? Major concepts are often the basis of essay questions. Be sure you know the major concepts, details, and relationships.

2. Listen to your teacher's directions carefully. The directions may include hints that will help you to answer the questions.

3. Be aware of time. Plan the amount of time you can spend answering the essay questions.

4. Read the question carefully. You won't be able to answer it correctly if you don't understand it.

5. Before you start to answer the question, organize or outline your facts. You may do this in the margin or on the back of the paper. A simple idea list of main ideas and details, which will form the structure of your essay, can be helpful. Number the ideas in the order in which you will present them. Be careful that you don't spend so much time organizing your essay that you don't have enough time to write it.

6. If you are not sure of some of the information you need to put in your essay, don't panic. Key your mind on the main ideas you've identified and think about how these ideas are related to other ideas. Finding relationships can often help you to sort through "fuzzy" information.

7. Start your essay with an opening, build to your body, and end with a conclusion. All main ideas should be supported with details and examples. A good opening rephrases the question, and a good conclusion briefly summarizes your main points.

8. Be sure to use complete sentences, write neatly, and use transitions between paragraphs and ideas. Attention to such details will result in strong writing that communicates your ideas clearly.

9. Keep your writing concise and simple. Don't try to impress your teacher with long-winded writing. He or she will be most impressed with good ideas.

10. If there is time, proofread your essay to catch any errors or oversights in mechanics.

MINI-LESSON 99:
READERS AND THE INTERNET

As the importance of personal computers to business, education, and the home has grown, so has the internet, exploding into a vast resource of ideas and information. Although many people think of the internet in terms of communication, research, and entertainment, not so many are aware of its rich material and resources for readers.

Procedure:

- Explain that the *internet* describes the lines of communication that connect countless computers, owned by various companies, organizations, and individuals. There is no central control. The internet is as big as the number of computers connected by modern data lines.

- You might wish to explain that the internet was originally developed by the military as a means to connect military computers. Later the network was expanded to include researchers, colleges, and universities, and, in time, anyone who had a computer and equipment capable of tapping into the system. Today, companies (usually referred to as online service providers or internet service providers) offer access to the internet for a fee.

- Explain that some online service providers—for example, America Online—offer various resources of interest to readers, including dictionaries, encyclopedias, literary references, and book reviews. Biographies of noted authors are also available. This is in addition to the internet, which contains thousands of websites of interest to readers. Many groups interested in reading and particular authors maintain websites, in which individuals can communicate over the internet and share their ideas.

- Note that many newspapers and magazines can be accessed online. Many contain search features, making it easy to find articles and information.

- Mention that the search engines of online service providers can help readers find information on countless topics. Identifying key words is crucial to locating information on the internet.

- Mention that as the internet continues to grow, it's likely that the opportunities it offers readers will also expand.

Activities:

1. Distribute copies of Worksheet 99–1, "Vocabulary for the Internet," to acquaint your students with common online terms. It's likely that some of your students will be familiar with the internet, and you may ask these students to share some of their experiences in using the World Wide Web, particularly in regard to reading and research.

2. If your school has a computer room and maintains access to the internet, schedule time for your class to meet there. Have students log on, and suggest that they use key words such as "literature," "novels," "authors," etc. If you have access to America Online, select "References" from the main menu

and explore information under "Literature" and related subjects. You may also explore the internet. (*Note:* Be sure to monitor how your students use the internet. Savvy kids will be able to find a lot of information that has nothing to do with reading.)

Writing Activity:

• Instruct students to write an essay on the topic: "The Internet and Its Effect on Reading." Do students feel that, over the long term, the internet will have a positive effect on reading, or a negative one? Will the interactive nature of the internet reduce the need for people to read? Or will it require greater skills in reading? Will the internet, in time, make reading obsolete? These questions are far-reaching in scope and raise some serious concerns.

   Prior to the writing, you might wish to conduct a discussion or brainstorming session to help your students generate and clarify ideas. Be sure to display the essays upon completion of the activity.

Name _____ Date _____ Section _____

Vocabulary for the Internet

Knowing the following internet words will help to make you "internet literate."

BAUD   The "baud" rate of a modem refers to how many units of information (measured in bits) it can send or receive per second. For example, a 28.8 modem can move 28,800 bits per second.

BBS (BULLETIN BOARD SYSTEM)   This is a computerized system that allows people to conduct discussions, download and upload files, and post announcements. Countless BBSs are maintained around the world.

BIT   The smallest unit of data used by computers.

BROWSER   Software that allows its user to search for and find information on the internet.

BYTE   A set of bits that represents a single character.

CYBERSPACE   The World Wide Web, which you access through your computer.

E-MAIL   Electronic mail. E-mail is a message, usually in the form of text, that an individual, company, or organization can send to someone else over the internet.

FTP (FILE TRANSFER PROTOCOL)   A method of moving files between internet sites.

HTML (HYPERTEXT MARKUP LANGUAGE)   The computer language used to create hypertext documents for the World Wide Web.

HTTP (HYPERTEXT TRANSPORT PROTOCOL)   The protocol used for moving hypertext files throughout the internet.

HYPERTEXT   Text that contains links to other documents. By clicking your mouse on a link, you are connected to other documents or sites online.

INTERNET   A vast assortment of computers linked over high-speed data transmission lines. The internet extends throughout the world.

KILOBYTE   Generally described as a thousand bytes, but actually is 1,024 bytes.

Worksheet 99–1 *(Continued)*

MEGABYTE   A million bytes.

MODEM   A device that is connected to your computer (either internally or externally), which enables your computer to communicate with other computers over telephone lines. A modem is essential to connecting to online services and the internet.

NETSITE   A site, or address, maintained by a business, school, organization, or individual on the World Wide Web.

NETWORK   A connection between two more computers which allows them to share data.

ONLINE   Term referring to your computer being connected via its modem and telephone line to other computers.

SEARCH ENGINE   One of the various software programs that enables you to search the internet and find topics of interest.

SERVER   A computer or software package that provides a particular service to software running on other computers.

URL (UNIFORMED RESOURCE LOCATOR)   The standard for giving the address of a site on the World Wide Web.

WWW (WORLD WIDE WEB)   All of the resources that make up the internet.

MINI-LESSON 100:
READING FOR ENJOYMENT

One of your goals as a reading teacher is to help your students experience the value and joy of reading. Reading is a marvelous way for people to learn, gain insight, and be entertained. It can stimulate and excite the imagination with new ideas that might never be considered otherwise. If, at the end of the year when your students leave your classroom, they think of themselves as readers, you will have achieved the greatest success.

Procedure:

- Explain that most people read for enjoyment or to obtain information. (Be willing to concede that in school some students read only because material is assigned to them; however, this does not comprise the majority of readers.)

- Explain that reading for pleasure may take many forms. People read to pass time, to relax, or as an escape from pressures or responsibilities. Reading allows people to learn about countless subjects, places, and other people. Reading enables people to find solutions to problems and explore the worlds—fictional and real—of others.

- Emphasize that people become good readers by reading. Remind your students to become active readers, searching for the author's purpose, analyzing what they read and comparing the information to what they know of life, making inferences and drawing conclusions. If they do these things, your students will discover the beauty and power of words, and their imaginations will grow sharp, filled with the scenes and images that spring alive from the pages of books.

Activity:

- Distribute copies of Worksheet 100–1, "End-of-the-year Reading Summary," and ask your students to answer the questions. Suggest they read the questionnaire first, and if they don't feel comfortable putting their names on the sheet, leave their names off. This questionnaire will provide you with information on how you might improve your reading workshop, and also offer students a chance to reflect on their experiences in reading during the year. When students are done, you might like to conduct a general discussion of the workshop.

Writing Activity:

- Ask your students to write a summary of their experiences in your reading workshop. Encourage them to include the highs, lows, and suggestions on how you might improve the workshop for next year.

Name _____ Date _____ Section _____

End-of-the-year
Reading Summary

Directions: Answer the questions below about your reading workshop. Use another sheet of paper if you need more space.

1. What books did you enjoy most this year? _____

_____

_____

_____

2. Who was your favorite author this year? _____

_____

Why was he or she your favorite? _____

_____

_____

3. What new things did you learn about reading this year? _____

_____

_____

_____

_____

4. How did your understanding or impressions of

reading change this year? _____

_____

_____

_____

_____

_____

Suggested Reading List

While the following list by no means includes all of the good books available for quality reading programs, it certainly includes enough titles to support a well-rounded curriculum. (Note that additional titles are provided with many of the mini-lessons of this book.)

Grades 5–8

Bridge to Terabithia by Katherine Paterson

Rascal by Sterling North

Island of the Blue Dolphins by Scott O'Dell

My Side of the Mountain by Jean Craighead George

Dear Mr. Henshaw by Beverly Cleary

Mrs. Frisby and the Rats of NIMH by Robert C. O'Brien

The Great Gilly Hopkins by Katherine Paterson

The House of Dies Drear by Virginia Hamilton

Johnny Tremain by Esther Forbes

The Cat Ate My Gymsuit by Paula Danziger

Hatchet by Gary Paulsen

A Wrinkle in Time by Madeleine L'Engle

Where the Red Fern Grows by Wilson Rawls

The Borrowers by Mary Norton

Number the Stars by Lois Lowry

Tuck Everlasting by Natalie Babbitt

The Dark Is Rising by Susan Cooper

The Sign of the Beaver by Elizabeth Speare

Across Five Aprils by Irene Hunt

Sounder by William H. Armstrong

Charlie and the Chocolate Factory by Roald Dahl

My Brother Sam Is Dead by James Lincoln Collier and Christopher Collier

Sing Down the Moon by Scott O'Dell

The Summer of the Swans by Betsy Byars

Tiger Eyes by Judy Blume

The Red Pony by John Steinbeck

Homecoming by Cynthia Voigt

The Sword in the Stone by T.H. White

Julie of the Wolves by Jean Craighead George

One Fat Summer by Robert Lipsyte

The Outsiders by S.E. Hinton

Diary of a Young Girl by Anne Frank

Fifteen by Beverly Cleary

Summer of My German Soldier by Bette Greene

The Contender by Robert Lipsyte

A Wizard of Earthsea by Ursula K. Le Guin

Durango Street by Frank Bonham

Shabanu: Daughter of the Wind by Suzanne Fisher Staples

The Upstairs Room by Johanna Reiss

The Slave Dancer by Paula Fox

I Will Call It Georgie's Blues by Suzanne Newton

Roll of Thunder, Hear My Cry by Mildred Taylor

Home before Dark by Sue Ellen Bridges

The Moves Make the Man by Bruce Brooks

The Last Unicorn by Peter S. Beagle

All Together Now by Sue Ellen Bridges

Enchanter's End Game by David Eddings

Tom Sawyer by Mark Twain

Sword of Shannara by Terry Brooks

The Pigman by Paul Zindel

Farewell to Manzanar by Jeanne Wakatsuki Houston

Divorce Express by Paula Danziger

P.S., I Love You by Barbara Conklin

Grades 9–12

Dicey's Song by Cynthia Voigt

Dragonwings by Laurence Yep

The Adventures of Huckleberry Finn by Mark Twain

Running Loose by Chris Crutcher

The House on Mango Street by Sandra Cisneros

Sheila's Dying by Alden R. Carter

The Pearl by John Steinbeck

I Know Why the Caged Bird Sings by Maya Angelou

Something Wicked This Way Comes by Ray Bradbury

The Miracle Worker (play) by William Gibson

To Kill a Mockingbird by Harper Lee

Of Mice and Men by John Steinbeck

Eight Plus One (short stories) by Robert Cormier

Animal Farm by George Orwell

The Hitchhiker's Guide to the Galaxy by Douglas Adams

A Tale of Two Cities by Charles Dickens

A Separate Peace by John Knowles

I Never Promised You a Rose Garden by Joanne Greenberg

Night by Elie Wiesel

Flowers for Algernon by Daniel Keyes

The Catcher in the Rye by J.D. Salinger

Hiroshima by John Hersey

After the First Death by Robert Cormier

Brave New World by Aldous Huxley

Lord of the Flies by William Golding

A Little Love by Virginia Hamilton

Fahrenheit 451 by Ray Bradbury

Remembering the Good Times by Richard Peck

Memory by Margaret Mahy

Dune by Frank Herbert

A Raisin in the Sun (play) by Lorraine Hansberry

Native Son by Richard Wright

One Flew Over the Cuckoo's Nest by Ken Kesey

Fallen Angels by Walter Dean Myers

The Scarlet Letter by Nathaniel Hawthorne

Watership Down by Richard Adams

Gone with the Wind by Margaret Mitchell

Dinner at the Homesick Restaurant by Anne Tyler

Hamlet by William Shakespeare

All Quiet on the Western Front by Erich Maria Remarque

Slaughterhouse-Five by Kurt Vonnegut, Jr.

Black Voices (anthology of poetry, short stories, nonfiction) edited by
　　Abraham Chapman